THE ALMANAC OF
WOMEN AND MINORITIES IN
AMERICAN POLITICS

THE ALMANAC
OF WOMEN
AND MINORITIES
IN AMERICAN
POLITICS

Mart Martin

foreword by
Paula D. McClain

Westview Press
A Member of the Perseus Books Group

Author's Note

The author and editors of this work have added value to the underlying factual material herein through one or more of the following: unique and original selection; coordination; presentation; expression; arrangement; and classification of the information.

Copyright © 1999 by Westview Press, A Member of the Perseus Books Group

Published in 1999 in the United States of America by Westview Press, 5500 Central Avenue, Boulder, Colorado 80301-2877, and in the United Kingdom by Westview Press, 12 Hid's Copse Road, Cumnor Hill, Oxford OX2 9JJ

Library of Congress Cataloging-in-Publication Data
Martin, Mart, 1944–
    The almanac of women and minorities in American politics / Mart Martin.
        p. cm.
    Includes bibliographical references and index.
    ISBN 0-8133-6870-7
    1. Women in politics—United States—Handbooks, manuals, etc.
2. Women politicians—United States—Handbooks, manuals, etc.
3. Minorities—United States—Political activity—Handbooks,
manuals, etc.   4. Gays—United States—Political activity—
Handbooks, manuals, etc.   I. Title.
HQ1236.5.U6M3778   1999
306.2'082'0973—dc21   98-15202
                                                                                         CIP

Design by Heather Hutchison

The paper used in this publication meets the requirements of the American National Standard for Permanence of Paper for Printed Library Materials Z39.48-1984.

10   9   8   7   6   5   4   3   2   1

Dedicated to
Martin Clifton, Audra Clifton, Michael Tran, Bonnie Yen,
Bryant Tran, Brandon Tran, Darren Yen

Through their veins flow the blood of the Cambodians,
the Chinese, the English, the Germans, the Irish,
the Native Americans, the Scots, and the Vietnamese.

Seven young Americans who prove that our country is
truly an international melting pot for the peoples of the world.

Contents

3   Hispanics in American Politics   173

4   Asian Americans in American Politics   205

5   Native Minorities in American Politics   227

Foreword

Alexis de Tocqueville, an early French visitor to the United States who wrote *Democracy in America* (1835), believed that the essence of America was the uniquely free and egalitarian ideas that abounded at the founding. Nonetheless, de Tocqueville noted that the treatment of blacks and Indians in the United States contradicted the American passion for democracy. Despite the universality of the language used by the founders in the documents they produced, they did not intend for these concepts to be universally applied. When Thomas Jefferson, in the Declaration of Independence, wrote the words, "All men are created equal," he should have added an asterisk with a note that read, "Does not apply to American Indians, blacks, and white women residing in the new nation." As a result of this initial exclusion of a majority of the American population, the political history of the United States has been the struggle of a polity to make accurate the words of Jefferson. As a student of American politics, I have always taken the position that one cannot truly understand the American political system without also understanding the politics of those groups initially excluded from participation in the system.

Despite the growing importance and volume of scholarship on the politics of African Americans, Latinos, Asian Americans, American Indians, and women of all colors, oftentimes we are unable to reconstruct easily the political histories of these groups. More often, we are unable to answer such specific questions as: 1) Who was the first black American nominated for a statewide office in United States? 2) What was the first state to grant women the right to vote? 3) When was the first Latina (female) elected to a state legislature in the United States? or 4) Who was the first Asian American woman to vote in a presidential election and in what year? Although we know the answers to these questions exist, we also know that finding them requires many hours in the library. Not anymore!

The Almanac of Women and Minorities in American Politics is the reference book students of American politics in general and those who study the politics of women and racial minorities have needed for years. In addition to historical information, it provides detailed data not readily available anywhere else. Moreover, the "Gays and Lesbians in American Politics" section highlights the intersection of race, gender, and sexual identity for several political firsts. Mart Martin and his colleagues provide a valuable service with this volume, one I plan to draw heavily on, especially when it is time for the third edition of *"Can We All Get Along?" Racial and Ethnic Minorities in American Politics, Second Edition* (Westview, 1998). This volume also means we will no longer dread those important, yet difficult questions to answer. By the way, the answers to the questions posed earlier are: 1) Frederick Douglass, 1855 in New York; 2) New Jersey in 1776; 3) Fedelina Lucero Gallegos, 1930 in New Mexico; and 4) Tye Leung, 1912 in San Francisco.

Paula D. McClain
University of Virginia

Acknowledgments

I am deeply grateful for the many people who assisted in one way or another with this book. My agent, Mitchell Rose, who always understands my determination, stepped in just when he was needed the most. Leo Wiegman, executive editor, who saw a comprehensive book hidden in a two-page proposal. Project editor Kristin Milavec deserves a special tip of the hat for the skillful manner in which she handled every little thing, along with Jane Raese and Heather Hutchison in composition, who worked magic with an unwieldy format. Jon Taylor Howard was simply the best copy editor I have ever encountered.

Particular thanks go to a group of people who help keep me on a firm basis every day: Jasmine Amper, John Chen, Karen Combs, Kenneth Fox, Bob Gillespie, Reg Hsu, Dean Jameson, Scott Roe, AnnMarie Thurmond, Michael Wagenhoffer, and Lon Wright. Plus, my guardian angel, who chides me daily about spending too much time in front of a computer and not enough doing chores. Then there are the women and men whose names and feats are mentioned herein. Without your collective ventures in American politics, winning and losing, this book would have no meaning; it was an honor to mention each and every one of your names. Finally, to those others who may have been omitted: Perhaps someone will bring it to our attention so your name will appear here in the future.

MART MARTIN

THE ALMANAC OF
WOMEN AND MINORITIES IN
AMERICAN POLITICS

Women in American Politics

A Brief Chronology

1655 First woman to cast a vote in the New World

Deborah Moody, who resided in what was then known as New Netherlands (most of which later became the state of New York), is reputed to have been the first woman to cast a vote in the New World. Moody's right to vote, first exercised in 1655, was a privilege conferred by virtue of a land grant registered in her name.

1776 First state to grant women the right to vote

New Jersey adopted the first state constitution that granted women the right to vote in 1776. In 1807, the all-male state legislature revoked their right, citing a lack of interest by women in voting, despite the fact that a large number of the state's women had done so in the recent presidential elections of 1800 and 1804.

1792 First woman appointed to a federal post after the adoption of the U.S. Constitution

Mrs. Sarah De Crow, appointed postmaster of Hartford, North Carolina.

1848 First meeting devoted to women's rights and suffrage

The first meeting devoted exclusively to women's rights and suffrage was held during 1848 in Seneca Falls, New York, under the leadership of early feminists Elizabeth Cady Stanton and Lucretia Mott. Frederick Douglass, at the time the leading African American spokesman for the abolition of slavery, was one of the speakers addressing the gathering.

1859 Women granted the right to vote—again

Kansas, then a territory, granted women the right to vote in school elections in 1859.

1866 First woman to run for a seat in the U.S. Congress

Elizabeth Cady Stanton, who sought a seat in the U.S. House of Representatives (New York–8th) as an Independent. Even though she couldn't vote for herself—no other women could—Stanton still received twenty-four votes out of a total of more than 24,000 cast in the congressional election.

1869 Women granted the right to vote—again

Wyoming, known today as "The Equality State," granted women the right to vote in 1869 while yet a territory, twenty-one years before being admitted to the Union. When the U.S. Congress voted on Wyoming's statehood in 1890, much pressure was brought on the territory to remove female suffrage from its constitution, but the territorial government refused.

1

Eventually, Congress relented on the issue and Wyoming—along with its women voters—entered the Union.

1872   First female presidential candidate

Victoria Claflin Woodhull of New York was nominated by the National Women's Suffrage Association and ran on the ticket of the National Radical Reformers in 1872 as their presidential candidate; she lost overwhelmingly.

1887   First woman elected mayor

Susanna M. Salter was elected mayor of Orgonia, Kansas.

1889   First all-female elected local government

Mayor Wilhelmina D. Morgan and an all-female town council were elected in Cottonwood Falls, Kansas. It is also possible that an all-female local government was elected in Oskaloosa, Kansas, near the same time, as some records indicate.

1893   First female candidate for the U.S. Senate

Mary Elizabeth Lease, the candidate of the Populist Party in Kansas, was the first female candidate for the U.S. Senate. This was during the period when U.S. senators were still elected by the state legislatures rather than by popular vote.

First woman elected to statewide office by male and female voters

Laura J. Eisenhuth, elected as North Dakota's superintendent of public instruction in 1893, was the first woman elected to statewide office by both male and female voters.

1894   First women elected to a state legislature

Clara Cressingham, **Carrie C. Holly,** and **Frances Klock**, all Republicans, were elected to Colorado's house of representatives.

1896   First woman elected to a state senate

Martha Hughes (Cannon), (D) Utah, elected to Utah's state senate.

1907   First woman elected to statewide office by a male-only electorate

Kate Barnard, (D) Oklahoma, elected to the post of commissioner of charities and collections by Oklahoma's male-only voters in 1907.

1916   First woman to be nominated for the Electoral College

Catharine W. McCullock, (D) Illinois, the first woman nominated as an elector for the presidential Electoral College in 1916. Since the Democrats did not carry Illinois in the November 1916 election, McCullock did not get to cast her vote in the Electoral College.

1917   First female sworn into the U.S. House of Representatives

Jeannette Rankin, (R) Montana, elected to one of Montana's two seats in the U.S. House in November 1916 was sworn into office when Congress convened in March 1917.

First women to vote as electors in the Electoral College

Mrs. W. C. Tyler, Mrs. Spinks, and **Mrs. Wylie**, all Democrats of California, cast their votes in the Electoral College for Pres. Woodrow Wilson after the Democratic Party carried California in the November 1916 presidential election.

1920 Women granted the right to vote

The 19th Amendment to the U.S. Constitution, which became effective after being ratified by Tennessee in August 1920, was supposed to guarantee women the right to vote. The amendment stated that the rights of U.S. citizens to vote should not be denied or abridged on account of sex. But other factors, such as "grandfather" clauses and restrictive poll taxes, continued to deny many women the right to vote.

First woman to reach a federal subcabinet-level position

Annette Abbott Adams, (R) California, appointed assistant attorney general in 1920, the first woman to hold a federal subcabinet-level position.

1922 First female sworn in as a U.S. senator

Rebecca Felton, (D) Georgia, sworn in as a U.S. senator for a temporary appointment that lasted only two days.

First woman to serve on a state supreme court

Florence Ellinwood Allen, (D), elected an associate justice of the Ohio Supreme Court in November 1922.

1924 First woman governor

Nellie Tayloe Ross, (D) Wyoming, chosen by the state legislature to succeed her deceased husband and complete the two years remaining in his term of office.

1926 First female mayor of a large city

Bertha Knight Landes elected mayor of Seattle, Washington, after having previously served on the city council.

1928 First female federal judge

Genevieve Cline, Ohio, sworn in as a judge for the U.S. Customs Court.

1932 First woman popularly elected to the U.S. Senate

Hattie Caraway, (D) Arkansas, elected by popular vote to succeed her deceased husband, Thaddeus, in the U.S. Senate.

1933 First woman appointed to a presidential cabinet

Frances Perkins, New York, appointed secretary of labor by Pres. Franklin D. Roosevelt in 1933, the first woman to hold a presidential cabinet post.

1949 First woman to bear the diplomatic rank of U.S. ambassador

Eugenie A. Anderson, appointed U.S. ambassador to Denmark by Pres. Harry S. Truman, was the first woman to hold the diplomatic rank of U.S. ambassador.

1964 First woman to have name formally placed into nomination for president at the Republican convention

Margaret Chase Smith, U.S. senator from Maine, was formally nominated for president at the 1964 Republican National Convention in San Francisco, California, but received less than thirty delegate votes on the first (and only) ballot.

1965 First female chief justice of a state supreme court

Lorna Lockwood, Arizona, elected chief justice of that state's supreme court.

1972 First woman to head a major national political party

Jean Westwood, Utah, selected by Democratic presidential nominee Sen. George McGovern to become chair of the National Democratic Party.

1981 First female U.S. Supreme Court justice

Sandra Day O'Connor, (R) Arizona, appointed an associate justice of the U.S. Supreme Court by Pres. Ronald Reagan.

1984 First female vice presidential candidate on a major-party ticket

Geraldine Ferraro, New York, a three-term member of the U.S. House of Representatives, was tapped by Democratic presidential nominee Walter Mondale as his vice presidential running mate.

1987 First woman to head a major presidential campaign

Susan Estrich, Massachusetts, chosen by Democratic presidential nominee Gov. Michael Dukakis of Massachusetts to head his presidential campaign.

1991 First state supreme court to have a majority of female justices

Minnesota, which already had three women sitting on its seven-member state supreme court, swore in a fourth female justice, which made it the first state to have a supreme court with a majority of female justices.

1993 First two women to represent a state concurrently in the U.S. Senate

Dianne Feinstein and **Barbara Boxer**, both Democrats of California, were elected to seats in the U.S. Senate in November 1992. Feinstein, replacing an appointed senator, was sworn in shortly after the election. With Boxer's oath of office in 1993, California became the first state to be represented concurrently by two women in the U.S. Senate.

First time that women hold more than 10 percent of the seats in the U.S. House of Representatives

After all the women who were elected to the U.S. House of Representatives in 1992 were sworn into office in January 1993, females held more than 10 percent of the seats in that body for the first time since the founding of the nation.

1994 First state legislature to convene where both legislative chambers are headed by women

Alaska, which opened its legislative session with **Gail Phillips** (R) as speaker of the state house and **Drue Pearce** (R) as state senate president pro tem, became the first state to convene a legislature where both chambers were headed by women.

1997 Highest number of women to serve concurrently in the U.S. Senate

The swearing-in of two new female U.S. senators brought that body to the highest number of women to serve concurrently—nine seats (or 9 percent) out of a total of 100 members.

1998 First state with all-female line of sucession

Arizona elected women to all five of its top constitutional offices (governor, secretary of state, attorney general, treasurer, superintendent of public instruction), making it the first state with an all-female line of succession.

Women and Political Power

The following chart (by state) details the total number of women who have served their states in three of the most powerful positions in U.S. politics: governor, U.S. Senate (both appointed and elected), and U.S. House of Representatives.

State	Governor	U.S. Senate	U.S. House
Alabama	1	2	1
Alaska	-	-	-
Arizona	2	-	2
Arkansas	-	2	4
California	-	2	24
Colorado	-	-	2
Connecticut	1	-	6
Delaware	-	-	-
Florida	-	1	6
Georgia	-	1	4
Hawaii	-	-	2
Idaho	-	-	2
Illinois	-	1	11
Indiana	-	-	5
Iowa	-	-	-
Kansas	1	2	3
Kentucky	1	-	2
Louisiana	-	3	2
Maine	-	3	2
Maryland	-	1	7

Massachusetts	-	-	3
Michigan	-	-	6
Minnesota	-	1	1
Mississippi	-	-	-
Missouri	-	-	5
Montana	-	-	1
Nebraska	1	2	1
Nevada	-	-	2
New Hampshire	1	-	-
New Jersey	1	-	5
New Mexico	-	-	2
New York	-	-	18
North Carolina	-	-	3
North Dakota	-	1	-
Ohio	-	-	6
Oklahoma	-	-	1
Oregon	1	1	4
Pennsylvania	-	-	4
Rhode Island	-	-	1
South Carolina	-	-	5
South Dakota	-	2	-
Tennessee	-	-	4
Texas	2	1	5
Utah	-	-	3
Vermont	1	-	-
Virginia	-	-	1
Washington	1	1	6
West Virginia	-	-	1
Wisconsin	-	-	1
Wyoming	1	-	1
Total Women Who Have Served	15	27	175

Best State for Women Achieving Power

Maryland, which had a delegation to the U.S. House in the 1970s with two women (out of eight seats total). Female representation later rose to 50 percent (four seats out of eight) during the late 1980s. The state has also had a female U.S. senator since 1986 (reelected 1992 and 1998), and female candidates competed in two other U.S. Senate contests. Although Maryland has never elected a female governor,[1] women have carried the banner for the two major parties three times in the past twenty years.

---

[1]Ellen Sauerbrey, the Republican candidate in 1994, came within 5,883 votes of victory. She filed suit asking that her opponent's election victory be invalidated for voting irregularities or that another election be ordered; both requests came to naught, and her Democratic opponent assumed office.

Worst States for Women Achieving Power

In four states—**Alaska**, **Delaware**, **Iowa**, and **Mississippi**—a woman has never served as governor or represented the state in either the U.S. House or Senate.

Women in the U.S. Cabinet

The President's Cabinet

The first female member of a U.S. presidential cabinet was Frances Perkins (see below), appointed in 1933.

Secretary of State

Madeleine K. Albright, 1997– , appointed by Bill Clinton

Attorney General

Janet Reno, 1993– , appointed by Bill Clinton

Secretary of Labor

Frances Perkins, 1933–1945, appointed by Franklin D. Roosevelt
Ann D. McLaughlin, 1987–1989, appointed by Ronald Reagan
Elizabeth H. Dole, 1989–1991, appointed by George Bush
Lynn Martin,[2] 1991–1993, appointed by George Bush
Alexis Herman, 1997– , appointed by Bill Clinton

Secretary of Commerce

Juanita M. Krebs, 1977–1979, appointed by Jimmy Carter
Barbara H. Franklin, 1992–1993, appointed by George Bush

Secretary of Housing and Urban Development

Carla A. Hills, 1975–1977, appointed by Gerald Ford
Patricia Roberts Harris, 1977–1979, appointed by Jimmy Carter

---

[2]Martin had previously served five terms (1981–1991) in the U.S. House.

Secretary of Transportation

Elizabeth H. Dole, 1983–1987, appointed by Ronald Reagan

Secretary of Energy

Hazel R. O'Leary, 1993–1997, appointed by Bill Clinton

Secretary of Health, Education, and Welfare

Oveta Culp Hobby, 1953–1955, appointed by Dwight Eisenhower
Patricia Roberts Harris, 1979, appointed by Jimmy Carter

Secretary of Health and Human Services

Patricia Roberts Harris, 1979–1981, appointed by Jimmy Carter
Margaret M. Heckler,[3] 1983–1985, appointed by Ronald Reagan
Donna E. Shalala, 1993– , appointed by Bill Clinton

Secretary of Education

Shirley Huffstedler, 1979–1981, appointed by Jimmy Carter

Federal Cabinet Statistics

Only two women have served in more than one position in the Federal Cabinet:

Elizabeth H. Dole headed the Departments of Transportation and Labor.
Patricia Roberts Harris headed the Departments of Housing and Urban Development and Health and Human Services (which was named Health, Education, and Welfare when she was appointed).

A woman has never served as the secretary of the following departments:

Agriculture
Defense
Interior
Treasury
Veterans Affairs

---

[3]Heckler had previously served eight terms (1967–1983) in the U.S. House.

Women in the Executive Branch

Notable Firsts: 1993

Sheila Widnall, appointed by Pres. Bill Clinton, became the first female secretary of the U.S. Air Force.

Jocelyn Elders, (D) Arkansas, appointed by Pres. Bill Clinton, became the first African American female to hold the position of surgeon general.

Notable First: 1990

Antonia C. Novello, appointed by Pres. George Bush, became both the first female and the first Hispanic to hold the position of surgeon general.

Notable Firsts: 1977

Bette B. Anderson, (D) Georgia, appointed by Pres. Jimmy Carter as undersecretary of the treasury, became the first female appointed to an undersecretary position in that department.

Eleanor Holmes Norton, (D) District of Columbia, appointed by Pres. Jimmy Carter as the first female to chair the Equal Employment Opportunity Commission.

Notable Firsts: 1976

Juanita Ashcroft, (R) California, named by Pres. Gerald Ford as assistant secretary of the U.S. Air Force, the first woman to hold the position in the Department of Defense.

Shirley Temple Black, (R) California, named by Pres. Gerald Ford as the first female chief of protocol.

Notable First: 1969

Virginia Mae Brown, (D) West Virginia, appointed by Pres. Lyndon B. Johnson in 1964 as the first female to sit on the Interstate Commerce Commission, accedes to the chair of that commission. She became the first female to head an independent federal administrative agency.

Notable First: 1968

Barbara Watson, appointed by Pres. Lyndon B. Johnson as assistant secretary of state, the first female (and first African American) appointed to an undersecretary position in that department.

Notable First: 1967

Dorothy Jackson, (D) Minnesota, appointed by Pres. Lyndon B. Johnson as an assistant secretary of agriculture, the first woman to hold a federal subcabinet-level position in that department.

Notable First: 1959

Cecil Harden, (R) Indiana, appointed by Pres. Dwight D. Eisenhower as a special assistant to the postmaster general, the first woman to hold a high office in the Department of the Post Office.

Notable First: 1950

Anna M. Rosenberg, appointed by Pres. Harry S. Truman as assistant secretary of defense, the first woman to hold a federal subcabinet-level position in that department.

Notable First: 1949

Georgia Neese Clark, (D) Kansas, appointed by Pres. Harry S. Truman as treasurer of the United States. She was the first female to hold that position, and also the first female whose signature appeared on U.S. currency.

Notable First: 1948

Frieda B. Hennock, appointed by Pres. Harry S. Truman to the Federal Communications Commission, the first woman to serve on an independent regulatory agency.

Notable First: 1946

Eleanor Roosevelt, (D) New York, named by Pres. Harry S. Truman as the first female delegate to the United Nations.

Notable First: 1934

Josephine Roche, (D) Colorado, appointed by Pres. Franklin D. Roosevelt as an assistant secretary of the treasury, the first woman to reach federal subcabinet-level position in that department.

Notable First: 1933

Nellie Tayloe Ross, (D) Wyoming, the nation's first female governor, named by Pres. Franklin D. Roosevelt as the first female director of the U.S. Mint.

Notable Firsts: 1920

Annette Abbott Adams, (R) California, appointed assistant attorney general, the first woman to
   hold federal subcabinet-level office in the U.S.
Helen H. Gardner, named by Pres. Woodrow Wilson to the U.S. Civil Service Commission, the
   first woman to sit on that body.
Estelle V. Collier, (D) Utah, appointed by Pres. Woodrow Wilson as collector of customs in Treasury, the first woman to achieve a high rank in that federal department.

Notable First: 1913

Mrs. J. Borden (Florence) Harriman, named a member of the U.S. Industrial Commission, the first female federal commissioner.

Notable First: 1912

Julia C. Lathrop, (R) Illinois, named by Pres. William H. Taft as head of the Children's Bureau, the first woman to head a major federal bureau.

Women at the National Party Level

Notable Firsts: 1988

Lenora Fulani, (National Alliance Party) New York, became the first African American woman to appear on the presidential ballot in all fifty states.

Susan Estrich was tapped by Democratic presidential nominee Gov. Michael Dukakis of Massachusetts to head his campaign, the first woman to head a major presidential campaign.

Notable First: 1984

Geraldine Ferraro, (D) New York, a three-term member of the U.S. House of Representatives, was tapped by Democratic presidential nominee Walter Mondale as his choice for vice president. Despite the excitement generated by the first woman on a major party's national ticket, the Mondale-Ferraro team lost the election. They won only thirteen electoral votes, compared to 525 for the Reagan-Bush team, although they did win 41 percent of the popular vote.

Notable Firsts: 1976

Corinne Clairborne "Lindy" Boggs, Louisiana, a two-term member of the U.S. House of Representatives, became the first woman to preside as chair of the Democratic National Convention.

Barbara Jordan, Texas, a two-term member of the U.S. House of Representatives, was the first woman and African American to deliver the keynote speech at the Democratic National Convention.

Notable Firsts: 1972

Shirley B. Chisholm, New York, a two-term member of the U.S. House of Representatives and a contender during the Democratic primary season in twelve states, had her name formally placed in nomination for president at the Democratic National Convention. In doing so, she became the first African American woman accorded that honor, but she received only 152 delegate votes on the first (and only) convention ballot.

Frances "Sissy" Farenthold, Texas, placed second to winner Sen. Thomas Eagleton of Missouri during the balloting for the vice presidential slot at the Democratic National Convention.

Anne L. Armstrong, Texas, delivered the keynote address at the Republican National Convention, the first woman to do so at the national convention of either major party.

Jean Westwood, Utah, tapped by Democratic presidential nominee Sen. George McGovern of South Dakota to chair the National Democratic Party, the first woman to head a major national political party in the U.S.

Patsy Takemoto Mink, Hawaii, a four-term member of the U.S. House of Representatives, ran in the Oregon primary for the Democratic presidential nomination. Although she was the first Asian American woman to seek the presidential nomination of either major party, she received only 2 percent of the Oregon Democratic primary vote.

Notable First: 1964

Margaret Chase Smith, Maine, a three-term member of the U.S. Senate, had her name formally placed in nomination for president at the Republican National Convention; despite receiving less than thirty delegate votes, she became the first woman accorded that honor in either national party.

Notable Firsts: 1952

Carlotta A. Bass, New York, the first African American woman to appear on the national presidential ballot as a vice presidential candidate, ran on the Progressive ticket.

India Edwards and **Judge Sarah Hughes**, both of Texas, had their names proposed for the vice presidential nomination at the Democratic National Convention, which eventually went by acclamation to Sen. John Sparkman of Alabama.

Notable First: 1928

Mrs. William Maulsly, Iowa, temporarily assumed control of the Democratic Party in Iowa, the first woman to head the state branch of a major national political party.

Notable First: 1924

Mrs. Springs, South Carolina, chair of the Credentials Committee, had her name placed in nomination for the vice presidential slot at the Democratic National Convention, the first woman to be formally nominated for the position; she received thirty-eight votes. Earlier in the convention three woman had also received one or more votes from the floor for the presidential nomination.

Notable First: 1922

Emily Newell Blair, vice chair of the Democratic National Committee, the first woman to hold that position in either major party.

Notable First: 1917

Mrs. W. C. Tyler, **Mrs. Spinks**, and **Mrs. Wylie**, all Democrats of California, cast their electoral votes for Pres. Woodrow Wilson, after the Democratic Party carried California in the 1916 presidential election, the first women to vote as electors in the Electoral College.

Notable First: 1916

Catharine W. McCullock, Illinois, the first woman to be nominated as an elector in the Electoral College by the Democratic Party of her state. The Democratic ticket—headed by Pres. Woodrow

Wilson—did not carry Illinois in the 1916 election, thus McCullock was denied her chance to vote in the Electoral College.

Notable First: 1912

Tye Leung, San Francisco, California, voted in the 1912 presidential election, the first Chinese American woman to vote in a presidential election. She was able to do so because California had granted women the right to vote one year earlier, in 1911.

Notable First: 1900

One female delegate attended both the Republican and Democratic National Conventions, the first official female delegates to either party's national convention.

Notable First: 1872

Victoria Claflin Woodhull, New York, the first female presidential candidate, nominated by the National Women's Suffrage Association and candidate for the National Radical Reformers, with African American notable Frederick Douglass as her vice presidential running mate.

Female U.S. Senators in Chronological Order of Service

Senator	Party	State	Dates Served
1. Rebecca Latimer Felton	Democrat	Georgia	11/21/22–11/22/22
2. Hattie Wyatt Caraway	Democrat	Arkansas	11/13/31–01/02/45
3. Rose McConnell Long	Democrat	Louisiana	01/31/36–01/02/37
4. Dixie Bibb Graves	Democrat	Alabama	08/20/37–01/10/38
5. Gladys Pyle	Republican	South Dakota	11/09/38–01/03/39
6. Vera Cahalan Bushfield	Republican	South Dakota	10/06/48–12/26/48
7. Margaret Chase Smith	Republican	Maine	01/03/49–01/03/73
8. Eva Kelly Bowring	Republican	Nebraska	04/26/54–11/07/54
9. Hazel Hempel Abel	Republican	Nebraska	11/08/54–12/31/54
10. Maurine Brown Neuberger	Democrat	Oregon	11/08/60–01/02/67
11. Elaine Schwartzenburg Edwards	Democrat	Louisiana	08/07/72–11/13/72
12. Muriel Buck Humphrey	Democrat	Minnesota	02/06/78–11/07/78
13. Maryon Pittman Allen	Democrat	Alabama	06/08/78–11/07/78
14. Nancy Landon Kassebaum	Republican	Kansas	12/23/78–01/06/97
15. Paula Fickes Hawkins	Republican	Florida	01/01/81–01/03/87
16. *Barbara Ann Mikulski*	Democrat	Maryland	01/03/87–
17. Jocelyn Birch Burdick	Democrat	North Dakota	09/16/92–12/14/92
18. *Dianne Goldman Feinstein*	Democrat	California	11/10/92–

19. *Barbara Levy Boxer*	Democrat	California	01/05/93–
20. Carol Moseley-Braun	Democrat	Illinois	01/05/93–01/04/99
21. *Patricia Johns Murray*	Democrat	Washington	01/05/93–
22. *Kay Bailey Hutchison*	Republican	Texas	06/14/93–
23. *Olympia Jean Snowe*	Republican	Maine	01/04/95–
24. Sheila Sloan Frahm	Republican	Kansas	06/11/96–11/27/96
25. *Susan Margaret Collins*	Republican	Maine	01/07/97–
26. *Mary Loretta Landrieu*	Democrat	Louisiana	01/07/97–
27. *Blanche Lambert Lincoln*	Democrat	Arkansas	01/04/99–

Note: **Bold *italic*** denotes that senator is still serving.

How They Assumed Office

1. **Rebecca Latimer Felton,** (D) Georgia (Born: 1835; Died: 1930)
   Served: 11/21/22–11/22/22

   Received an interim appointment in early October 1922 from Gov. Thomas Hardwick (D) to fill the term of deceased Sen. Thomas E. Watson (D). Since an election was already scheduled for October 17, 1922, to replace Watson, and with the Senate in adjournment—leaving Felton unable to be sworn in—Hardwick thought she would remain a "titular" senator only. Immediately after the October election, Felton confounded his plan. She sought the help of Sen.-elect Walter B. George (D), impressing upon him the importance that the honor of her being the first female U.S. senator would bring to all women in the United States. George agreed to delay his own swearing-in by two days to permit her to briefly "hold" the office.

   Felton journeyed to Washington and appeared in the Senate when it reconvened on November 21, 1922. She was sworn in that same day, then served an additional day before relinquishing the seat to Senator-elect George. During her two-day tenure, the Senate cast no votes and had no quorum calls, thus she was unable to perform those formal senatorial duties. Felton did, however, deliver one short speech concerning the importance of her appointment to American women.

   Previous and subsequent elected political office: None

2. **Hattie Wyatt Caraway,** (D) Arkansas (Born: 1878; Died: 1950). Politically prominent spouse: Thaddeus H. Caraway (D), U.S. House 1912–1921, U.S. Senate 1921–1931
   Served: 11/13/31–01/02/45

   Received an interim appointment in early November 1931 from Gov. Harvey J. Parnell (D) to the seat of her recently deceased husband, Thaddeus H. Caraway (D). Meanwhile, a special election was scheduled for January 1932 to fill the remainder—one year—of his term. Mrs. Caraway ran and won that election, then made another successful run in November 1932 for a full six-year term of her own. She was reelected for another full term in 1938. Her Senate career ended when she was defeated for renomination to a third term in the 1944 Democratic primary, where she placed fourth and gathered only 13 percent of the vote.

Previous and subsequent elected political office: None

3. **Rose McConnell Long,** (D) Louisiana (Born: 1892; Died: 1970). Politically prominent
   spouse: Huey P. Long (D), governor 1928–1932, U.S. Senate 1932–1935
   Served: 01/31/36–01/02/37

   Received an interim appointment in early January 1936 from Gov. Richard W. Leche (D) to the
   seat of her assassinated husband, Huey P. "The Kingfish" Long. Her selection for the position
   was delayed for several months because fierce in-fighting had broken out among the cronies of
   Huey Long's political machine as to which of them would be heir to his considerable political
   power in the state. Mrs. Long did not run in the November 1936 special election to fill the remainder—three years—of the term.

   Previous and subsequent elected political office: None

4. **Dixie Bibb Graves,** (D) Alabama (Born: 1882; Died: 1965). Politically prominent spouse:
   Bibb Graves (D), governor 1927–1931, 1935–1939
   Served: 08/20/37–01/10/38

   Received an interim appointment on August 8, 1937, from her husband, Gov. Bibb Graves (D),
   to the seat of former Sen. Hugo Black (D), who had resigned to become a U.S. Supreme Court
   justice. Governor Graves came under strong pressure from several Alabama politicians for the
   Senate appointment. It was a tempting prize, because whoever received it would have been immediately established as the strongest candidate in two scheduled elections; one would fill the
   seat for the few months remaining in the term, the other was for a new full six-year term. To
   prevent any hard feelings and preserve good relations with all the competing political factions,
   Governor Graves chose to appoint a neutral party: his wife. Mrs. Graves did not run in the
   Democratic primaries to select the nominees for either the "short" or full terms.

   Previous and subsequent elected political office: None

5. **Gladys Pyle,** (R) South Dakota (Born: 1890; Died: 1989)
   Served: 11/09/38–01/03/39

   Elected on November 8, 1938, to serve the balance of deceased Sen. Peter Norbeck's (R) original term. Another election was held the same day for a full six-year term for the seat, but Miss
   Pyle did not run in that election. She resigned on January 3, 1939, to permit the new senator to
   be sworn in for that term. Even though the Senate was not in session during her tenure and she
   was not sworn in as a senator, she drove to Washington anyway to establish and operate her office. She was not a newcomer to the South Dakota statewide ballot. In 1930, Miss Pyle, who
   was already secretary of state, was a candidate in the Republican gubernatorial primary. She led
   the four other candidates—all male—but since she won less than the 35 percent required to receive the nomination, the final decision went to a state convention. At that meeting two of the
   other candidates reached a deal whereby one of them received the nomination, thus denying it
   to Miss Pyle. Back in 1922, she had already set a personal record when she became the first
   woman elected to South Dakota's house of representatives.

Previous elected political office:
  South Dakota House of Representatives, 1923–1927
  South Dakota Secretary of State, 1927–1931
Subsequent elected political office: None

6. **Vera Cahalan Bushfield,** (R) South Dakota (Born: 1889; Died: 1976). Politically prominent spouse: Harlan J. Bushfield (R), governor 1939–1943, 1943–1948.
Served: 10/06/48–12/26/48

Received an interim appointment on September 30, 1948, from Gov. George T. Mickelson (R) to the seat of her recently deceased husband, Sen. Harlan J. Bushfield (R), who was running for reelection when he died. She served until the new senator elected for the full six-year term was sworn in.

Previous and subsequent elected political office: None

7. **Margaret Chase Smith,** (R) Maine (Born: 1897; Died: 1995). Politically prominent spouse: Clyde H. Smith (R), U.S. House 1937–1940.
Served: 01/03/49–01/03/73

Elected to a full six-year term on November 2, 1948. Mrs. Smith had previously succeeded her deceased husband, Clyde, in his U.S. House seat when he died after serving two terms in that body. She won additional six-year terms in the U.S. Senate in 1954, 1960, and 1966. Seeking her fifth term in 1972, Mrs. Smith won the Republican nomination but was left wounded for the general election because her primary opponent had made her increasing age an issue. Softened by his attack, she was defeated by William D. Hathaway (D) in November 1972.

Previous elected political office:
  U.S. House of Representatives, 1941–1949
Subsequent elected political office: None

8. **Eva Kelly Bowring,** (R) Nebraska (Born: 1892; Died: 1985)
Served: 04/26/54–11/07/54
Received an interim appointment on April 16, 1954, from Gov. Robert B. Crosby (R) to the seat of deceased Sen. Dwight Griswold (R). She held the seat until two November special elections were held. One filled the seat until January 1, 1955; the other selected someone to fill the re-mainder—four years—of Griswold's term. Mrs. Bowring resigned immediately following the special elections so the winner of the "short" term could be sworn in.

Previous and subsequent elected political office: None

9. **Hazel Hempel Abel,** (R) Nebraska (Born: 1888; Died: 1966)
Served: 11/08/54–12/31/54

Elected on November 2, 1954, in a special election to fill a portion, until January 1, 1955, of deceased Sen. Dwight Griswold's term. On the same date as her special election, another one filled the seat for the remainder—four years—of Griswold's original term. She did not contest that election. In 1960, at age seventy-two, Mrs. Abel returned to Nebraska elective politics and sought the Republican nomination for governor. She lost, placing second in the primary.

Previous and subsequent elected political office: None

10. **Maurine Brown Neuberger,** (D) Oregon (Born: 1907). Politically prominent spouse: Richard L. Neuberger (D), U.S. Senate 1955–1960.
Served: 11/08/60–01/02/67

Elected on November 8, 1960, to both the remainder (November 8, 1960–January 3, 1961) of her deceased husband Richard Neuberger's (D) term and a full six-year term of her own. In 1966, shortly before the expiration of that term, Mrs. Neuberger, who had remarried, announced that she would retire and not seek reelection to a second full term.

Previous elected political office:
   Oregon House of Representatives, 1951–1955[4]
Subsequent elected political office: None

11. **Elaine Schwartzenburg Edwards,** (D) Louisiana (Born: 1929). Politically prominent spouse: Edwin Edwards (D), governor 1972–1980, 1984–1988, 1992–1997.
Served: 08/07/72–11/13/72

Received an interim appointment on August 1, 1972, from her husband, Gov. Edwin Edwards (D), to fill the seat of deceased Sen. Allen Ellender (D). Before naming his wife, Governor Edwards had been under strong pressure from several Louisiana politicians for the Senate appointment. Whoever received it would have been immediately established as the strongest candidate in the upcoming primary to select the Democratic nominee for the full six-year term, which Ellender had already filed for prior to his death. To prevent any hard feelings and preserve good relations with all the competing factions, the governor decided to appoint a neutral party to the seat and—by employing an option used thirty-six years before by another governor—named his own wife. Mrs. Edwards resigned immediately following the November general election so the winner could be sworn in early to the seat. Several years later, she and Edwin Edwards divorced.

Previous and subsequent elected political office: None

12. **Muriel Buck Humphrey,** (D) Minnesota (Born: 1912; Died: 1998). Politically prominent spouse: Hubert H. Humphrey (D), vice president 1965–1969, U.S. Senate 1949–1964, 1971–1978.
Served: 02/06/78–11/07/78

---

[4]During this term in the legislature, Neuberger and her husband, Richard, tied a record: They were the second married couple to serve concurrently in a state legislative body. Miles H. and Margaret Dustin, both Democrats, were the first; both were elected to the New Hamphire house in 1943.

Received an interim appointment on January 25, 1978, from Gov. Rudy Perpich (D) to the seat of her recently deceased husband, Hubert H. Humphrey, which ran until a November special election filled the remainder—four years—of his term. Mrs. Humphrey was not a candidate in that election and resigned immediately following it so the winner could be sworn in.

Previous and subsequent elected political office: None

13. **Maryon Pittman Allen,** (D) Alabama (Born: 1925; Died: 1998). Politically prominent spouse: James B. Allen (D), U.S. Senate 1969–1978.
Served: 06/08/78–11/07/78

Received an interim appointment in early June 1978 from Gov. George C. Wallace (D) to the seat of her recently deceased husband, James B. Allen (D), which ran until a November special election filled the remainder—two years—of his term. Mrs. Allen immediately filed as a candidate in hopes of keeping the seat. She placed first in the Democratic primary but lost the nomination in a runoff to a state senator, Donald Stewart (D). She resigned following the November special election so the winner could be sworn in.

Previous and subsequent elected political office: None

14. **Nancy Landon Kassebaum,** (R) Kansas (Born: 1932)
Served: 12/23/78–01/06/97

Elected on November 7, 1978, to a full six-year term. She won additional terms in 1984 and 1990. Mrs. Kassebaum, the daughter of 1936 Republican presidential nominee and Kansas governor (1933–1937) Alf Landon, decided to retire and declined to seek a fourth term in 1996. Shortly after leaving the U.S. Senate in 1997, she wed former Sen. Howard Baker (R) of Tennessee.

Previous and subsequent elected political office:
  Maize, Kansas, School Board, 1972–1975

15. **Paula Fickes Hawkins,** (R) Florida (Born: 1927)
Served: 01/01/81–01/03/87

Elected on November 4, 1980, to a full six-year term. She sought a second term in 1986 but was defeated in the November general election by Bob Graham (D), a popular governor whose term was ending. Hawkins had also been a primary candidate in 1974 for the Republican senatorial nomination for this same seat, but she narrowly lost that election to Jack Eckard, founder of a drugstore chain that bore his name.

Previous elected political office:
  Florida Public Service Commission, 1973–1979
Subsequent elected political office: None

16. **Barbara Ann Mikulski,** (D) Maryland (Born: 1936)
Served: 01/03/87–present

Elected on November 4, 1986, to a full six-year term. She won additional terms in 1992 and 1998.

Previous elected political office:
   Baltimore, Maryland, City Council, 1971–1976
   U.S. House of Representatives, 1977–1986

17. **Jocelyn Birch Burdick,** (D) North Dakota (Born: 1922). Politically prominent spouse: Quentin N. Burdick (D), U.S. House 1959–1960, U.S. Senate 1960–1992. Served: 09/16/92–12/14/92

Received an interim appointment on September 12, 1992, from Gov. George A. Sinner (D) to the seat of her recently deceased husband, Quentin Burdick (D), which lasted until a November special election filled the remainder—two years—of his term. Mrs. Burdick did not contest the seat in that election and resigned shortly afterward to allow the winner to be sworn in.

Previous and subsequent elected political office: None

18. **Dianne Goldman Feinstein**, (D) California (Born: 1933)
Served: 11/10/92–present

Elected on November 3, 1992, to the two years remaining in former Sen. Pete Wilson's (R) original six-year term. Wilson had resigned two years earlier when he was elected governor—his opponent in that election was Feinstein—then appointed John Seymour (R) to hold the seat until a special 1992 election. She won a full six-year term in 1994. In 1990 Feinstein had been the Democratic candidate for governor, but she lost the race to Pete Wilson.

Previous elected political office:
   San Francisco, California, Board of Supervisors, 1970–1978
   Mayor, San Francisco, California, 1978–1988

19. **Barbara Levy Boxer,** (D) California (Born: 1940)
Served: 01/05/93–present

Elected on November 3, 1992, to a full six-year term. Won an additional term in 1998.

Previous elected political office:
   Marin County, California, Board of Supervisors, 1976–1982
   U.S. House of Representatives, 1983–1992

20. **Carol Moseley-Braun,** (D) Illinois (Born: 1947)
Served: 01/05/93–01/04/99

Elected on November 3, 1992, to a full six-year term. Moseley-Braun won the Democratic nomination for the seat by upsetting two-term Sen. Alan Dixon (D), who had been expected to coast to reelection, in the primary. As both an African American and a woman, she was helped enormously—in both the primary and the general election—by the controversy over the treatment of Anita Hill during the Supreme Court confirmation hearings of Clarence Thomas in the U.S. Senate. Defeated for reelection to another term in 1998.

Previous elected political office:
   Illinois House of Representatives, 1978–1988
   Cook County, Illinois, Recorder of Deeds, 1989–1992

21. **Patricia Johns Murray**, (D) Washington (Born: 1950)
Served: 01/05/93–present

Elected on November 3, 1992, to a full six-year term. Won an additional term in 1998.

Previous elected political office:
   Shoreline, Washington, School Board, 1985–1989
   Washington State Senate, 1988–1992

22. **Kay Bailey Hutchison,** (R) Texas (Born: 1943)
Served: 06/14/93–present

Elected on June 7, 1993, in a special election when she defeated appointed Sen. Robert Krueger (D) to fill the remainder—one year—of former Sen. Lloyd Bentsen's original six-year term after he had resigned to join President Clinton's cabinet as secretary of the treasury. She won a full six-year term in 1994.

Previous elected political office:
   Texas House of Representatives, 1972–1976
   Texas State Treasurer, 1990–1993

23. **Olympia Jean Snowe,** (R) Maine (Born: 1947). Politically prominent spouse:
John R. McKernan Jr. (R), U.S. House 1983–1987, governor 1987–1995.
Served: 01/04/95–present

Elected on November 8, 1994, to a full six-year term.

Previous elected political office:
   Maine House of Representatives, 1973–1976
   Maine State Senate, 1976–1978
   U.S. House of Representatives, 1979–1995

24. **Sheila Sloan Frahm,** (R) Kansas (Born: 1945)
Served: 06/11/96–11/27/96

Received an interim appointment on May 24, 1996, from Gov. Bill Graves (R) to fill the seat resigned by Sen. Bob Dole, the Republican nominee for president. Mrs. Frahm was defeated by U.S. Rep. Sam Brownback (R) on August 6, 1996, in the Republican primary for the nomination to fill the remainder—two years—of the term.

Previous elected political office:
    Colby, Kansas, School Board, 1981–1985
    Kansas State Board of Education, 1985–1989
    Kansas State Senate, 1989–1995
    Lieutenant Governor, 1995–1996

25. **Susan Margaret Collins,** (R) Maine (Born: 1952)
Served: 01/07/97–present

Elected on November 5, 1996, to a full six-year term. Two years earlier, in 1994, Collins had been the Republican gubernatorial candidate when she placed third in the general election, being bested by both the Democratic candidate and the winning Independent candidate.

Previous elected political office: None

26. **Mary Loretta Landrieu,** (D) Louisiana (Born: 1955)
Served: 01/07/97–present

Elected on November 5, 1996, to a full six-year term.

Previous elected political office:
    Louisiana House of Representatives, 1979–1987
    Louisiana State Treasurer, 1987–1995

27. **Blanche Lambert Lincoln,** (D) Arkansas (Born: 1960)
Served: 01/04/99–present

Elected on November 3, 1998, to a full six-year term.

Previous elected political office:
    U.S. House of Representatives, 1993–1997

Female U.S. Senatorial Statistics

Shortest Tenure of a Female U.S. Senator

Rebecca L. Felton, (D) Georgia, who served for only two days: January 21 and 22, 1922.

Longest Tenure of a Female U.S. Senator

Margaret C. Smith, (R) Maine, who served for twenty-four years: four full six-year terms, from January 3, 1949, until January 3, 1973.

First Vote Cast in U.S. Senate by a Female

Cast by **Hattie W. Caraway**, (D) Arkansas, in December 1931 on a minor procedural matter.

First State Represented by More Than One Female U.S. Senator

South Dakota
11/09/38–01/02/39	Gladys Pyle (R)
10/06/48–12/26/48	Vera C. Bushfield (R)

First State Represented by Three Elected Female U.S. Senators

Maine
01/03/49–01/03/73	Margaret C. Smith (R)
01/02/95–	Olympia J. Snowe (R)
01/07/97–	Susan M. Collins (R)

Other State Represented by Three Female U.S. Senators

Louisiana
01/31/36–01/02/37	Rose M. Long (D)
08/01/72–11/13/72	Elaine S. Edwards (D)
01/07/97–	Mary L. Landrieu (D)

Other States Represented by More Than One Female U.S. Senator

Alabama
08/20/37–01/10/38	Dixie B. Graves (D)
07/01/78–11/08/78	Maryon P. Allen (D)

Arkansas
11/13/31–01/02/45	Hattie W. Carraway (D)
01/04/99–	Blanche L. Lincoln (D)

California
11/16/92–	Dianne G. Feinstein (D)
01/05/93–	Barbara L. Boxer (D)

Kansas
11/08/78–01/06/97	Nancy L. Kassebaum (R)
06/11/96–11/27/96	Sheila S. Frahm (R)

Nebraska
04/26/54–11/07/54	Eva K. Bowring (R)
11/08/54–12/31/54	Hazel H. Abel (R)

First State Represented by Two Female U.S. Senators Concurrently

California
    11/16/92–   Dianne G. Feinstein (D)
    01/05/93–   Barbara L. Boxer (D)

In June 1996 Kansas became the second state to have two female U.S. senators sitting concurrently when Sheila S. Frahm (R), who had received an interim appointment, joined Nancy L. Kassebaum (R) in representing that state. Maine, with the November 1996 election, became the second state to be represented by two *elected* female U.S. senators.

First Female Senator to Preside over the U.S. Senate

Hattie W. Caraway, (D) Arkansas, on May 9, 1932.

First Female Senator to Chair a Standing Committee in the U.S. Senate

Hattie W. Caraway, (D) Arkansas, who chaired the U.S. Senate Committee on Enrolled Bills from the 73rd Congress to the 78th Congress (1933–1945).

Female U.S. Senators Who Have Served in Both Houses of Congress

Margaret C. Smith, (R) Maine
Barbara A. Mikulski, (D) Maryland
Barbara L. Boxer, (D) California
Olympia J. Snowe, (R) Maine
Blanche L. Lincoln, (D) Arkansas

First Race Where Both Major-Party Candidates Were Female

There have been only three races for U.S. senator in which the candidates of both major parties were female. The first was in Maine in 1960, when incumbent **Margaret C. Smith** (R), seeking her third term, was challenged by **Lucia Cormier** (D), a former minority leader of the state house of representatives. After paying her opponent one ladylike compliment early in the campaign, Senator Smith virtually ignored her thereafter and coasted to a 62–38 percent victory. After completing that term, Senator Smith won one more, then went down to defeat in 1972 when she sought a fifth six-year term.

The next all-female contest did not occur again until 1986, in Maryland. **Barbara A. Mikulski** (D), a five-term member of the U.S. House of Representatives, sought to move up to the Senate seat being vacated by Charles "Mac" Mathias (R). Her opponent, **Linda Chavez** (R), a Hispanic member of the Reagan White House staff who had only recently moved into the state, was hard-pressed to make a good showing against Mikulski. She staved off Chavez's challenge easily, winning the seat 61–39 percent.

Election year 1998 saw another all-female contest for a U.S. Senate seat, this time in Washington. The contenders were incumbent **Patty Murray** (D), seeking a second term, and challenger

Linda Smith (R), a two-term member of the U.S. House. Murray was the victor, winning the race by a margin of 58–42 percent.

First Succession of One Female U.S. Senator by Another

November 8, 1954, when **Hazel H. Abel**, (R) Nebraska, was sworn in to complete the time remaining (November 8, 1954–December 31, 1954) in the term of deceased Sen. Dwight Griswold (R), marked the first instance when one female senator replaced another. When Griswold died in office on April 12, 1954, Gov. Robert B. Crosby (R) appointed **Eva K. Bowring** (R) to serve in the interim until an election could be held in November.

Nebraska law required that two elections be held that November. One was for the balance of the interim appointment (until the next Congress convened on January 1, 1955); the other was for the balance remaining of Griswold's original full six-year term. Ms. Abel sought and won the short-term election. As soon as she was elected, Ms. Bowring resigned the seat to allow her colleague to be sworn in.

First Women Elected Whose Husbands Had Not Preceded Them in the U.S. Senate

Gladys Pyle, (R) South Dakota, who was elected in 1938 to complete (until January 2, 1939) the term of deceased Sen. Peter Norbeck (R), was the first woman elected to the U.S. Senate whose husband had not served there before her. At that time, South Dakota law required that two elections be held concurrently for a vacant U.S. Senate seat. One was for the balance of the interim appointment until the convening of the next Congress (January 2, 1939); the other was for a new full six-year term. Pyle did not contest the election for a full six-year term.

When **Margaret C. Smith**, (R) Maine, won her November 1948 election she became the first woman elected to a full six-year term whose husband had not preceded her in the U.S. Senate for a full six-year term. Before her Senate election, Smith had served eight years in the U.S. House of Representatives (serving since 1940), where she succeeded her husband, Clyde.

Female Senators Preceded by Their Husbands in the U.S. Senate

With one exception, each of these women received the "interim" appointment to succeed her deceased husband, thus holding his Senate seat until the next election.

Hattie W. Caraway, (D) Arkansas, was preceded by her husband, Thaddeus H. Caraway (D), who had served March 4, 1921–November 16, 1931. Although she served a total of some thirteen years, Caraway sat quietly knitting in the Senate chamber, rarely speaking. She once said, "I haven't the heart to take a minute from the men. The poor dears love it so."

Rose M. Long, (D) Louisiana, was preceded by her husband, Huey P. Long (D), who had served from January 25, 1932, until his assassination on September 10, 1935.

Maurine B. Neuberger, (D) Oregon, was preceded by her husband, Richard Neuberger (D), who had served January 3, 1955–March 9, 1960. When he died, she was not given the interim appointment for his seat, because it was made by a Republican governor. In November 1960 Neuberger defeated former Gov. Elmo Smith (R) for a full six-year term.

Muriel B. Humphrey, (D) Minnesota, was preceded by her husband, Hubert H. Humphrey (D), who had served January 3, 1949–December 29, 1964, and again January 3, 1971–November 25, 1977. In 1988, their son, Hubert H. Humphrey III, was the Democratic senatorial nominee, but his election bid failed.

Maryon P. Allen, (D) Alabama, was preceded by her husband, James B. Allen (D), who had served January 3, 1969–June 8, 1978.

Jocelyn B. Burdick, (D) North Dakota, was preceded by her husband, Quentin Burdick (D), who had served August 8, 1960–September 6, 1992.

Only Father, Mother, and Son Who Served as U.S. Senators

In 1948 Huey P. and Rose M. Long's son, Russell Long (D), was elected to the U.S. Senate, where he served May 13, 1948–January 5, 1987. Russell's election made Huey, Rose, and Russell the only father-mother-son trio ever to have been U.S. senators.

Women Who Tried to Succeed Their Husbands in the U.S. Senate but Failed

Doloris Bridges, (R) New Hampshire, in 1962. Ms. Bridges wanted the interim appointment when her husband, Styles Bridges (R), died early in 1962. Instead, it went to Maurice Murphy (R). She, along with several other candidates, opposed Murphy in the Republican primary that followed shortly for the nomination for the balance of the six-year term, which was won by U.S. Rep. Perkins Bass (R). The animosity resulting from that primary race, plus Bridges's refusal to support Bass, caused the Republican nominee to lose the November general election to a Democrat. Bridges tried again for the nomination in the 1966 Republican primary but met with another defeat.

Maryon P. Allen, (D) Alabama, in 1978. After having received the interim appointment in July 1978, Allen was forced to immediately file and run in the Democratic primary for the nomination for the balance remaining (two years) of the full six-year term. She was defeated in the primary runoff by a state senator, Donald Stewart; two years later Stewart lost his own bid for renomination to a full six-year term for the seat.

Female U.S. Senators Who Were Defeated

After having served at least one full six-year term, the following four women were defeated in their reelection bids. One defeat was in a primary, three in the general election.

Hattie W. Caraway, (D) Arkansas, was defeated in the 1944 Democratic primary by J. William Fulbright when she sought reelection to a third six-year term. She received only 13 percent of the vote, placing fourth among the candidates.

Margaret C. Smith, (R) Maine, was defeated (53–47 percent) by William Hathaway (D) in 1972 when she sought reelection to a fifth six-year term.

Paula F. Hawkins, (R) Florida, was defeated (55–45 percent) by her opponent, Gov. Robert "Bob" Graham (D), in 1986 when she sought reelection to a second six-year term.

Carol Moseley-Braun, (D) Illinois, was defeated (51–47 percent) by her opponent, Peter Fitzgerald (R), in 1998 when she sought reelection to a second six-year term.

First Women to Defeat a Male Incumbent Senator

Carol Moseley-Braun, (D) Illinois, won the distinction for defeating an elected male U.S. senator, with her May 1992 Democratic primary victory, when she unexpectedly upset one-term Sen. Alan J. Dixon.

Dianne G. Feinstein, (D) California, won the distinction for defeating an *appointed* male U.S. senator, with her victory over Sen. John Seymour (R) in the November 1992 election for the interim (until January 3, 1995) of former Sen. Pete Wilson's full six-year term. In a bizarre twist, Wilson himself had defeated Feinstein only two years earlier in their contest for California governor.

First Female U.S. Senator to Be Defeated in a General Election

Margaret C. Smith, (R) Maine, when she lost in November 1972, became the first female senator to be defeated in a general election. **Paula F. Hawkins**, (R) Florida, became the second female U.S. senator to suffer a loss, when she was defeated in the November 1986 general election.

First Female Former U.S. Senator to Marry Another Former U.S. Senator

Nancy L. Kassebaum, (R) Kansas, who married former U.S. Sen. Howard Baker, (R) Tennessee (January 3, 1967–January 2, 1985), in 1997 after she had left office.

Female U.S. Senatorial Election Statistics

The following section provides voting statistics on female senators who contested elections, including primaries, primary runoffs, and general elections. Since many female senators were appointed, they did not face elections for their seats. Names in this section appear in chronological order by senatorial service, from earliest to most recent.

Hattie Wyatt Caraway, (D) Arkansas

1944	Democratic Primary	J. William Fulbright	67,228	36.2%
		Homer Adkins	49,795	26.6%
		T. H. Barton	43,053	23.2%
		Hattie W. Caraway	24,881	13.4%
1938	General	Hattie W. Caraway (D)	183,795	89.5%
		C. D. Atkinson (R)	14,240	10.4%
1938	Democratic Primary	Hattie W. Caraway	145,472	51.0%
		John L. McClellan	134,708	47.3%
1932	General	Hattie W. Caraway (D)	183,795	89.5%
		John W. White (R)	21,597	10.5%
1932	Democratic Primary	Hattie W. Caraway	127,702	44.7%
		O. L. Bodenhammer	63,858	22.4%
		Vincent Miles	30,423	10.7%

		Two others	47,655	16.7%
1932	Special Election	Hattie W. Caraway (D)	31,133	91.6%
		Rex Floyd (I)	1,752	5.2%

Gladys Pyle, (R) South Dakota

1938	Special Election	Gladys Pyle (R)	155,292	58.1%
		John T. McCullum Sr. (D)	112,177	41.9%

Margaret Chase Smith, (R) Maine

1972	General	William D. Hathaway (D)	224,270	53.2%
		Margaret C. Smith (R)	197,040	46.8%
1966	General	Margaret C. Smith (R)	188,291	59.0%
		Elmer H. Violette (D)	131,136	41.1%
1960	General	Margaret C. Smith (R)	256,890	61.7%
		Lucia M. Cormier (D)	159,809	38.4%
1954	General	Margaret C. Smith (R)	144,530	58.6%
		Paul A. Fullam (D)	102,075	41.4%
1948	General	Margaret C. Smith (R)	159,182	71.3%
		Adrian H. Scolten (D)	64,074	28.7%

Hazel Hempel Abel, (R) Nebraska

1954	Special Election	Hazel H. Abel (R)	233,589	57.8%
		William H. Meier (D)	170,828	40.2%

Maurine Brown Neuberger, (D) Oregon

1960	General	Maurine B. Neuberger (D)	412,757	55.0%
		Elmo Smith (R)	343,009	45.0%
1960	Special Election	Maurine B. Neuberger (D)	422,024	55.0%
		Elmo Smith (R)	345,464	45.0%

Maryon Pittman Allen, (D) Alabama

1978	Primary Runoff	Donald Stewart	502,346	57.0%
		Maryon P. Allen	375,894	43.0%
1978	Democratic Primary	Maryon P. Allen	334,758	45.0%
		Donald Stewart	259,795	35.0%

Nancy Landon Kassebaum, (R) Kansas

1990	General	Nancy L. Kassebaum (R)	578,605	74.0%
		Dick Williams (D)	207,491	26.0%
1990	Republican Primary	Nancy L. Kassebaum	267,946	87.0%
		R. Gregory Walstrom	39,379	13.0%
1984	General	Nancy L. Kassebaum (R)	757,402	76.0%
		James Maher (D)	211,664	21.0%
1978	General	Nancy L. Kassebaum (R)	403,354	56.0%
		William "Bill" Roy (D)	317,602	44.0%

1978	Republican Primary	Nancy L. Kassebaum	67,324	31.0%
		Wayne Angell	54,161	25.0%
		Sam Hardage	30,248	14.0%
		Two others	68,309	32.0%

Paula Fickes Hawkins, (R) Florida

1986	General	Robert "Bob" Graham (D)	1,877,231	55.0%
		Paula F. Hawkins (R)	1,551,888	45.0%
1980	General	Paula F. Hawkins (R)	1,822,460	52.0%
		Bill Gunter (D)	1,705,409	48.0%
1980	Primary Runoff	Paula F. Hawkins	293,600	62.0%
		Lou Frey Jr.	182,911	38.0%
1980	Republican Primary	Paula F. Hawkins	209,856	48.0%
		Lou Frey Jr.	119,834	27.0%
		Andy Crenshaw	54,767	13.0%
1974	Republican Primary	Jack Eckard	175,000	56.8%
		Paula F. Hawkins	150,000	43.2%

Barbara Ann Mikulski, (D) Maryland

1998	General	Barbara A. Mikulski (D)	1,034,814	71.0%
		Ross Pierpont (R)	426,499	29.0%
1998	Democratic Primary	Barbara A. Mikulski	326,157	84.0%
		Ann Mallory	41,020	11.0%
		Kauko Kokkonen	20,750	5.0%
1992	General	Barbara A. Mikulski (D)	1,307,610	71.0%
		Alan L. Keyes (R)	533,688	29.0%
1992	Democratic Primary	Barbara A. Mikulski	376,444	77.0%
		Five others	119,253	23.0%
1986	General	Barbara A. Mikulski (D)	675,225	61.0%
		Linda Chavez (R)	437,411	39.0%
1986	Democratic Primary	Barbara A. Mikulski	307,876	50.0%
		Michael Barnes	195,086	31.0%
		Harry Hughes	88,908	14.0%
1974	General	Charles "Mac" Mathias (R)	503,223	57.0%
		Barbara A. Mikulski (D)	374,563	43.0%

Dianne Goldman Feinstein, (D) California

1994	General	Dianne G. Feinstein (D)	3,976,885	46.8%
		Michael Huffington (R)	3,811,232	44.9%
1992	General	Dianne G. Feinstein (D)	5,853,621	54.0%
		John Seymour (R)	4,093,488	38.0%
		Five others	832,531	8.0%
1992	Democratic Primary	Dianne G. Feinstein	1,775,730	58.0%
		Gray Davis	1,009,761	33.0%
		Two others	289,328	9.0%

Barbara Levy Boxer, (D) California

1998	General	Barbara L. Boxer (D)	3,910,987	53.0%
		Matt K. Fong (R)	3,154,036	43.0%
		Others		4.0%
1998	Primary	Barbara L. Boxer (D)	2,328,749	44.0%
		Matt K. Fong (R)	1,163,685	22.0%
		Darrell Issa (R)	1,031,000	19.0%
		Frank Riggs (R)	267,209	5.0%
		John Pinkerton (D)	201,044	4.0%
		Others		6.0%
1992	General	Barbara L. Boxer (D)	5,173,443	48.0%
		Bruce Herschensohn (R)	4,644,139	43.0%
1992	Democratic Primary	Barbara L. Boxer	1,339,126	44.0%
		Leo McCarthy	935,209	31.0%
		Mel Levine	667,359	22.0%

Carol Moseley-Braun, (D) Illinois

1998	General	Peter Fitzgerald (R)	1,691,994	51.0%
		Carol Moseley-Braun (D)	1,565,265	47.0%
		Dan Torgersen (Reform)	85,527	2.0%
1998	Democratic Primary	Carol Moseley-Bruan	unopposed	
1992	General	Carol Moseley-Braun (D)	2,631,229	53.0%
		Richard S. Williamson (R)	2,126,833	43.0%
1992	Democratic Primary	Carol Moseley-Braun	557,694	38.0%
		Alan J. Dixon	504,077	35.0%
		Albert F. Hofeld	394,497	27.0%

Patricia Johns Murray, (D) Washington

1998	General	Patricia J. Murray (D)	807,499	58.0%
		Linda Smith (R)	576,674	42.0%
1998	General Primary[5]	Patricia J. Murray (D)	331,463	46.25%
		Linda Smith (R)	229,837	32.07%
		Chris Bayley (R)	104,257	14.55%
		Others		7.13%
1992	General	Patricia J. Murray (D)	1,197,973	54.0%
		Rod Chandler (R)	1,020,829	46.0%
1992	General Primary	Patricia J. Murray (D)	318,455	28.0%
		Rod Chandler (R)	228,083	20.0%
		Don Bonker (D)	208,321	19.0%
		Leo K. Thorsness (R)	185,498	16.0%

---

[5]Washington law requires all candidates to compete in a single ("jungle") primary ballot, regardless of party affiliation. If no candidate wins a majority, the two highest vote winners from different parties meet as candidates in the November general election.

| | | Tim Hill (R) | 128,232 | 11.0% |
| | | Six others | 56,042 | 5.0% |

Kay Bailey Hutchison, (R) Texas

1994	General	Kay B. Hutchison (R)	2,604,218	61.0%
		Richard Fisher (D)	1,639,615	38.0%
1994	Republican Primary	Kay B. Hutchison	467,975	84.0%
		Stephen Hopkins	34,703	6.0%
		Others	52,660	9.0%
1993	Special Runoff	Kay B. Hutchison (R)	1,188,716	67.0%
		Bob Kreuger (D)	576,538	33.0%
1993	Special[6]	Kay B. Hutchison (R)	593,479	29.0%
		Bob Krueger (D)	592,982	29.0%
		Joe L. Barton (R)	284,135	14.0%
		Jack M. Fields (R)	277,560	14.0%
		Richard Fisher (D)	165,564	8.0%
		Nineteen others	131,923	6.0%

Olympia Jean Snowe, (R) Maine

| 1994 | General | Olympia J. Snowe (R) | 308,244 | 60.0% |
| | | Thomas Andrews (D) | 186,042 | 40.0% |

Susan Margaret Collins, (R) Maine

1996	General	Susan M. Collins (R)	298,422	49.0%
		Joseph Brennan (D)	266,226	44.0%
		Others	42,129	7.0%
1996	Republican Primary	Susan M. Collins	53,339	55.5%
		W. John Hathaway	29,792	31.0%
		Robert Monks	12,943	13.5%

Mary Loretta Landrieu, (D) Louisiana

1996	General	Mary L. Landrieu (D)	852,925	50.1%
		Woody Jenkins (R)	847,157	49.9%
1996	Primary[7]	Woody Jenkins (R)	322,244	26.0%
		Mary L. Landrieu (D)	264,268	22.0%
		Richard Ieyoub (D)	250,682	20.0%
		David Duke (R)	141,489	12.0%
		Jimmy Hayes (R)	71,699	6.0%
		Bill Linder (R)	58,243	5.0%
		Others	119,934	10.0%

[6]For special elections Texas law requires all candidates to compete on a single ("jungle") primary ballot, regardless of party affiliation. If no candidate wins a majority, the two highest vote winners, regardless of party affiliation, meet as candidates in a runoff.

[7]In Louisiana all candidates, regardless of party affiliation, are listed on one ballot. If no candidate wins a majority, the two highest vote winners, regardless of party affiliation, meet as candidates in the general election.

Blanche Lambert Lincoln, (D) Arkansas

1998	General	Blanche L. Lincoln (D)	386,822	55.0%
		Fay Boozman (R)	294,139	42.0%
		Charley Heffley (Reform)	18,919	3.0%
1998	Special Runoff	Blanche L. Lincoln	135,612	63.0%
		Winston Bryant	79,599	37.0%
1998	Democratic Primary	Blanche L. Lincoln	144,849	45.0%
		Winston Bryant	87,038	27.0%
		Scott Ferguson	44,768	14.0%
		Nate Coulter	41,802	13.0%
		Others		1.0%

Chronology of Major Female Candidates for U.S. Senate
(denotes winner)*

1893	Mary Elizabeth Lease	Populist	Kansas
1918	Martha E. Bean	Socialist	Oregon
	Anne H. Martin	Independent	Nevada
	Jeannette Rankin[8]	Independent	Montana
1920	Josephine Bennett	National Farmer-Labor	Connecticut
	Leah Cobb Marion	Progressive	Pennsylvania
	Anne H. Martin	Independent	Nevada
	Ella A. Poole	Progressive	New York
	Rose Schneiderman	Labor	New York
1922	Jessie Jack Hooper	Democrat	Wisconsin
	Anna Dickie Oleson	Democrat	Minnesota
	Rachel Robinson	Progressive	Pennsylvania
1930	Ruth Hanna McCormick[9]	Republican	Illinois
	Thelma Parkinson	Democrat	New Jersey
1931	*Hattie W. Caraway	Democrat	Arkansas
1932	*Hattie W. Caraway	Democrat	Arkansas
1938	*Hattie W. Caraway	Democrat	Arkansas
	*Gladys Pyle	Republican	South Dakota
1940	Ona S. Searles	Democrat	Vermont
1948	*Margaret C. Smith[10]	Republican	Maine
1950	Helen Gahagan Douglas[11]	Democrat	California
1954	*Hazel H. Abel	Republican	Nebraska
	*Margaret C. Smith	Republican	Maine

---

[8]Jeannette Rankin was the first woman elected to the U.S. House, where she served one term (1917–1919) as a Republican. Years later, she was reelected to the House for another single term (1941–1943).

[9]McCormick had previously served one term (1929–1931) in the U.S. House.

[10]Smith had previously served four terms (1941–1949) in the U.S. House.

[11]Douglas had previously served three (1945–1951) terms in the U.S. House.

1958	Hazel Palmer	Republican	Missouri
	Louise O. Wenzel	Independent	Virginia
1960	Lucia Cormier	Democrat	Maine
	*Maurine B. Neuberger	Democrat	Oregon
	*Margaret C. Smith	Republican	Maine
1962	Gracie Pfost[12]	Democrat	Idaho
1964	Genevieve Blatt	Democrat	Pennsylvania
	Elly Peterson	Republican	Michigan
1966	Ruth Briggs	Republican	Rhode Island
	*Margaret C. Smith	Republican	Maine
1968	Katherine Peden	Democrat	Kentucky
1970	Lenore Romney	Republican	Michigan
1972	Louise Leonard	Republican	West Virginia
	Margaret C. Smith	Republican	Maine
1974	Gwenyfred Bush	Republican	South Carolina
	Barbara Keating	Conservative	New York
	Barbara A. Mikulski	Democrat	Maryland
	Barbara H. Roberts[13]	Democrat	Oregon
1976	Gloria Schaffer	Democrat	Connecticut
1978	Jane Eskind	Democrat	Tennessee
	*Nancy L. Kassebaum	Republican	Kansas
1980	Mary Estill Buchanan	Republican	Colorado
	Mary Louise Foust	Republican	Kentucky
	Mary Gojack	Democrat	Nevada
	*Paula F. Hawkins	Republican	Florida
	Elizabeth Holtzman[14]	Democrat	New York
1982	Millicent Fenwick[15]	Republican	New Jersey
	Florence Sullivan	Republican	New York
	Harriet Woods	Democrat	Missouri
1984	Nancy Dick	Democrat	Colorado
	Joan Growe	Democrat	Minnesota
	Edyth C. Harrison	Democrat	Virginia
	Margie Hendriksen	Democrat	Oregon
	Nancy Hoch	Republican	Nebraska
	*Nancy L. Kassebaum	Republican	Kansas
	Barbara Leonard	Democrat	Rhode Island
	Elizabeth Mitchell	Democrat	Maine
	Mary Mochary	Republican	New Jersey

[12]Pfost had previously served five terms (1953–1963) in the U.S. House.

[13]Roberts was elected governor of Oregon in 1990 and held that office 1991–1995.

[14]Holtzman had previously served four terms (1973–1981) in the U.S. House.

[15]Fenwick had previously served four terms (1975–1983) in the U.S. House.

	Judy Pratt	Democrat	New Mexico
1986	Linda Chavez	Republican	Maryland
	Paula F. Hawkins	Republican	Florida
	Judy Koehler	Republican	Illinois
	Jill Long[16]	Democrat	Indiana
	*Barbara A. Mikulski[17]	Democrat	Maryland
	Harriet Woods	Democrat	Missouri
1988	Susan Engeleiter	Republican	Wisconsin
	Maria Hustace	Republican	Hawaii
1990	M. Jane Brady	Republican	Delaware
	Josie Heath	Democrat	Colorado
	Kathy Helling	Democrat	Wyoming
	Lynn Martin[18]	Republican	Illinois
	Patricia F. Saiki[19]	Republican	Hawaii
	Claudine Schneider[20]	Republican	Rhode Island
	Christine T. Whitman[21]	Republican	New Jersey
1992	*Barbara L. Boxer[22]	Democrat	California
	*Dianne G. Feinstein[23]	Democrat	California
	Charlene Haas	Republican	South Dakota
	Jean Lloyd-Jones	Democrat	Iowa
	*Barbara A. Mikulski	Democrat	Maryland
	*Carol Moseley-Braun	Democrat	Illinois
	*Patricia J. Murray	Democrat	Washington
	Gloria O'Dell	Democrat	Kansas
	Geri Rothman-Serot	Democrat	Missouri
	Claire Sargent	Democrat	Arizona
	Lynn Yeakel	Democrat	Pennsylvania
1993	*Kay B. Hutchison	Republican	Texas
1994	Jan Bachus	Democrat	Vermont
	Bernadette Castro	Republican	New York
	*Dianne Feinstein	Democrat	California
	Maria Hustace	Republican	Hawaii
	*Kay B. Hutchison	Republican	Texas

---

[16]Long was later elected to the U.S. House and served three terms (1989–1995).

[17]Mikulski had previously served five terms (1977–1987) in the U.S. House.

[18]Martin had previously served five terms (1981–1991) in the U.S. House.

[19]Saiki had previously served two terms (1987–1991) in the U.S. House. Unsuccessful in the 1994 election as Republican nominee for governor.

[20]Schneider had previously served five terms (1981–1991) in the U.S. House.

[21]Whitman was elected governor in 1993.

[22]Boxer had previously served five terms (1983–1993) in the U.S. House.

[23]Feinstein was unsuccessful in 1990 as Democratic nominee for governor.

	Linda Kushner	Democrat	Rhode Island
	*Olympia J. Snowe[24]	Republican	Maine
	Jan Stoney	Republican	Nebraska
	Ann Wynia	Democrat	Minnesota
1996	Betty Burks	Republican	West Virginia
	*Susan M. Collins[25]	Republican	Maine
	Jill Docking	Democrat	Kansas
	Kathy Karpan [26]	Democrat	Wyoming
	*Mary L. Landrieu	Democrat	Louisiana
	Nancy J. Mayer	Republican	Rhode Island
	Theresa Obermeyer	Democrat	Alaska
	Ronna Romney	Republican	Michigan
	Rebecca "Becky" Shaw	Reform	Montana
	Sally Thompson	Democrat	Kansas
1998	*Barbara Boxer	Democrat	California
	Mary Boyle	Democrat	Ohio
	*Blanche Lambert-Lincoln[27]	Democrat	Arkansas
	Dottie Lamm	Democrat	Colorado
	*Barbara Mikulski	Democrat	Maryland
	Carol Moseley-Braun	Democrat	Illinois
	*Patty Murray	Democrat	Washington
	Donna Nalewja	Republican	North Dakota
	Linda Smith[28]	Republican	Washington
	Crystal Young	Republican	Hawaii

Women and Their Seniority in the U.S. Senate

Compiling a combined seniority roster for the U.S. Senate is difficult for three reasons. First, Democrats and Republicans use slightly different methods in calculating seniority for members of their respective parties. Second, by tradition the seniority roster for the majority party takes precedence. The third factor is that custom decrees that when new members are sworn in on the same day, those with prior political experience are ranked higher. Counted as political experience, in order of importance: previous senatorial service, service as vice president, service in the U.S. House, service in a presidential cabinet, a gubernatorial term, and the size of the home state's population. After all that is taken into consideration, final ranking may need to be alphabetical by last name.

---

[24]Snowe had previously served six terms (1983–1995) in the U.S. House.

[25]Collins was unsuccessful in 1994 as the Republican nominee for governor.

[26]Karpan was unsuccessful in 1994 as the Democratic nominee for governor.

[27]Lambert-Lincoln had previously served two terms (1993–1997) in the U.S. House.

[28]Smith had previously served two terms (1995–1999) in the U.S. House.

In the list below, the names of female senators are ***bold italic*** for greater emphasis.

1	11/07/56	Thurmond, Strom (R) South Carolina
2	01/03/59	Byrd, Robert (D) West Virginia
3	11/07/62	Kennedy, Edward (D) Massachusetts
4	01/03/63	Inouye, Daniel (D) Hawaii
5	11/09/66	Hollings, Ernest (D) South Carolina
6	12/24/68	Stevens, Ted (R) Alaska
7	01/01/71	Roth, William (R) Delaware
8	01/03/73	Biden, Joseph (D) Delaware
9	01/03/73	Domenici, Peter (R) New Mexico
10	01/03/73	Helms, Jesse (R) North Carolina
11	01/03/75	Leahy, Patrick (D) Vermont
12	12/29/76	Chafee, John (R) Rhode Island
13	01/03/77	Hatch, Orrin (R) Utah
14	01/03/77	Lugar, Richard (R) Indiana
15	01/04/77	Sarbanes, Paul (D) Maryland, ex-Representative, 3 terms
16	01/04/77	Moynihan, Daniel (D) New York
17	12/15/78	Baucus, Max (D) Montana
18	12/27/78	Cochran, Thad (R) Mississippi
19	01/02/79	Warner, John (R) Virginia
20	01/15/79	Levin, Sander (D) Michigan
21	01/05/81	Grassley, Charles (R) Iowa, ex-Representative, 3 terms
22	01/05/81	Murkowski, Frank (R) Alaska
23	01/05/81	Nickles, Don (R) Oklahoma
24	01/05/81	Specter, Arlen (R) Pennsylvania
25	01/15/81	Dodd, Christopher (D) Connecticut
26	12/27/82	Lautenberg, Frank (D) New Jersey
27	01/03/83	Bingaman, Jeff (D) New Mexico
28	01/02/85	Kerry, John (D) Massachusetts
29	01/03/85	Harkin, Tom (D) Iowa, ex-Representative, 5 terms
30	01/03/85	Gramm, Phil (R) Texas, ex-Representative, 2 terms
31	01/03/85	McConnell, Mitch (R) Kentucky
32	01/15/85	Rockefeller, John J. (D) West Virginia
33	01/03/87	***Mikulski, Barbara A. (D) Maryland***
34	01/06/87	Breaux, John (D) Louisiana, ex-Representative, 8 terms
35	01/06/87	Daschle, Tom (D) South Dakota, ex-Representative, 4 terms
36	01/06/87	Shelby, Richard (R) Alabama, ex-Representative, 4 terms
37	01/06/87	McCain, John (R) Arizona, ex-Representative, 2 terms
38	01/06/87	Reid, Harry (D) Nevada, ex-Representative, 2 terms
39	01/06/87	Bond, Christopher (R) Missouri, ex-Governor
40	01/06/87	Graham, Robert (D) Florida, ex-Governor
41	01/06/87	Conrad, Kent (D) North Dakota
42	01/03/89	Gorton, Slade (R) Washington, ex-Senator, also served 1981–87
43	01/03/89	Lott, Trent (R) Mississippi, ex-Representative, 8 terms

44	01/03/89	Jeffords, James (R) Vermont, ex-Representative, 7 terms
45	01/03/89	Mack, Connie (R) Florida, ex-Representative, 3 terms
46	01/03/89	Bryan, Richard (D) Nevada, ex-Governor
47	01/03/89	Kerrey, Robert (D) Nebraska, ex-Governor
48	01/03/89	Robb, Charles (D) Virginia, ex-Governor
49	01/03/89	Burns, Conrad (R) Montana
50	01/03/89	Kohl, Herbert (D) Wisconsin
51	01/03/89	Lieberman, Joseph (D) Connecticut
52	04/28/90	Akaka, Daniel (D) Hawaii
53	12/07/90	Smith, Robert C. (R) New Hampshire
54	01/03/91	Craig, Larry (R) Idaho, ex-Representative, 5 terms
55	01/03/91	Wellstone, Paul (D) Minnesota
56	11/10/92	*Feinstein, Dianne G. (D) California*
57	12/15/92	Dorgan, Bryan (D) North Dakota, ex-Representative, 6 terms
58	01/05/93	*Boxer, Barbara L. (D) California, ex-Representative, 5 terms*
59	01/05/93	Gregg, Judd (R) New Hampshire, ex-Representative, 4 terms
60	01/05/93	Campbell, Ben Nighthorse (R) Colorado, ex-Representative, 3 terms
61	01/05/93	Bennett, Robert F. (R) Utah
62	01/05/93	Coverdell, Paul (R) Georgia
63	01/05/93	Feingold, Russell (D) Wisconsin
64	01/05/93	*Murray, Patricia J. (D) Washington*
65	06/06/93	*Hutchison, Kay B. (R) Texas*
66	11/17/94	Inhofe, James (R) Oklahoma
67	12/02/94	Thompson, Fred (R) Tennessee
68	01/04/95	*Snowe, Olympia J. (R) Maine, ex-Representative, 6 terms*
69	01/04/95	DeWine, Michael (R) Ohio, ex-Representative, 4 terms
70	01/04/95	Kyl, John (R) Arizona, ex-Representative, 4 terms
71	01/04/95	Thomas, Craig (R) Wyoming, ex-Representative, 3 terms
72	01/04/95	Santorum, Rick (R) Pennsylvania, ex-Representative, 2 terms
73	01/04/95	Grams, Ron (R) Minnesota, ex-Representative, 1 term
74	01/04/95	Ashcroft, John (R) Missouri, ex-Governor
75	01/04/95	Abraham, Spencer (R) Michigan
76	01/04/95	Frist, Bill (R) Tennessee
77	02/05/96	Wyden, Ron (D) Oregon
78	11/27/96	Brownback, Sam (R) Kansas
79	01/07/97	Roberts, Pat (R) Kansas, ex-Representative, 8 terms
80	01/07/97	Durbin, Richard (D) Illinois, ex-Representative, 7 terms
81	01/07/97	Toricelli, Bob (D) New Jersey, ex-Representative, 7 terms
82	01/07/97	Johnson, Tim (D) South Dakota, ex-Representative, 5 terms
83	01/07/97	Allard, Wayne (R) Colorado, ex-Representative, 3 terms
84	01/07/97	Reed, Jack (D) Rhode Island, ex-Representative, 3 terms
85	01/07/97	Hutchinson, Tim (R) Arkansas, ex-Representative, 2 terms
86	01/07/97	Cleland, Max (D) Georgia

87	01/07/97	*Collins, Susan M. (R) Maine*
88	01/07/97	Enzi, Mike (R) Wyoming
89	01/07/97	Hagel, Chuck (R) Nebraska
90	01/07/97	*Landrieu, Mary L. (D) Louisiana*
91	01/07/97	Sessions, Jeff (R) Alabama
92	01/07/97	Smith, Gordon (R) Oregon
93	01/04/99	Schumer, Charles (D) New York, ex-Representative, 9 terms
94	01/04/99	Bunning, Jim (R) Kentucky, ex-Representative, 6 terms
95	01/04/99	Crapo, Mike (R) Idaho, ex-Representative, 3 terms
96	01/04/99	*Lincoln, Blanche L. (D) Arkansas, ex-Representative, 2 terms*
97	01/04/99	Bayh, Evan (D) Indiana, ex-Governor
98	01/04/99	Voinovich, George (R) Ohio, ex-Governor
99	01/04/99	Fitzgerald, Peter (R) Illinois
100	01/04/99	Edwards, John (D) North Carolina

Women Serving in the U.S. House of Representatives

106th Congress (1999–2001)

State	District	Name	Party Affiliation
California	6	Lynn Woolsey	Democrat
California	9	Barbara Lee	Democrat
California	8	Nancy Pelosi	Democrat
California	10	Ellen Tauscher	Democrat
California	14	Anna G. Eshoo	Democrat
California	16	Zoe Lofgren	Democrat
California	22	Lois Capps	Democrat
California	33	Lucille Roybal-Allard	Democrat
California	34	Grace Napolitano	Democrat
California	35	Maxine Waters	Democrat
California	37	Juanita Millender-McDonald	Democrat
California	44	Mary Bono	Republican
California	46	Loretta Sanchez (Brixley)	Democrat
Colorado	1	Diana Degette	Democrat
Connecticut	3	Rosa L. De Lauro	Democrat
Connecticut	6	Nancy L. Johnson	Republican
Florida	3	Corrine Brown	Democrat
Florida	4	Tillie Fowler	Republican
Florida	5	Karen L. Thurman	Democrat
Florida	17	Carrie Meek	Democrat
Florida	18	Ileana Ros-Lehtinen	Republican
Georgia	4	Cynthia McKinney	Democrat
Hawaii	2	Patsy Takemoto Mink	Democrat

Idaho	1	Helen Chenoweth	Republican
Illinois	9	Janice Schakowsky	Democrat
Illinois	13	Judy Biggert	Republican
Indiana	10	Julia Carson	Democrat
Kentucky	3	Anne Northup	Republican
Maryland	8	Constance A. Morella	Republican
Michigan	8	Debbie Stabenow	Democrat
Michigan	13	Lynn Rivers	Democrat
Michigan	15	Carolyn C. Kilpatrick	Democrat
Missouri	5	Karen McCarthy	Democrat
Missouri	6	Patsy Ann Danner	Democrat
Missouri	8	Jo Ann Emerson	Republican
Nevada	1	Shelley Berkley	Democrat
New Jersey	5	Marge Roukema	Republican
New Mexico	1	Heather Wilson	Republican
New York	4	Carolyn McCarthy	Democrat
New York	12	Nydia M. Velazquez	Democrat
New York	14	Carolyn B. Maloney	Democrat
New York	18	Nita M. Lowey	Democrat
New York	19	Sue W. Kelly	Republican
New York	28	Louise M. Slaughter	Democrat
North Carolina	1	Eva Clayton	Democrat
North Carolina	9	Sue Myrick	Republican
Ohio	9	Marcy Kaptur	Democrat
Ohio	11	Stephanie Tubbs-Jones	Democrat
Ohio	15	Deborah Pryce	Republican
Oregon	5	Darlene Hooley	Democrat
Texas	12	Kay Granger	Republican
Texas	18	Sheila Jackson-Lee	Democrat
Texas	30	Eddie Bernice Johnson	Democrat
Washington	8	Jennifer Dunn	Republican
Wisconsin	2	Tammy Baldwin	Democrat
Wyoming	AL	Barbara Cubin	Republican

Total Women Serving
56 (39 Democrats, 17 Republicans)

Best Representation by State

| Wyoming | 100% (1 of 1) |
| Hawaii | 50.0% (1 of 2) |

| Idaho | 50.0% (1 of 2) |
| Nevada | 50.0% (1 of 2) |

Minority Representation

12 African Americans

California	9	Barbara Lee	Democrat
California	35	Maxine Waters	Democrat
California	37	Juanita Millender-McDonald	Democrat
Florida	3	Corrine Brown	Democrat
Florida	17	Carrie Meek	Democrat
Georgia	4	Cynthia McKinney	Democrat
Indiana	10	Julia Carson	Democrat
Michigan	15	Carolyn C. Kilkpatrick	Democrat
North Carolina	1	Eva Clayton	Democrat
Ohio	11	Stephanie Tubbs-Jones	Democrat
Texas	18	Sheila Jackson-Lee	Democrat
Texas	30	Eddie Bernice Johnson	Democrat

5 Hispanics

California	33	Lucille Roybal-Allard	Democrat
California	34	Grace Napolitano	Democrat
California	46	Loretta Sanchez (Brixley)	Democrat
Florida	18	Ileana Ros-Lehtinen	Republican
New York	12	Nydia M. Velazquez	Democrat

1 Asian American

Hawaii	2	Patsy Takemoto Mink	Democrat

Senior Female Member

The senior member of all the women elected in November 1998 is **Marge Roukema**, (R) New Jersey–7th, who was first elected in 1980 and is now serving her tenth term.

Achieving Power

No women hold committee chairs in the 106th Congress.

Losing Female Candidates

In addition to the women elected to the 106th Congress, the two major political parties fielded a total of 119 female candidates. The Democrats had thirty-five who failed in their bid to be elected, and the Republicans had twenty-eight.

One of the more interesting losing challengers was **Marjorie McKeithen,** (D) Louisiana, grand-daughter of former governor John McKeithen and daughter of the Louisiana's current secretary of state, a Republican.

Notable First

Wisconsin elects its first woman to the U.S. House, leaving only eight states (Alaska, Delaware, Iowa, Mississippi, New Hampshire, North Dakota, South Dakota, and Vermont) that have never had female representation in that body.

Female Incumbents Not Returning from the 105th Congress

Four female incumbents did not seek reelection, with three choosing instead to run for other offices:

Jane Harman, (D) California–36th, lost her bid for the Democratic gubernatorial nomination.
Barbara Bailey Kennelly, (D) Connecticut–1st, lost her race as the Democratic nominee for governor.
Linda Smith, (R) Washington–3rd, lost her race as Republican nominee for U.S. Senate.

One decided to retire and not seek reelection:

Elizabeth Furse, (D) Oregon–1st

105th Congress (1997–1999)

State	District	Name	Party Affiliation
California	6	Lynn Woolsey	Democrat
California	8	Nancy Pelosi	Democrat
California	9	Barbara Lee[29]	Democrat
California	10	Ellen Tauscher	Democrat
California	14	Anna G. Eshoo	Democrat
California	16	Zoe Lofgren	Democrat
California	22	Lois Capps[30]	Democrat
California	33	Lucille Roybal-Allard	Democrat
California	35	Maxine Waters	Democrat
California	36	Jane Harman	Democrat
California	37	Juanita Millender-McDonald	Democrat
California	44	Mary Bono[31]	Republican
California	46	Loretta Sanchez (Brixley)	Democrat
Colorado	1	Diana Degette	Democrat
Connecticut	1	Barbara Bailey Kennelly	Democrat
Connecticut	3	Rosa L. De Lauro	Democrat

[29]Lee was elected in a special April 7, 1998, election to replace Ronald Dellums, who had resigned.

[30]Capps was elected in a special March 10, 1998, election to replace her husband, Walter, who died in October 1997.

[31]Bono was elected in a special April 7, 1998, election to replace her husband, Sonny, who died on January 5, 1998.

Connecticut	6	Nancy L. Johnson	Republican
Florida	3	Corrine Brown	Democrat
Florida	4	Tillie Fowler	Republican
Florida	5	Karen L. Thurman	Democrat
Florida	17	Carrie Meek	Democrat
Florida	18	Ileana Ros-Lehtinen	Republican
Georgia	4	Cynthia McKinney	Democrat
Hawaii	2	Patsy Takemoto Mink	Democrat
Idaho	1	Helen Chenoweth	Republican
Indiana	10	Julia Carson	Democrat
Kentucky	3	Anne Northup	Republican
Maryland	8	Constance A. Morella	Republican
Michigan	8	Debbie Stabenow	Democrat
Michigan	13	Lynn Rivers	Democrat
Michigan	15	Carolyn C. Kilpatrick	Democrat
Missouri	5	Karen McCarthy	Democrat
Missouri	6	Patsy Ann Danner	Democrat
Missouri	8	Jo Ann Emerson	Republican[32]
New Jersey	5	Marge Roukema	Republican
New Mexico	1	Heather Wilson[33]	Republican
New York	4	Carolyn McCarthy	Democrat
New York	12	Nydia M. Velazquez	Democrat
New York	13	Susan Molinari[34]	Republican
New York	14	Carolyn B. Maloney	Democrat
New York	18	Nita M. Lowey	Democrat
New York	19	Sue W. Kelly	Republican
New York	28	Louise M. Slaughter	Democrat
North Carolina	1	Eva Clayton	Democrat
North Carolina	9	Sue Myrick	Republican
Ohio	9	Marcy Kaptur	Democrat
Ohio	15	Deborah Pryce	Republican
Oregon	1	Elizabeth Furse	Democrat
Oregon	5	Darlene Hooley	Democrat
Texas	12	Kay Granger	Republican
Texas	18	Sheila Jackson-Lee	Democrat
Texas	30	Eddie Bernice Johnson	Democrat
Washington	3	Linda Smith	Republican

---

[32]Emerson, the widow of 8th District Rep. William Emerson, filed and won as an Independent because her husband died after the filing date for the Republican nomination had closed.

[33]Wilson was elected in a special June 23, 1998, election to replace Steven Schriff, who died March 24, 1998.

[34]Molinari resigned her seat on August 1, 1997.

| Washington | 8 | Jennifer Dunn | Republican |
| Wyoming | AL | Barbara Cubin | Republican |

Total Women Serving

55 (37 Democrats, 18 Republicans)

Best Representation by State

Wyoming	100% (1 of 1)
Connecticut	50.0% (3 of 6)
Hawaii	50.0% (1 of 2)
Idaho	50.0% (1 of 2)

Minority Representation

11 African Americans

California	9	Barbara Lee	Democrat
California	35	Maxine Waters	Democrat
California	37	Juanita Millender-McDonald	Democrat
Florida	3	Corrine Brown	Democrat
Florida	17	Carrie Meek	Democrat
Georgia	4	Cynthia McKinney	Democrat
Indiana	10	Julia Carson	Democrat
Michigan	15	Carolyn C. Kilpatrick	Democrat
North Carolina	1	Eva Clayton	Democrat
Texas	18	Sheila Jackson-Lee	Democrat
Texas	30	Eddie Bernice Johnson	Democrat

4 Hispanics

California	33	Lucille Roybal-Allard	Democrat
California	46	Loretta Sanchez (Brixley)	Democrat
Florida	18	Ileana Ros-Lehtinen	Republican
New York	12	Nydia M. Velazquez	Democrat

1 Asian American

| Hawaii | 2 | Patsy Takemoto Mink | Democrat |

Senior Female Member

The senior member of all the women elected in November 1996 is **Marge Roukema**, (R) New Jersey–7th, who was first elected in 1980 and is now serving her ninth term.

Achieving Power

No women held committee chairs in the 105th Congress.

Losing Female Candidates

In addition to the women elected to the 105th Congress, the two major political parties fielded a total of 120 female candidates. The Democrats had forty-seven who failed in their bid to be elected, and the Republicans had thirty.

One of the more interesting losing challengers was **Georgianna Lincoln**, (D) Alaska, a native Alaskan minority (Athabascan), who sought that state's at-large House seat. She was only the second Native American woman to receive a major party's congressional nomination.

Female Incumbents Not Returning from the 104th Congress

Six female incumbents retired and did not seek reelection:

Cardiss Collins, (D) Illinois–7th
Blanche Lambert-Lincoln, (D) Arkansas–1st
Jan Meyers, (R) Kansas–3rd
Patricia Schroeder, (D) Colorado–1st
Barbara Vucanovich, (R) Nevada–1st
Enid Waldholtz, (R) Utah–2nd

One was defeated in the Democratic primary in her district:

Barbara-Rose Collins, Michigan–15th

One was defeated in the general election:

Andrea Seastrand, (R) California–22nd

104th Congress (1995–1997)

State	District	Name	Party Affiliation
Arkansas	1	Blanche Lambert-Lincoln	Democrat
California	6	Lynn Woolsey	Democrat
California	8	Nancy Pelosi	Democrat
California	14	Anna G. Eshoo	Democrat
California	16	Zoe Lofgren	Democrat
California	22	Andrea Seastrand	Republican
California	33	Lucille Roybal-Allard	Democrat
California	35	Maxine Waters	Democrat
California	36	Jane Harman	Democrat
California	37	Juanita Millender-McDonald[35]	Democrat
Colorado	1	Patricia Schroeder	Democrat

[35]Millender-McDonald was elected in a special March 19, 1996, election to replace Walter Tucker III, who had resigned.

Connecticut	1	Barbara Bailey Kennelly	Democrat
Connecticut	3	Rosa L. De Lauro	Democrat
Connecticut	6	Nancy L. Johnson	Republican
Florida	3	Corrine Brown	Democrat
Florida	4	Tillie Fowler	Republican
Florida	5	Karen L. Thurman	Democrat
Florida	17	Carrie Meek	Democrat
Florida	18	Ileana Ros-Lehtinen	Republican
Georgia	11	Cynthia McKinney	Democrat
Hawaii	2	Patsy Takemoto Mink	Democrat
Idaho	1	Helen Chenoweth	Republican
Illinois	7	Cardiss Collins	Democrat
Kansas	3	Jan Meyers	Republican
Maryland	8	Constance A. Morella	Republican
Michigan	13	Lynn Rivers	Democrat
Michigan	15	Barbara-Rose Collins	Democrat
Missouri	5	Karen McCarthy	Democrat
Missouri	6	Patsy Ann Danner	Democrat
Nevada	2	Barbara F. Vucanovich	Republican
New Jersey	5	Marge Roukema	Republican
New York	12	Nydia M. Velazquez	Democrat
New York	13	Susan Molinari	Republican
New York	14	Carolyn B. Maloney	Democrat
New York	18	Nita M. Lowey	Democrat
New York	19	Sue W. Kelly	Republican
New York	28	Louise M. Slaughter	Democrat
North Carolina	1	Eva Clayton	Democrat
North Carolina	9	Sue Myrick	Republican
Ohio	9	Marcy Kaptur	Democrat
Ohio	15	Deborah Pryce	Republican
Oregon	1	Elizabeth Furse	Democrat
Texas	18	Sheila Jackson-Lee	Democrat
Texas	30	Eddie Bernice Johnson	Democrat
Utah	2	Enid Waldholtz[36]	Republican
Washington	3	Linda Smith	Republican
Washington	8	Jennifer Dunn	Republican
Wyoming	AL	Barbara Cubin	Republican

---

[36]During this session of Congress Waldholtz became only the second member of Congress to give birth to a child, or, as she put it, "the first Republican" to do so. Later in 1996 two other female representatives—Susan Molinari, (R) New York, and Blanche Lambert-Lincoln, (D) Arkansas—also gave birth to children, making a total of four children born to mothers serving in Congress, probably a record that will stand for some time. Yvonne Braithwaite Burke, (D) California, was the first congressional "mother" when she gave birth to her daughter, Autumn, during the 93rd Congress in 1973.

Total Women Serving

48 (31 Democrats, 17 Republicans)

Best Representation by State

Wyoming	100% (1 of 1)
Connecticut	50.0% (3 of 6)
Hawaii	50.0% (1 of 2)
Idaho	50.0% (1 of 2)
Nevada	50.0% (1 of 2)
Utah	33.3% (1 of 3)

Minority Representation

10 African Americans

California	35	Maxine Waters	Democrat
California	37	Juanita Millender-McDonald	Democrat
Florida	3	Corrine Brown	Democrat
Florida	17	Carrie Meek	Democrat
Georgia	11	Cynthia McKinney	Democrat
Illinois	7	Cardiss Collins	Democrat
Michigan	15	Barbara-Rose Collins	Democrat
North Carolina	1	Eva Clayton	Democrat
Texas	18	Sheila Jackson-Lee	Democrat
Texas	30	Eddie Bernice Johnson	Democrat

3 Hispanics

California	33	Lucille Roybal-Allard	Democrat
Florida	18	Ileana Ros-Lehtinen	Republican
New York	12	Nydia M. Velazquez	Democrat

1 Asian American

Hawaii	2	Patsy Takemoto Mink	Democrat

Senior Female Member

Patricia Schroeder, (D) Colorado–1st, first elected in 1972.

Achieving Power

Jan Meyers, (R) Kansas–3rd, became chair of U.S. House Committee on Small Business.
Nancy Johnson, (R) Connecticut–6th, became chair of the U.S. House Ethics Committee.

Susan Molinari, (R) New York–13th, was elected vice chair and **Barbara Vucanovich**, (R) Nevada–2nd, was elected secretary of the U.S. House Republican conference, the first women to serve in the elected House leadership of either party.

Losing Female Candidates

In addition to the women elected to the 104th Congress, the two major political parties also fielded other female candidates. The Democrats had thirty-five who failed in their bid to be elected, and the Republicans had nineteen.

Female Incumbents Not Returning from the 103rd Congress

Nine female incumbents, all Democrats, lost their seats to Republican challengers in the general election:

Karen English, Arizona–6th
Lynn Schenk, California–49th
Jill Long, Indiana–4th
Marjorie Margolies-Mezvinsky, Pennsylvania–13th
Karen Shepherd, Utah–2nd
Leslie A. Byrne, Virginia–11th
Maria Cantwell, Washington–1st
Jolene Unsoeld, Washington–3rd
Catherine Webber, Oregon–5th

Three other female incumbents did not return to the House for various reasons:

Olympia J. Snowe, (R) Maine–2nd, was elected to the U.S. Senate.
Helen Delich Bentley, (R) Maryland–2nd, lost a primary run for the gubernatorial nomination.
Marilyn Lloyd, (D) Tennessee–3rd, retired and did not seek reelection.

103rd Congress (1993–1995)

State	District	Name	Party Affiliation
Arizona	6	Karen English	Democrat
Arkansas	1	Blanche Lambert	Democrat
California	6	Lynn Woolsey	Democrat
California	8	Nancy Pelosi	Democrat
California	14	Anna G. Eshoo	Democrat
California	33	Lucille Roybal-Allard	Democrat
California	35	Maxine Waters	Democrat
California	36	Jane Harman	Democrat
California	49	Lynn Schenk	Democrat
Colorado	1	Patricia Schroeder	Democrat
Connecticut	1	Barbara Bailey Kennelly	Democrat

Connecticut	3	Rosa L. De Lauro	Democrat
Connecticut	6	Nancy L. Johnson	Republican
Florida	3	Corrine Brown	Democrat
Florida	4	Tillie Fowler	Republican
Florida	5	Karen L. Thurman	Democrat
Florida	17	Carrie Meek	Democrat
Florida	18	Ileana Ros-Lehtinen	Republican
Georgia	11	Cynthia McKinney	Democrat
Hawaii	2	Patsy Takemoto Mink	Democrat
Illinois	7	Cardiss Collins	Democrat
Indiana	4	Jill L. Long	Democrat
Kansas	3	Jan Meyers	Republican
Maine	2	Olympia J. Snowe	Republican
Maryland	2	Helen Delich Bentley	Republican
Maryland	8	Constance A. Morella	Republican
Michigan	15	Barbara-Rose Collins	Democrat
Missouri	6	Patsy Ann Danner	Democrat
Nevada	2	Barbara F. Vucanovich	Republican
New Jersey	5	Marge Roukema	Republican
New York	12	Nydia M. Velazquez	Democrat
New York	13	Susan Molinari	Republican
New York	14	Carolyn F. Maloney	Democrat
New York	18	Nita M. Lowey	Democrat
New York	28	Louise M. Slaughter	Democrat
North Carolina	1	Eva Clayton	Democrat
Ohio	9	Marcy Kaptur	Democrat
Ohio	15	Deborah Pryce	Republican
Oregon	1	Elizabeth Furse	Democrat
Pennsylvania	13	Marjorie Margolies-Mezvinsky	Democrat
Tennessee	3	Marilyn Lloyd	Democrat
Texas	30	Eddie Bernice Johnson	Democrat
Utah	2	Karen Shepherd	Democrat
Virginia	11	Leslie A. Byrne	Democrat
Washington	1	Maria Cantwell	Democrat
Washington	3	Jolene Unsoeld	Democrat
Washington	8	Jennifer Dunn	Republican

Total Women Serving

47 (35 Democrats, 12 Republicans)

Notable Firsts

Women became more than 10 percent of total U.S. House membership for the first time.

In July 1994, **Susan Molinari**, (R) New York–13th, married **Bill Paxon**, (R) New York–27th. They became the first U.S. representatives from the same state to marry while both were serving in Congress.

Best Representation by State

Connecticut	50.0% (3 of 6)
Hawaii	50.0% (1 of 2)
Maine	50.0% (1 of 2)
Nevada	50.0% (1 of 2)
Utah	33.3% (1 of 3)
Washington	33.3% (3 of 9)

Minority Representation

8 African Americans

California	35	Maxine Waters	Democrat
Florida	3	Corrine Brown	Democrat
Florida	17	Carrie Meek	Democrat
Georgia	11	Cynthia McKinney	Democrat
Illinois	7	Cardiss Collins	Democrat
Michigan	15	Barbara-Rose Collins	Democrat
North Carolina	1	Eva Clayton	Democrat
Texas	30	Eddie Bernice Johnson	Democrat

3 Hispanics

California	33	Lucille Roybal-Allard	Democrat
Florida	18	Ileana Ros-Lehtinen	Republican
New York	12	Nydia M. Velazquez	Democrat

1 Asian American

| Hawaii | 2 | Patsy Takemoto Mink | Democrat |

Senior Female Member

Patricia Schroeder, (D) Colorado–1st, first elected in 1972.

Losing Female Candidates

In addition to the women elected to the 103rd Congress, the two major political parties also fielded other female candidates. The Democrats had thirty-five who failed in their bid to be elected, and the Republicans had twenty-five.

One of the most unusual losing female challengers was **Ada Deer**, (D) Wisconsin, a Native American (Menominee) who sought a seat from Wisconsin's 2nd Congressional District.

Female Incumbents Not Returning from the 102nd Congress

Three female incumbents, all Democrats, lost their seats to Republican challengers in the general election:

Joan Kelly Horn, Missouri–2nd
Mary Rose Oakar, Ohio–10th
Elizabeth J. Patterson, South Carolina–4th

Two other female incumbents did not return to the House for various reasons:

Barbara L. Boxer, (D) California–6th, was elected to the U.S. Senate.
Beverly Byron, (D) Maryland–6th, was defeated by a challenger in the Democratic primary.

102nd Congress (1991–1993)

State	District	Name	Party Affiliation
California	5	Nancy Pelosi	Democrat
California	6	Barbara L. Boxer	Democrat
California	29	Maxine Waters	Democrat
Colorado	1	Patricia Schroeder	Democrat
Connecticut	1	Barbara Bailey Kennelly	Democrat
Connecticut	3	Rosa L. DeLauro	Democrat
Connecticut	6	Nancy L. Johnson	Republican
Florida	18	Ileana Ros-Lehtinen	Republican
Hawaii	2	Patsy Takemoto Mink	Democrat
Illinois	7	Cardiss Collins	Democrat
Indiana	4	Jill Long	Democrat
Kansas	3	Jan Meyers	Republican
Maine	2	Olympia J. Snowe	Republican
Maryland	2	Helen Delich Bentley	Republican
Maryland	6	Beverly B. Byron	Democrat
Maryland	8	Constance A. Morella	Republican
Michigan	13	Barbara-Rose Collins	Democrat
Missouri	2	Joan Kelly Horn	Democrat
Nevada	2	Barbara Vucanovich	Republican
New Jersey	7	Marge Roukema	Republican
New York	14	Susan Molinari	Republican
New York	20	Nita M. Lowey	Democrat
New York	30	Louise M. Slaughter	Democrat
Ohio	9	Marcy Kaptur	Democrat

Ohio	22	Mary Rose Oakar	Democrat
South Carolina	4	Elizabeth Patterson	Democrat
Tennessee	3	Marilyn Lloyd	Democrat
Washington	3	Jolene Unsoeld	Democrat

Total Women Serving

28 (19 Democrats, 9 Republicans)

Minority Representation

3 African American

California	29	Maxine Waters	Democrat
Illinois	6	Cardiss Collins	Democrat
Michigan	13	Barbara-Rose Collins	Democrat

1 Hispanic

| Florida | 18 | Ileana Ros-Lehtinen | Republican |

1 Asian American

| Hawaii | 2 | Patsy Takemoto Mink | Democrat |

Senior Female Member

Patricia Schroeder, (D) Colorado–1st, first elected in 1972.

Losing Female Candidates

In addition to the women elected to the 102nd Congress, the two major political parties also fielded other female candidates. The Democrats had eighteen who failed in their bid to be elected, and the Republicans had nineteen.

One of the most unusual losing female challengers was **Joan Dennison** (D), seeking Michigan's 10th Congressional District seat, who was described as an "admirer" of radical politician Lyndon LaRouche.

Incumbents Not Returning from the 101st Congress

Corinne "Lindy" Boggs, (D) Louisiana–2nd, retired and did not seek reelection.
Lynn Martin, (R) Illinois–16th, was defeated in a bid for the U.S. Senate.
Patricia F. Saiki, (R) Hawaii–1st, was defeated in a bid for the U.S. Senate.
Claudine Schneider, (R) Rhode Island–2nd, was defeated in a bid for the U.S. Senate.
Virginia Smith, (R) Nebraska–3rd, retired and did not seek reelection.

101st Congress (1989–1991)

State	District	Name	Party Affiliation
California	5	Nancy Pelosi	Democrat
California	6	Barbara L. Boxer	Democrat
Colorado	1	Patricia Schroeder	Democrat
Connecticut	1	Barbara Bailey Kennelly	Democrat
Connecticut	6	Nancy L. Johnson	Republican
Florida	18	Ileana Ros-Lehtinen[37]	Republican
Hawaii	1	Patricia F. Saiki	Republican
Hawaii	2	Patsy Takemoto Mink[38]	Democrat
Illinois	7	Cardiss Collins	Democrat
Illinois	16	Lynn Martin	Republican
Indiana	4	Jill Long[39]	Democrat
Kansas	3	Jan Meyers	Republican
Louisiana	2	Corinne "Lindy" Boggs	Democrat
Maine	2	Olympia J. Snowe	Republican
Maryland	2	Helen Delich Bentley	Republican
Maryland	6	Beverly B. Byron	Democrat
Maryland	8	Constance A. Morella	Republican
Nebraska	3	Virginia Smith	Republican
Nevada	2	Barbara Vucanovich	Republican
New Jersey	7	Marge Roukema	Republican
New York	14	Susan Molinari[40]	Republican
New York	20	Nita M. Lowey	Democrat
New York	30	Louise M. Slaughter	Democrat
Ohio	9	Marcy Kaptur	Democrat
Ohio	22	Mary Rose Oakar	Democrat
Rhode Island	2	Claudine Schneider	Republican
South Carolina	4	Elizabeth Patterson	Democrat
Tennessee	3	Marilyn Lloyd	Democrat
Washington	3	Jolene Unsoeld	Democrat

Total Women Serving

29 (16 Democrats, 13 Republicans)

---

[37]Ros-Lehtinen was selected in a special August 1989 election to fill the seat of a deceased incumbent.

[38]Mink was elected in a special September 1990 election to fill the seat of an incumbent who had resigned. She had previously served six terms (1965–1977) in the U.S. House.

[39]Long was selected in a special March 28, 1989, election to fill the seat of an incumbent who had been appointed to the U.S. Senate.

[40]Molinari was elected in a special March 1990 election to the seat from which her father had resigned. In winning his seat she became only the second daughter to succeed her father in the U.S. House. Winnifred Mason Huck of the 67th Congress (1921–1923) was the first.

Minority Representation

1 African American

Illinois	6	Cardiss Collins	Democrat

1 Hispanic

Florida	18	Ileana Ros-Lehtinen	Republican

2 Asian Americans

Hawaii	1	Patricia F. Saiki	Republican
Hawaii	2	Patsy Takemoto Mink	Democrat

Notable First

Ileana Ros-Lehtinen, a Cuban American representing Florida's 18th Congressional District as a Republican, became the first Hispanic woman elected to the U.S. House of Representatives. This occurred only sixty-six years after the first Hispanic woman attempted to win a seat in the U.S. House of Representatives. (See the **68th Congress** for details.) In 1982, when she was first elected to the Florida house, Ros-Lehtinen set another record in becoming the first Hispanic elected to Florida's legislature.

Notable First

In 1989 **Olympia J. Snowe**, (R) Maine–2nd, married Gov. John McKernan, (R) Maine. Snowe, a widow, and McKernan, who was divorced and had previously represented Maine's 1st Congressional District in the U.S. House, had fallen in love while serving in Congress together. Snowe became the first sitting member of Congress to marry an incumbent governor while in office.

Senior Female Member

Patricia Schroeder, (D) Colorado–1st, first elected in 1972.

Losing Female Candidates

In addition to the women elected to the 101st Congress, the two major political parties also fielded other female candidates. The Democrats had nineteen who failed in their bid to be elected, and the Republicans had fourteen.

One of the most unusual losing female challengers was **Adeline Roemer** (D), mother of newly elected Louisiana Gov. Buddy Roemer. She sought to fill Louisiana's 4th Congressional District seat previously occupied by her son, the first instance when a mother tried to succeed a son in Congress.

Incumbents Not Returning from the 100th Congress

All incumbents from the 100th Congress were returned to office and there were no retirements.

100th Congress (1987–1989)

State	District	Name	Party Affiliation
California	5	Nancy Pelosi	Democrat
California	6	Barbara L. Boxer	Democrat
Colorado	1	Patricia Schroeder	Democrat
Connecticut	1	Barbara Bailey Kennelly	Democrat
Connecticut	6	Nancy L. Johnson	Republican
Hawaii	1	Patricia F. Saiki	Republican
Illinois	7	Cardiss Collins	Democrat
Illinois	16	Lynn Martin	Republican
Kansas	3	Jan Meyers	Republican
Louisiana	2	Corinne "Lindy" Boggs	Democrat
Maine	2	Olympia J. Snowe	Republican
Maryland	2	Helen Delich Bentley	Republican
Maryland	6	Beverly B. Byron	Democrat
Maryland	8	Constance A. Morella	Republican
Nebraska	3	Virginia Smith	Republican
Nevada	2	Barbara Vucanovich	Republican
New Jersey	7	Marge Roukema	Republican
New York	30	Louise M. Slaughter	Democrat
Ohio	9	Marcy Kaptur	Democrat
Ohio	22	Mary Rose Oakar	Democrat
Rhode Island	2	Claudine Schneider	Republican
South Carolina	4	Elizabeth Patterson	Democrat
Tennessee	3	Marilyn Lloyd	Democrat

Total Women Serving

23 (12 Democrats, 11 Republicans)

Minority Representation

1 African American

Illinois	6	Cardiss Collins	Democrat

1 Asian American

Hawaii	1	Patricia F. Saiki	Republican

Senior Female Member

Patricia Schroeder, (D) Colorado–1st, first elected in 1972.

Notable First

In 1987 **Barbara Vucanovich**, (R) Nevada–2nd, became the first great-grandmother to serve in the U.S. Congress when her granddaughter gave birth to a son, Brandon.

Losing Female Candidates

In addition to the women who won their races in the November 1986 general election, the Democrats had eighteen other female candidates, and the Republicans twenty-two, who lost their races for a seat in the U.S. House of Representatives.

Two of the more interesting losing female candidates were **Kathleen Kennedy Townsend,** (D) Maryland, and **Bella Abzug,** (D) New York. Townsend, the daughter of Robert Kennedy and the first female Kennedy to venture into electoral politics, ran against a female Republican incumbent in Maryland's 2nd Congressional District. Abzug, who had previously served in the House for three terms (1971–1977), then left seeking a U.S. Senate nomination, tried to return from New York's 20th Congressional District in suburban Westchester County.

Incumbents Not Returning from the 99th Congress

Bobbi Fiedler, (R) California–21st, lost a primary race for a U.S. Senate nomination.
Marjorie Holt, (R) Maryland–4th, retired and did not seek reelection.
Cathy Long, (D) Louisiana–8th, did not seek election to a full term.
Barbara A. Mikulski, (D) Maryland–3rd, won a seat in the U.S. Senate.

99th Congress (1985–1987)

State	*District*	*Name*	*Party Affiliation*
California	5	Sala Burton	Democrat
California	5	Nancy Pelosi[41]	Democrat
California	6	Barbara L. Boxer	Democrat
California	21	Bobbi Fiedler	Republican
Colorado	1	Patricia Schroeder	Democrat
Connecticut	1	Barbara Bailey Kennelly	Democrat
Connecticut	6	Nancy L. Johnson	Republican
Illinois	7	Cardiss Collins	Democrat
Illinois	16	Lynn Martin	Republican
Kansas	3	Jan Meyers	Republican
Louisiana	2	Corinne "Lindy" Boggs	Democrat

[41]Pelosi was selected in a special June 2, 1987, election to fill the seat of deceased incumbent Sala Burton. In doing so she became the first woman to replace another woman as a result of a special election.

Louisiana	8	Cathy Long[42]	Democrat
Maine	2	Olympia J. Snowe	Republican
Maryland	2	Helen Delich Bentley	Republican
Maryland	3	Barbara A. Mikulski	Democrat
Maryland	4	Marjorie Holt	Republican
Maryland	6	Beverly B. Byron	Democrat
Nebraska	3	Virginia Smith	Republican
Nevada	2	Barbara Vucanovich	Republican
New Jersey	7	Marge Roukema	Republican
Ohio	9	Marcy Kaptur	Democrat
Ohio	22	Mary Rose Oakar	Democrat
Rhode Island	2	Claudine Schneider	Republican
Tennessee	3	Marilyn Lloyd	Democrat

Total Women Serving

24 (13 Democrats, 11 Republicans)

Minority Representation

1 African American

| Illinois | 6 | Cardiss Collins | Democrat |

Senior Female Member

Patricia Schroeder, (D) Colorado–1st, first elected in 1972.

Losing Female Candidates

In addition to the women who won their races in the November 1984 general election, the Democrats had six other female candidates, and the Republicans thirteen, who lost their races for a seat in the U.S. House of Representatives.

One of the most interesting losing female candidates was **Nancy Kulp** (D), who contested Pennsylvania's 9th Congressional District. She was familiar to television viewers nationwide from the years she spent in the 1960s playing the role of Miss Jane Hathaway on *The Beverly Hillbillies*. Her former costar and head of the Clampett clan in the series, Buddy Ebsen, made some campaign commercials for her opponent, the Republican incumbent.

Another female candidate of note who lost was **Peggy Begich** (D), seeking Alaska's single at-large seat. Her husband, Nick, had held the seat years before and was campaigning for another term when he was killed in a small-plane crash thirteen years earlier. After Begich lost her 1984 try for the seat, she tried again—and lost—in 1986.

---

[42]Long was selected in a special March 30, 1985, election to fill the seat of her deceased husband.

Incumbents Not Returning from the 98th Congress

Geraldine Ferraro, (D) New York–9th, lost her bid to become the first female vice president of the United States.

Katie Hall, (D) Indiana–1st, was beaten by a challenger in the Democratic primary.

98th Congress (1983–1985)

State	District	Name	Party Affiliation
California	5	Sala Burton[43]	Democrat
California	6	Barbara L. Boxer	Democrat
California	21	Bobbi Fiedler	Republican
Colorado	1	Patricia Schroeder	Democrat
Connecticut	1	Barbara Bailey Kennelly	Democrat
Connecticut	6	Nancy L. Johnson	Republican
Illinois	7	Cardiss Collins	Democrat
Illinois	16	Lynn Martin	Republican
Indiana	1	Katie Hall	Democrat
Louisiana	2	Corinne "Lindy" Boggs	Democrat
Maine	2	Olympia J. Snowe	Republican
Maryland	3	Barbara A. Mikulski	Democrat
Maryland	4	Marjorie Holt	Republican
Maryland	6	Beverly B. Byron	Democrat
Nebraska	3	Virginia Smith	Republican
Nevada	2	Barbara Vucanovich	Republican
New Jersey	7	Marge Roukema	Republican
New York	9	Geraldine Ferraro	Democrat
Ohio	9	Marcy Kaptur	Democrat
Ohio	22	Mary Rose Oakar	Democrat
Rhode Island	2	Claudine Schneider	Republican
Tennessee	3	Marilyn Lloyd	Democrat

Total Women Serving

22 (13 Democrats, 9 Republicans)

Minority Representation

2 African Americans

Illinois	6	Cardiss Collins	Democrat
Indiana	1	Katie Hall	Democrat

---

[43]Burton was selected in a special June 21, 1983, election to fill the seat of her deceased husband.

Senior Female Member

Patricia Schroeder, (D) Colorado–1st, first elected in 1972.

Losing Female Candidates

In addition to the women who won their races in the November 1982 general election, the Democrats had fifteen other female candidates, and the Republicans eighteen, who lost their races for a seat in the U.S. House of Representatives.

One of the most interesting losing female candidates was **Cynthia "Cissy" Baker** (R), who contested Tennessee's 4th Congressional District. She was the daughter of then–Senate Majority Leader Howard Baker, (R) Tennessee.

Incumbents Not Returning from the 97th Congress

Jean Ashbrook, (R) Ohio–17th, did not seek a full term.
Shirley Chisholm, (D) New York–12th, retired and did not seek reelection.
Millicent Fenwick, (R) New Jersey–5th, lost the general election for a U.S. Senate seat.
Margaret M. Heckler, (R) Massachusetts–10th, lost the general election when her district was combined with another during redistricting.

97th Congress (1981–1983)

State	District	Name	Party Affiliation
California	21	Bobbi Fiedler	Republican
Colorado	1	Patricia Schroeder	Democrat
Connecticut	1	Barbara Bailey Kennelly[44]	Democrat
Illinois	7	Cardiss Collins	Democrat
Illinois	16	Lynn Martin	Republican
Indiana	1	Katie Hall[45]	Democrat
Louisiana	2	Corinne "Lindy" Boggs	Democrat
Maine	2	Olympia J. Snowe	Republican
Maryland	3	Barbara A. Mikulski	Democrat
Maryland	4	Marjorie Holt	Republican
Maryland	5	Gladys Noon Spellman[46]	Democrat
Maryland	6	Beverly B. Byron	Democrat
Massachusetts	10	Margaret M. Heckler	Republican
Nebraska	3	Virginia Smith	Republican

[44]Kennnelly was selected in a special 1982 election to fill the seat of a deceased incumbent.

[45]Hall was selected in a special election to fill the seat of a deceased incumbent.

[46]Spellman had a heart attack in October 1980 but was easily reelected the following month. After she went into an irreversible coma, her seat was declared vacant in early 1981. Her husband, Reuben, was a candidate to fill her vacant seat, but he was narrowly defeated in the Democratic primary. Had he been victorious, Reuben Spellman would have been the first husband to succeed his wife in the U.S. House of Representatives.

New Jersey	5	Millicent Fenwick	Republican
New Jersey	7	Marge Roukema	Republican
New York	9	Geraldine Ferraro	Democrat
New York	12	Shirley Chisholm	Democrat
Ohio	17	Jean Ashbrook[47]	Republican
Ohio	22	Mary Rose Oakar	Democrat
Rhode Island	2	Claudine Schneider	Republican
Tennessee	3	Marilyn Lloyd Bouquard	Democrat

Total Women Serving

22 (12 Democrats, 10 Republicans)

Minority Representation

3 African Americans

Illinois	6	Cardiss Collins	Democrat
Indiana	1	Katie Hall	Democrat
New York	12	Shirley Chisholm	Democrat

Senior Female Member

Margaret M. Heckler, (R) Massachusetts–10th, first elected in 1966.

Losing Female Candidates

In addition to the women who won their races in the November 1980 general election, the Democrats had sixteen other female candidates, and the Republicans fifteen, who lost their races for a seat in the U.S. House of Representatives.

One of the most interesting—nay, unusual—losing female candidates was in California's 34th Congressional District. Running as a Democrat, she appeared on the November ballot only as **Simone**. Her mononame failed to enchant the district's voters, as she lost 72–24 percent.

Incumbents Not Returning from the 96th Congress

Elizabeth Holtzman, (D) New York–16th, lost her bid as the Democratic nominee for the U.S. Senate.

96th Congress (1979–1981)

State	District	Name	Party Affiliation
Colorado	1	Patricia Schroeder	Democrat
Illinois	7	Cardiss Collins	Democrat
Louisiana	2	Corinne "Lindy" Boggs	Democrat

---

[47]Ashbrook was selected in a special 1982 election to fill the seat of her deceased husband.

Maine	2	Olympia J. Snowe	Republican
Maryland	3	Barbara A. Mikulski	Democrat
Maryland	4	Marjorie Holt	Republican
Maryland	5	Gladys Noon Spellman	Democrat
Maryland	6	Beverly B. Byron[48]	Democrat
Massachusetts	10	Margaret M. Heckler	Republican
Nebraska	3	Virginia Smith	Republican
New Jersey	5	Millicent Fenwick	Republican
New York	9	Geraldine Ferraro	Democrat
New York	16	Elizabeth Holtzman	Democrat
New York	12	Shirley Chisholm	Democrat
Ohio	22	Mary Rose Oakar	Democrat
Tennessee	3	Marilyn Lloyd Bouquard	Democrat

Total Women Serving

16 (11 Democrats, 5 Republicans)

Minority Representation

2 African Americans

Illinois	6	Cardiss Collins	Democrat
New York	12	Shirley Chisholm	Democrat

Senior Female Member

Margaret M. Heckler, (R) Massachusetts–10th, first elected in 1966.

Notable First

When **Beverly B. Byron** carried Maryland's 6th Congressional District, she joined three other women representing the state of Maryland in the U.S. House. This was the first time a state had elected four female U.S. representatives concurrently.

Losing Female Candidates

In addition to the women who won their races in the November 1978 general election, the Democrats had fourteen other female candidates, and the Republicans thirteen, who lost their races for a seat in the U.S. House of Representatives.

Two of the most interesting losing female candidates were **Marge Roukema** (R), who contested New Jersey's 7th Congressional District, and **Claudine Schneider** (R), who contested Rhode Is-

---

[48]Byron was preceded representing her district in the U.S. House by her husband, her mother-in-law, and her father-in-law. This is the only incident of its kind. In addition to this family political lineage, Byron's mother-in-law's grandfather also served in the U.S. House. (See 77th Congress, 1941–1943, for more details.)

land's 2nd Congressional District. Both women ran strong races, then returned in 1980 for another challenge against their same male opponents—and won.

Incumbents Not Returning from the 95th Congress

Yvonne B. Burke, (D) California–28th, sought another office—attorney general of California—as the Democratic nominee for the post; she lost that election 53–43 percent.
Barbara Jordan, (D) Texas–18th, retired and did not seek reelection.
Martha Keys, (D) Kansas–2nd, was defeated in the general election.
Helen Meyner, (D) New Jersey–18th, was defeated in the general election.
Shirley Pettis, (R) California–37th, retired and did not seek reelection.

95th Congress (1977–1979)

State	District	Name	Party Affiliation
California	28	Yvonne B. Burke	Democrat
California	37	Shirley Pettis	Republican
Colorado	1	Patricia Schroeder	Democrat
Illinois	7	Cardiss Collins	Democrat
Kansas	2	Martha Keys	Democrat
Louisiana	2	Corinne "Lindy" Boggs	Democrat
Maryland	3	Barbara A. Mikulski	Democrat
Maryland	4	Marjorie Holt	Republican
Maryland	5	Gladys Noon Spellman	Democrat
Massachusetts	10	Margaret M. Heckler	Republican
Nebraska	3	Virginia Smith	Republican
New Jersey	5	Millicent Fenwick	Republican
New Jersey	13	Helen Meyner	Democrat
New York	16	Elizabeth Holtzman	Democrat
New York	12	Shirley Chisholm	Democrat
Ohio	22	Mary Rose Oakar	Democrat
Tennessee	3	Marilyn Lloyd	Democrat
Texas	18	Barbara Jordan	Democrat

Total Women Serving

18 (13 Democrats, 5 Republicans)

Minority Representation

4 African Americans

California	28	Yvonne B. Burke	Democrat

Illinois	6	Cardiss Collins	Democrat
New York	12	Shirley Chisholm	Democrat
Texas	18	Barbara Jordan	Democrat

Senior Female Member

Margaret M. Heckler, (R) Massachusetts–10th, first elected in 1966.

Notable First

In 1977, after she had won reelection, **Martha Keys**, (D) Kansas–2nd, married U.S. Representative **Andy Jacobs**, (D) Indiana–11th, making them the first U.S. representatives from different states to marry while both were still serving. Keys was defeated in the next general election, and the couple later divorced. It is also worth noting that Keys was the sister-in-law of onetime U.S. senator—and presidential candidate—**Gary Hart**, (D) Colorado.

Losing Female Candidates

In addition to the women who won their races in the November 1976 general election, the Democrats had twenty-one other female candidates, and the Republicans fifteen, who lost their races for a seat in the U.S. House of Representatives.

One of the most interesting losing female candidates was **Patty Lear Corman** (D), who contested California's 20th Congressional District. She was the daughter of the inventor of the Lear jet and the wife of U.S. Rep. James Corman (D), who represented California's 21st Congressional District. Her husband didn't want her to run, but she did anyhow and got only 33 percent of the vote. Shortly thereafter, their marriage broke up, and she contested the seat again in 1978, losing a second time.

Incumbents Not Returning from the 94th Congress

Bella Abzug, (D) New York–20th, lost the Democratic primary for nomination to the U.S. Senate.
Patsy Takemoto Mink, (D) Hawaii–2nd, lost the Democratic primary for nomination to the U.S. Senate.
Leonor K. Sullivan, (D) Missouri–3rd, retired and did not seek reelection.

94th Congress (1975–1977)

State	District	Name	Party Affiliation
California	28	Yvonne B. Burke	Democrat
California	37	Shirley Pettis[49]	Republican
Colorado	1	Patricia Schroeder	Democrat
Hawaii	2	Patsy Takemoto Mink	Democrat

---

[49]Pettis was selected in a special April 29, 1975, election to fill the seat of her deceased husband.

Illinois	7	Cardiss Collins	Democrat
Kansas	2	Martha Keys	Democrat
Louisiana	2	Corinne "Lindy" Boggs	Democrat
Maryland	4	Marjorie Holt	Republican
Maryland	5	Gladys Noon Spellman	Democrat
Massachusetts	10	Margaret M. Heckler	Republican
Missouri	3	Leonor K. Sullivan	Democrat
Nebraska	3	Virginia Smith	Republican
New Jersey	5	Millicent Fenwick	Republican
New Jersey	13	Helen Meyner[50]	Democrat
New York	10	Elizabeth Holtzman	Democrat
New York	12	Shirley Chisholm	Democrat
New York	20	Bella Abzug	Democrat
Tennessee	3	Marilyn Lloyd[51]	Democrat
Texas	18	Barbara Jordan	Democrat

Total Women Serving

19 (14 Democrats, 5 Republicans)

Minority Representation

4 African Americans

California	28	Yvonne B. Burke	Democrat
Illinois	6	Cardiss Collins	Democrat
New York	12	Shirley Chisholm	Democrat
Texas	18	Barbara Jordan	Democrat

1 Asian American

| Hawaii | 2 | Patsy Takemoto Mink | Democrat |

Senior Female Member

Leonor K. Sullivan, (D) Missouri–3rd, first elected in 1952.

Wielding Power

Leonor K. Sullivan, (D) Missouri–3rd, was chair of the House Committee on Merchant Marine and Fisheries.

---

[50]Meyner's husband, Robert, was governor of New Joersey (1955–1963) well before she began her congressional career; she was also the first cousin of two-time presidential candidate Adlai Stevenson.

[51]Lloyd received the Democratic nomination for her seat and won the November 1974 general election after her husband, Mort Lloyd, who had won the nomination in the Democratic primary, died while campaigning for the seat.

Losing Female Candidates

In addition to the women who won their races in the November 1974 general election, the Democrats had fourteen other female candidates, and the Republicans eleven, who lost their races for a seat in the U.S. House of Representatives.

One of the most interesting losing female candidates was **Judy Petty** (R), who contested Arkansas's 2nd Congressional District. She ran against Wilbur Mills (D), powerful chair of the House Ways and Means Committee, after he was embroiled in a scandal with a stripper who jumped from a car and plunged into a Washington, D.C., fountain.

Incumbents Not Returning from the 93rd Congress

Ella T. Grasso, (D) Connecticut–6th, was elected governor of Connecticut.
Edith Green, (D) Oregon–3rd, retired and did not seek reelection.
Martha W. Griffiths,[52] (D) Michigan–17th, retired and did not seek reelection.
Julia Butler Hansen, (D) Washington–3rd, retired and did not seek reelection.

93rd Congress (1973–1975)

State	District	Name	Party Affiliation
California	28	Yvonne B. Burke	Democrat
Colorado	1	Patricia Schroeder	Democrat
Connecticut	6	Ella T. Grasso	Democrat
Hawaii	2	Patsy Takemoto Mink	Democrat
Illinois	6	Cardiss Collins[53]	Democrat
Louisiana	2	Corinne "Lindy" Boggs[54]	Democrat
Maryland	4	Marjorie Holt	Republican
Massachusetts	10	Margaret M. Heckler	Republican
Michigan	17	Martha W. Griffiths	Democrat
Missouri	3	Leonor K. Sullivan	Democrat
New York	10	Elizabeth Holtzman[55]	Democrat
New York	12	Shirley Chisholm	Democrat
New York	20	Bella Abzug	Democrat
Oregon	3	Edith Green	Democrat
Texas	18	Barbara Jordan	Democrat
Washington	3	Julia Butler Hansen	Democrat

Total Women Serving

16 (14 Democrats, 2 Republicans)

---

[52]In 1982 Griffith reentered elective politics, winning office as lieutenant governor of Michigan.

[53]Collins was selected in a special June 5, 1973, election to fill the seat of her deceased husband.
[54]Boggs was selected in a special March 20, 1973, election to fill the seat of her deceased husband.
[55]Holtzman, born August 11, 1941, was the youngest woman ever elected to the U.S. Congress.

Notable First

Barbara Jordan, (D) Texas–18th, became the first African American woman elected to Congress from the old states of the Confederacy.

Yvonne B. Burke, (D) California–28th, became the first member of Congress to give birth to a child when her daughter, Autumn Roxanne, was born on November 23, 1973. To highlight the significance of the event, Burke asked for and the House passed a special maternity-leave resolution for her.

Minority Representation

4 African Americans

California	28	Yvonne B. Burke	Democrat
Illinois	6	Cardiss Collins	Democrat
New York	12	Shirley Chisholm	Democrat
Texas	18	Barbara Jordan	Democrat

1 Asian American

Hawaii	2	Patsy Takemoto Mink	Democrat

Senior Female Member

Leonor K. Sullivan, (D) Missouri–3rd, first elected in 1952.

Achieving Power

Leonor K. Sullivan, (D) Missouri–3rd, became chair of the House Committee on Merchant Marine and Fisheries.

Losing Female Candidates

In addition to the women who won their races in the November 1972 general election, the Democrats also had nine other female candidates and the Republicans six, who lost their race for a seat in the U.S. House of Representatives.

One of the most interesting losing female candidates was **Jane Pickens Langley** (R), who contested New York's 18th Congressional District. She had been well known during the 1940s throughout the U.S. appearing regularly on radio as one of the singing Pickens Sisters.

Incumbents Not Returning from the 92nd Congress

Elizabeth Andrews, (D) Alabama–3rd, did not seek a full term.

Florence P. Dwyer, (R) New Jersey–12th, retired and did not seek reelection.
Louise Day Hicks, (D) Massachusetts–9th, was defeated in the general election.

92nd Congress (1971–1973)

State	District	Name	Party Affiliation
Alabama	3	Elizabeth Andrews[56]	Democrat
Connecticut	6	Ella T. Grasso	Democrat
Hawaii	AL	Patsy Takemoto Mink	Democrat
Illinois	15	Charlotte T. Reid[57]	Republican
Massachusetts	9	Louise Day Hicks	Democrat
Massachusetts	10	Margaret M. Heckler	Republican
Michigan	17	Martha W. Griffiths	Democrat
Missouri	3	Leonor K. Sullivan	Democrat
New Jersey	12	Florence P. Dwyer	Republican
New York	12	Shirley Chisholm	Democrat
New York	20	Bella Abzug	Democrat
Oregon	3	Edith Green	Democrat
Washington	3	Julia Butler Hansen	Democrat

Total Women Serving

13 (10 Democrats, 3 Republicans)

Minority Representation

1 African American

New York	12	Shirley Chisholm	Democrat

1 Asian American

Hawaii	AL	Patsy Takemoto Mink	Democrat

Senior Female Member

Leonor K. Sullivan, (D) Missouri–3rd, first elected in 1952.

Losing Female Candidates

In addition to the women who won their races in the November 1970 general election, the Democrats also had six other female candidates and the Republicans six, who lost their race for a seat in the U.S. House of Representatives.

---

[56]Andrews won a special 1972 election to fill the seat of her deceased husband.

[57]Reid resigned in 1971 to accept an appointment by President Nixon to the FCC.

Two of the most interesting losing female candidates were **Myrlie Evers** (D), wife of slain Mississippi civil rights leader Medgar Evers, who challenged a John Birch Society member in California's Republican-leaning 24th Congressional District. **Phyllis Schlafly** (R), an extremely vocal foe of the "feminist" movement, lost in Illinois's 22nd Congressional District.

Incumbent Not Returning from the 91st Congress

Catherine May, (R) Washington–4th, was defeated in the general election.

91st Congress (1969–1971)

State	District	Name	Party Affiliation
Hawaii	AL	Patsy Takemoto Mink	Democrat
Illinois	15	Charlotte T. Reid	Republican
Massachusetts	10	Margaret M. Heckler	Republican
Michigan	17	Martha W. Griffiths	Democrat
Missouri	3	Leonor K. Sullivan	Democrat
New Jersey	12	Florence P. Dwyer	Republican
New York	12	Shirley Chisholm	Democrat
Oregon	3	Edith Green	Democrat
Washington	3	Julia Butler Hansen	Democrat
Washington	4	Catherine May	Republican

Total Women Serving

10 (6 Democrats, 4 Republicans)

Senior Female Member

Leonor K. Sullivan, (D) Missouri–3rd, first elected in 1952.

Notable First

Shirley Chisholm, (D) New York–12th, became the first African American female elected to the U.S. House.

Incumbents Not Returning from the 90th Congress

Frances P. Bolton, (R) Ohio–22nd, was defeated in the general election.
Edna F. Kelly, (D) New York–12th, was defeated in the Democratic primary for another district after her district was eliminated during redistricting.

90th Congress (1967–1969)

State	District	Name	Party Affiliation
Hawaii	AL	Patsy Takemoto Mink	Democrat
Illinois	15	Charlotte T. Reid	Republican
Massachusetts	10	Margaret M. Heckler	Republican
Michigan	17	Martha W. Griffiths	Democrat
Missouri	3	Leonor K. Sullivan	Democrat
New Jersey	12	Florence P. Dwyer	Republican
New York	12	Edna F. Kelly	Democrat
Ohio	22	Frances P. Bolton	Republican
Oregon	3	Edith Green	Democrat
Washington	3	Julia Butler Hansen	Democrat
Washington	4	Catherine May	Republican

Total Women Serving

11 (6 Democrats, 5 Republicans)

Senior Female Member

Frances P. Bolton, (R) Ohio–22nd, first elected in 1940.

Incumbent Not Returning from the 89th Congress

Lera M. Thomas, (D) Texas–8th, did not seek a full term.

89th Congress (1965–1967)

State	District	Name	Party Affiliation
Hawaii	AL	Patsy Takemoto Mink	Democrat
Illinois	15	Charlotte T. Reid	Republican
Michigan	17	Martha W. Griffiths	Democrat
Missouri	3	Leonor K. Sullivan	Democrat
New Jersey	12	Florence P. Dwyer	Republican
New York	10	Edna F. Kelly	Democrat
Ohio	22	Frances P. Bolton	Republican
Oregon	3	Edith Green	Democrat
Texas	8	Lera M. Thomas[58]	Democrat
Washington	3	Julia Butler Hansen	Democrat
Washington	4	Catherine May	Republican

[58]Thomas was selected in a special March 1966 election to fill the seat of her deceased husband.

Total Women Serving

11 (7 Democrats, 4 Republicans)

Senior Female Member

Frances P. Bolton, (R) Ohio–22nd, first elected in 1940.

Notable First

Patsy Takemoto Mink, (D) Hawaii–AL, became the first Asian American woman elected to the U.S. House. In 1956 she had already established another notable first: With her election to Hawaii's territorial legislature, she was the first Japanese American woman elected to a state or territorial legislature.

Incumbents Not Returning from the 88th Congress

Irene Baker, (R) Tennessee–1st, did not seek a full term.

Elizabeth Kee, (D) West Virginia–5th, retired and did not seek reelection. She was succeeded by her son in the seat, the same one in which she had originally succeeded her husband in 1951.

Katharine St. George, (R) New York–27th, was defeated in the general election.

88th Congress (1963–1965)

State	District	Name	Party Affiliation
Illinois	15	Charlotte T. Reid[59]	Republican
Michigan	17	Martha W. Griffiths	Democrat
Missouri	3	Leonor K. Sullivan	Democrat
New Jersey	12	Florence P. Dwyer	Republican
New York	10	Edna F. Kelly	Democrat
New York	28	Katharine St. George	Republican
Ohio	22	Frances P. Bolton	Republican
Oregon	3	Edith Green	Democrat
Tennessee	2	Irene H. Baker[60]	Republican
Washington	3	Julia Butler Hansen	Democrat
Washington	4	Catherine May	Republican
West Virginia	5	Elizabeth Kee	Democrat

Total Women Serving

12 (6 Democrats, 6 Republicans)

---

[59]Reid received the Republican nomination and won the November 1962 general election after her husband, Frank Reid Jr., who had won the nomination in the Republican primary, died while campaigning for the seat.

[60]Baker won a special 1964 election to fill the seat of her deceased husband. She is also the stepmother of Howard Baker Jr., a former Tennessee senator and Senate majority leader.

Senior Female Member

Frances P. Bolton, (R) Ohio–22nd, first elected in 1940.

Incumbents Not Returning from the 87th Congress

Iris F. Blitch, (D) Georgia–8th, retired and did not seek reelection.
Marguerite Stitt Church, (R) Illinois–13th, retired and did not seek reelection.
Kathryn Granahan, (D) Pennsylvania–2nd, had been appointed treasurer of the U.S. and did not seek reelection.
Catherine D. Norrell, (D) Arkansas–6th, did not seek a full term.
Gracie Pfost, (D) Idaho–1st, lost her race as the Democratic nominee for a U.S. Senate seat.
Louise Goff Reece, (R) Tennessee–1st, did not seek a full term.
Corinne Boyd Riley, (D) South Carolina–2nd, did not seek a full term.
Jessica Weiss, (R) New York–38th, retired and did not seek reelection.

87th Congress (1961–1963)

State	District	Name	Party Affiliation
Arkansas	6	Catherine D. Norrell[61]	Democrat
Georgia	8	Iris F. Blitch	Democrat
Idaho	1	Gracie Pfost	Democrat
Illinois	13	Marguerite Stitt Church	Republican
Michigan	17	Martha W. Griffiths	Democrat
Missouri	3	Leonor K. Sullivan	Democrat
New Jersey	12	Florence P. Dwyer	Republican
New York	10	Edna F. Kelly	Democrat
New York	28	Katharine St. George	Republican
New York	38	Jessica Weiss	Republican
Ohio	22	Frances P. Bolton	Republican
Oregon	3	Edith Green	Democrat
Pennsylvania	2	Kathryn Granahan	Democrat
South Carolina	2	Corinne Boyd Riley[62]	Democrat
Tennessee	1	Louise Goff Reece[63]	Republican
Washington	3	Julia Butler Hansen	Democrat
Washington	4	Catherine May	Republican
West Virginia	5	Elizabeth Kee	Democrat

---

[61]Norrell won a special 1961 election to fill the seat of her deceased husband.

[62]Riley won a special 1962 election to fill the seat of her deceased husband.

[63]Reece won a special May 1961 election to fill the seat of her deceased husband. She had also been preceded in Congress by both her grandfather, Nathan Goff, (R) West Virginia, who served in the U.S. House (1883–1889) and Senate (1913–1919), and her father, Guy D. Goff, (R) West Virginia, who served in the U.S. Senate (1925–1931).

Total Women Serving

18 (11 Democrats, 7 Republicans)

Senior Female Member

Frances P. Bolton, (R) Ohio–22nd, first elected in 1940.

Achieving Power

Katharine St. George, (R) New York–28th, was the first woman named to the House Committee on Rules, considered to be the most powerful committee in the U.S. House.

Incumbents Not Returning from the 86th Congress

Edith Nourse Rogers, (R) Massachusetts–5th, died in September 1960 shortly before she was to begin campaigning for a new term. Rogers's tenure in the U.S. House, thirty-five years—from June 1925 until September 1960–is the record for a woman.

Edna Simpson, (R) Illinois–20th, retired and did not seek reelection.

86th Congress (1959–1961)

State	District	Name	Party Affiliation
Georgia	8	Iris F. Blitch	Democrat
Idaho	1	Gracie Pfost	Democrat
Illinois	13	Marguerite Stitt Church	Republican
Illinois	20	Edna Simpson	Republican
Massachusetts	5	Edith Nourse Rogers	Republican
Michigan	17	Martha W. Griffiths	Democrat
Missouri	3	Leonor K. Sullivan	Democrat
New Jersey	12	Florence P. Dwyer	Republican
New York	10	Edna F. Kelly	Democrat
New York	28	Katharine St. George	Republican
New York	38	Jessica Weiss	Republican
Ohio	22	Frances P. Bolton	Republican
Oregon	3	Edith Green	Democrat
Pennsylvania	2	Kathryn Granahan	Democrat
Washington	3	Julia Butler Hansen	Democrat
Washington	4	Catherine May	Republican
West Virginia	5	Elizabeth Kee	Democrat

Total Women Serving

17 (9 Democrats, 8 Republicans)

Senior Female Member

Edith Nourse Rogers, (R) Massachusetts–5th, first elected in 1925.

Notable First

When **Jessica Weiss** (R) carried New York's 38th Congressional District and joined fellow New Yorkers **Katharine St. George** (R) and **Edna F. Kelly** (D) in the U.S. House, New York thereby became the first state to elect three women concurrently to its U.S. House delegation.

Incumbents Not Returning from the 85th Congress

Cecil M. Harden, (R) Indiana–6th, was defeated in the general election.
Coya Knutson, (D) Minnesota–9th, was defeated in the general election. She holds the dubious distinction of being the only incumbent Democratic House member defeated during the Democratic "sweep" of the November 1958 general elections.

85th Congress (1957–1959)

State	District	Name	Party Affiliation
Georgia	8	Iris F. Blitch	Democrat
Idaho	1	Gracie Pfost	Democrat
Illinois	13	Marguerite Stitt Church	Republican
Indiana	6	Cecil M. Harden	Republican
Massachusetts	5	Edith Nourse Rogers	Republican
Michigan	17	Martha W. Griffiths	Democrat
Minnesota	9	Coya Knutson	Democrat
Missouri	3	Leonor K. Sullivan	Democrat
New Jersey	12	Florence P. Dwyer	Republican
New York	10	Edna F. Kelly	Democrat
New York	28	Katharine St. George	Republican
Ohio	22	Frances P. Bolton	Republican
Oregon	3	Edith Green	Democrat
Pennsylvania	2	Kathryn Granahan	Democrat
West Virginia	5	Elizabeth Kee	Democrat

Total Women Serving

15 (9 Democrats, 6 Republicans)

Senior Female Member

Edith Nourse Rogers, (R) Massachusetts–5th, first elected in 1925.

Incumbent Not Returning from the 84th Congress

Ruth Thompson, (R) Michigan–9th, was defeated by a challenger in the Republican primary.

84th Congress (1955–1957)

State	District	Name	Party Affiliation
Georgia	8	Iris F. Blitch	Democrat
Idaho	1	Gracie Pfost	Democrat
Illinois	13	Marguerite Stitt Church	Republican
Indiana	6	Cecil M. Harden	Republican
Massachusetts	5	Edith Nourse Rogers	Republican
Michigan	9	Ruth Thompson	Republican
Michigan	17	Martha W. Griffiths	Democrat
Minnesota	9	Coya Knutson	Democrat
Missouri	3	Leonor K. Sullivan	Democrat
New York	10	Edna F. Kelly	Democrat
New York	28	Katharine St. George	Republican
Ohio	22	Frances P. Bolton	Republican
Oregon	3	Edith Green	Democrat
Pennsylvania	2	Kathryn Granahan[64]	Democrat
Pennsylvania	33	Vera D. Buchanan[65]	Democrat
West Virginia	5	Elizabeth Kee	Democrat

Total Women Serving

16 (10 Democrats, 6 Republicans)

Senior Female Member

Edith Nourse Rogers, (R) Massachusetts–5th, first elected in 1925.

83rd Congress (1953–1955)

State	District	Name	Party Affiliation
Idaho	1	Gracie Pfost	Democrat

---

[64]Granahan was selected in a special May 1956 election to succeed her deceased husband.

[65]Buchanan died in office on November 26, 1959.

Illinois	13	Marguerite Stitt Church	Republican
Indiana	6	Cecil M. Harden	Republican
Massachusetts	5	Edith Nourse Rogers	Republican
Michigan	9	Ruth Thompson	Republican
Missouri	3	Leonor K. Sullivan	Democrat
New York	10	Edna F. Kelly	Democrat
New York	28	Katharine St. George	Republican
Ohio	22	Frances P. Bolton[66]	Republican
Pennsylvania	33	Vera D. Buchanan	Democrat
West Virginia	5	Elizabeth Kee	Democrat

Total Women Serving

11 (6 Republicans, 5 Democrats)

Senior Female Member

Edith Nourse Rogers, (R) Massachusetts–5th, first elected in 1925.

Achieving Power

Edith Nourse Rogers, (R) Massachusetts–5th, became chair of the House Committee on Veterans Affairs.

Incumbent Not Returning from the 82nd Congress

Reva Beck Bosone, (D) Utah–2nd, was defeated in the general election.

82nd Congress (1951–1953)

State	District	Name	Party Affiliation
Illinois	13	Marguerite Stitt Church	Republican
Indiana	6	Cecil M. Harden	Republican
Massachusetts	5	Edith Nourse Rogers	Republican
Michigan	9	Ruth Thompson	Republican
New York	10	Edna F. Kelly	Democrat
New York	28	Katharine St. George	Republican
Ohio	22	Frances P. Bolton	Republican
Pennsylvania	33	Vera D. Buchanan[67]	Democrat
Utah	2	Reva Beck Bosone	Democrat
West Virginia	5	Elizabeth Kee[68]	Democrat

[66]Bolton's son, Oliver, was sworn in also for the 83rd Congress, representing Ohio's 11th District, making them the only mother-son team to ever serve concurrently in Congress.

[67]Buchanan was selected in a special 1951 election to fill the seat of her deceased husband.

[68]Kee was selected in a special 1951 election to fill the seat of her deceased husband.

Total Women Serving

10 (6 Republicans, 4 Democrats)

Senior Female Member

Edith Nourse Rogers, (R) Massachusetts–5th, first elected in 1925.

Incumbents Not Returning from the 81st Congress

Helen Gahagan Douglas, (D) California–14th, was defeated as the Democratic nominee in her bid
for a U.S. Senate seat; her victorious opponent was U.S. Representative Richard M. Nixon.
Mary T. Norton, (D) New Jersey–13th, retired and did not seek reelection.
Chase Going Woodhouse, (D) Connecticut–2nd, was defeated in the general election.

81st Congress (1949–1951)

State	District	Name	Party Affiliation
California	14	Helen Gahagan Douglas	Democrat
Connecticut	2	Chase Going Woodhouse	Democrat
Indiana	6	Cecil M. Harden	Republican
New Jersey	13	Mary T. Norton	Democrat
Massachusetts	5	Edith Nourse Rogers	Republican
New York	10	Edna F. Kelly[69]	Democrat
New York	29	Katharine St. George	Republican
Ohio	22	Frances P. Bolton	Republican
Utah	2	Reva Beck Bosone	Democrat

Total Women Serving

9 (5 Democrats, 4 Republicans)

Senior Female Member

Mary T. Norton, (D) New Jersey–13th, first elected in 1924.

Wielding Power

Mary T. Norton, (D) New Jersey–13th, was chair of the House Committee on House Administration.

---

[69]Kelly was selected in a special November 1949 election to fill the seat of a deceased incumbent.

Notable Firsts

When **Cecil M. Harden** (R) carried Indiana's 6th Congressional District, it became the first congressional district to elect a second woman to represent it in the House of Representatives. Previously (1933–1939), it had been represented by **Virginia E. Jenckes** (D).

When **Chase Going Woodhouse** (D) carried Connecticut's 2nd Congressional District and returned to the U.S. House, she became the first woman to be elected, defeated, then reelected to the U.S. House. She had served one previous term (1945–1947) but had been defeated when she sought reelection in 1946.

Incumbents Not Returning from the 80th Congress

Georgia L. Lusk, (D) New Mexico–AL, was defeated by a challenger in the Democratic primary.
Margaret Chase Smith, (R) Maine–2nd, was elected to the U.S. Senate.

80th Congress (1947–1949)

State	District	Name	Party Affiliation
California	14	Helen Gahagan Douglas	Democrat
Maine	2	Margaret Chase Smith	Republican
Massachusetts	5	Edith Nourse Rogers	Republican
New Jersey	13	Mary T. Norton	Democrat
New Mexico	AL	Georgia L. Lusk	Democrat
New York	29	Katharine St. George[70]	Republican
Ohio	22	Frances P. Bolton	Republican

Total Women Serving

7 (4 Republicans, 3 Democrats)

Senior Female Member

Mary T. Norton, (D) New Jersey–13th, first elected in 1924.

Wielding Power

Edith Nourse Rogers, (R) Massachusetts–5th, was chair of the House Committee on Veterans Affairs.

Notable First

In 1948, the **Reverend Annalee Stewart**, an ordained Methodist minister, offered the daily opening prayer in the U.S. House of Representatives. She was the first female minister since the founding of the United States—159 years before—to be accorded the honor.

---

[70]St. George was a first cousin to Pres. Franklin D. Roosevelt on the side of his mother, Sara Delano.

Incumbents Not Returning from the 79th Congress

Helen Douglas Mankin, (D) Georgia–5th, was defeated by a challenger in the Democratic primary.

Emily Taft Douglas, (D) Illinois–AL, was defeated in the general election.

Clare Booth Luce, (R) Connecticut–4th, retired and did not seek reelection.

Jane Pratt, (D) North Carolina–8th, did not seek a full term.

Jessie Sumner, (R) Illinois–18th, retired and did not seek reelection.

Chase Going Woodhouse, (D) Connecticut–2nd, was defeated in the general election.

79th Congress (1945–1947)

State	District	Name	Party Affiliation
California	14	Helen Gahagan Douglas	Democrat
Connecticut	2	Chase Going Woodhouse	Democrat
Connecticut	4	Clare Booth Luce	Republican
Georgia	5	Helen Douglas Mankin	Democrat
Illinois	AL	Emily Taft Douglas	Democrat
Illinois	18	Jessie Sumner	Republican
Maine	2	Margaret Chase Smith	Republican
Massachusetts	5	Edith Nourse Rogers	Republican
New Jersey	13	Mary T. Norton	Democrat
North Carolina	8	Jane Pratt[71]	Democrat
Ohio	22	Frances P. Bolton	Republican

Total Women Serving

11 (6 Democrats, 5 Republicans)

Senior Female Member

Mary T. Norton, (D) New Jersey–13th, first elected in 1924.

Wielding Power

Mary T. Norton, (D) New Jersey–13th, was chair of the House Committee on Labor.

Notable Firsts

Connecticut became the first state to elect two women concurrently to its U.S. House delegation for full terms (see 71st Congress) when **Chase Going Woodhouse** carried the 2nd Congressional District and **Clare Booth Luce** carried the 4th Congressional District.

---

[71]Pratt was selected in a special May 1946 election to fill the seat of a deceased incumbent.

Connecticut's 4th Congressional District became the first district to witness a House race where both major-party candidates were female. Incumbent Republican **Clare Booth Luce** won the contest over her Democratic opponent, **Margaret Connor,** by the narrowest of margins—49.9–48.9 percent.

With her election to her seat in the U.S. House, **Emily Taft Douglas**, (D) Illinois–AL, became the first woman to *precede* her husband in Congress; her spouse, Paul Douglas, was elected to the U.S. Senate in November 1948.

Incumbents Not Returning from the 78th Congress

Willa L. Fulmer, (D) South Carolina–2nd, did not seek a full term.
Winifred C. Stanley, (R) New York–AL, retired and did not seek reelection when her statewide, at-large district was abolished.

78th Congress (1943–1945)

State	District	Name	Party Affiliation
Connecticut	4	Clare Booth Luce[72]	Republican
Illinois	18	Jessie Sumner	Republican
Maine	2	Margaret Chase Smith	Republican
Massachusetts	5	Edith Nourse Rogers	Republican
New Jersey	13	Mary T. Norton	Democrat
New York	AL	Winifred C. Stanley	Republican
Ohio	22	Frances P. Bolton	Republican
South Carolina	2	Willa L. Fulmer[73]	Democrat

Total Women Serving

8 (6 Republicans, 2 Democrats)

Senior Female Member

Mary T. Norton, (D) New Jersey–13th, first elected in 1924.

Wielding Power

Mary T. Norton, (D) New Jersey–13th, was chair of the House Committee on Labor.

---

[72]Luce's stepfather, Albert E. Austin, had held Connecticut's 4th District seat until he was defeated in November 1940. She became the first woman to succeed her stepfather in Congress.

[73]Fulmer was selected in a special November 1944 election to fill the seat of her deceased husband.

Notable First

On February 18, 1943, the U.S. House and Senate sat in a joint session to hear an address by **Madame Chiang Kai-shek**, wife of the president of the Republic of China, America's wartime ally. She was the first foreign woman to ever address a joint session of Congress.

Incumbents Not Returning from the 77th Congress

Veronica B. Boland, (D) Pennsylvania–11th, did not seek a full term.
Katharine E. Byron, (D) Maryland–6th, did not seek a full term.
Caroline O'Day, (D) New York–AL, retired and did not seek reelection.

77th Congress (1941–1943)

State	District	Name	Party Affiliation
Illinois	18	Jessie Sumner	Republican
Maine	2	Margaret Chase Smith	Republican
Massachusetts	5	Edith Nourse Rogers	Republican
Maryland	6	Katharine E. Byron[74]	Democrat
Montana	1	Jeannette Rankin	Republican
New Jersey	13	Mary T. Norton	Democrat
New York	AL	Caroline O'Day	Democrat
Ohio	22	Frances P. Bolton	Republican
Pennsylvania	11	Veronica B. Boland[75]	Democrat

Total Women Serving

9 (5 Republicans, 4 Democrats)

Senior Female Member

Mary T. Norton, (D) New Jersey–13th, first elected in 1924.

Wielding Power

Mary T. Norton, (D) New Jersey–13th, was chair of the House Committee on Labor.
Caroline O'Day, (D) New York–AL, was chair of the House Committee on the Election of the President.

---

[74]Byron was selected in a special election to fill the seat of her deceased husband. She had also been preceded in Congress by her grandfather, Louis E. McComas, (R) Maryland, who served in the U.S. House (1883–1891). Years later, in 1970, her son, Goodloe Byron, was elected to the U.S. House from this very same district. When he died in 1978 shortly before the general election, his wife, Beverly, was named the nominee and was elected. She held the seat 1979–1993, making the four of them the only husband-wife-son-wife quartet ever to serve in Congress.

[75]Boland was selected in a special election to fill the seat of her deceased husband.

Notable First

Jeannette Rankin, (R) Montana–1st, became the first woman elected for nonconsecutive terms in the U.S. House. Her previous term was 1917–1919 (65th Congress), when she was the first woman elected to the House. Rankin also gathered a more unusual distinction during this new term: She became the only member of Congress to vote against America's entry into *both* World War I and World War II. Those two votes created immense political problems for Rankin, ultimately causing her to be a one-term representative both times she was elected.

Incumbents Not Returning from the 76th Congress

Florence Reville Gibbs, (D) Georgia–8th, did not seek a full term.
Clara G. McMillan, (D) South Carolina–1st, did not seek a full term.

76th Congress (1939–1941)

State	District	Name	Party Affiliation
Georgia	8	Florence Reville Gibbs[76]	Democrat
Illinois	18	Jessie Sumner	Republican
Maine	2	Margaret Chase Smith[77]	Republican
Massachusetts	5	Edith Nourse Rogers	Republican
New Jersey	13	Mary T. Norton	Democrat
New York	AL	Caroline O'Day	Democrat
Ohio	22	Frances P. Bolton[78]	Republican
South Carolina	1	Clara G. McMillan[79]	Democrat

Total Women Serving

8 (4 Republicans, 4 Democrats)

Senior Female Member

Mary T. Norton, (D) New Jersey–13th, first elected in 1924.

Wielding Power

Mary T. Norton, (D) New Jersey–13th, was chair of the House Committee on Labor.

---

[76]Gibbs was selected in a special October 1940 election to fill the seat of her deceased husband.

[77]Smith was selected in a special June 1940 election to complete the term of her deceased husband.

[78]Bolton was selected in a special February 1940 election to complete the term of her deceased husband. She had also been preceded in Congress by her grandfather, Henry B. Payne, (R) Ohio, who served in the U.S. House (1875–1877) and Senate (1885–1891).

[79]McMillan was selected in a special November 1939 election to fill the seat of her deceased husband.

Caroline O'Day, (D) New York–AL, was chair of the House Committee on the Election of the President.

Incumbents Not Returning from the 75th Congress

Elizabeth H. Gasque, (D) South Carolina–6th, did not seek a full term.
Nan Wood Honeyman, (D) Oregon–3rd, was defeated in the general election.
Virginia E. Jenckes, (D) Indiana–6th, was defeated in the general election.

75th Congress (1937–1939)

State	District	Name	Party Affiliation
Indiana	6	Virginia E. Jenckes	Democrat
Massachusetts	5	Edith Nourse Rogers	Republican
New Jersey	13	Mary T. Norton	Democrat
New York	AL	Caroline O'Day	Democrat
Oregon	3	Nan Wood Honeyman	Democrat
South Carolina	6	Elizabeth H. Gasque[80]	Democrat

Total Women Serving

6 (5 Democrats, 1 Republican)

Senior Female Member

Mary T. Norton, (D) New Jersey–13th, first elected in 1924.

Achieving Power

Mary T. Norton, (D) New Jersey–13th, became chair of the House Committee on Labor.
Caroline O'Day, (D) New York–AL, became chair of the House Committee on the Election of the President.

Incumbents Not Returning from the 74th Congress

Isabella Greenway, (D) Arizona–AL, retired and did not seek reelection.
Florence P. Kahn, (R) California–4th, was defeated in the general election.

74th Congress (1935–1937)

State	District	Name	Party Affiliation
Arizona	AL	Isabella Greenway	Democrat

---

[80]Gasque was selected in a special election to complete the last four months of her deceased husband's term.

California	4	Florence P. Kahn	Republican
Indiana	6	Virginia E. Jenckes	Democrat
Massachusetts	5	Edith Nourse Rogers	Republican
New Jersey	13	Mary T. Norton	Democrat
New York	AL	Caroline O'Day	Democrat

Total Women Serving

6 (4 Democrats, 2 Republicans)

Senior Female Member

Mary T. Norton, (D) New Jersey–13th, who was first elected in 1924.

Wielding Power

Mary T. Norton, (D) New Jersey–13th, was chair of the House Committee on the District of Columbia.

Incumbents Not Returning from the 73rd Congress

Marian W. Clarke, (R) New York–34th, did not seek reelection to a full term.
Kathryn O'Loughlin McCarthy, (D) Kansas–6th, was defeated in the general election.

73rd Congress (1933–1935)

State	District	Name	Party Affiliation
Arizona	AL	Isabella Greenway	Democrat
California	4	Florence P. Kahn	Republican
Indiana	6	Virginia E. Jenckes	Democrat
Kansas	6	Kathryn O'Loughlin McCarthy	Democrat
Massachusetts	5	Edith Nourse Rogers	Republican
New Jersey	13	Mary T. Norton	Democrat
New York	34	Marian W. Clarke[81]	Republican

Total Women Serving

7 (4 Democrats, 3 Republicans)

Senior Female Member

Mary T. Norton, (D) New Jersey–13th, first elected in 1924.

---

[81]Clarke was selected in a special election to fill the seat of her deceased husband.

Wielding Power

Mary T. Norton, (D) New Jersey–13th, was chair of the House Committee on the District of Columbia.

Incumbents Not Returning from the 72nd Congress

Willa B. Eslick, (D) Tennessee–7th, did not seek a full term.
Ruth Bryan Owen, (D) Florida–4th, was defeated by a challenger in the Democratic primary.
Ruth Baker Pratt, (R) New York–17th, was defeated in the general election.
Effigene Wingo, (D) Arkansas–4th, retired and did not seek reelection.

Elected but Never Served

In 1933 Rep. Bolivar Kemp, (D) Louisiana–6th, died in office. The struggle to fill his vacant seat turned into a free-for-all, Louisiana-style. Sen. Huey Long (D) wanted Kemp's widow, Lallie Connor Kemp, to succeed her husband, but the district's community and county leaders had other plans. They "boycotted" the special election called to fill the seat, in which Mrs. Kemp received 99.8 percent of the vote, and managed to have the results thrown out, which necessitated another special election a few months later. Mrs. Kemp, disgusted by all the anti-Long and pro-Long maneuvering, chose not to run in that election.

72nd Congress (1931–1933)

State	District	Name	Party Affiliation
Arkansas	4	Effigene L. Wingo	Democrat
California	4	Florence P. Kahn	Republican
Florida	4	Ruth Bryan Owen	Democrat
Massachusetts	5	Edith Nourse Rogers	Republican
New Jersey	13	Mary T. Norton[82]	Democrat
New York	17	Ruth Baker Pratt	Republican
Tennessee	7	Willa B. Eslick[83]	Democrat

Total Women Serving

7 (4 Democrats, 3 Republicans)

Senior Female Member

Mary T. Norton, (D) New Jersey–13th, first elected in 1924.

---

[82]In 1932 Norton became the chair of the New Jersey State Democratic Party, the first female state chair of any national political party.

[83]Eslick won a special election to fill the seat of her deceased husband, Edward, after he had dropped dead on the floor of the House in 1932 while making a speech. He was the first member of the House to die on the floor of the chamber since 1834.

Achieving Power

Mary T. Norton, (D) New Jersey–13th, became chair of the House Committee on the District of Columbia.

Incumbents Not Returning from the 71st Congress

Katherine Langley, (R) Kentucky–10th, was defeated in the general election.
Ruth Hanna McCormick, (R) Illinois–AL, was defeated as the Republican nominee in her bid for
  a seat in the U.S. Senate.
Pearl Peden Oldfield, (D) Arkansas–2nd, did not seek reelection.

71st Congress (1929–1931)

State	District	Name	Party Affiliation
Arkansas	2	Pearl Peden Oldfield	Democrat
Arkansas	4	Effigene L. Wingo[84]	Democrat
California	4	Florence P. Kahn	Republican
Florida	4	Ruth Bryan Owen[85]	Democrat
Illinois	AL	Ruth Hanna McCormick[86]	Republican
Kentucky	10	Katherine Langley	Republican
Massachusetts	5	Edith Nourse Rogers	Republican
New Jersey	12	Mary T. Norton	Democrat
New York	17	Ruth Baker Pratt	Republican

Total Women Serving

9 (5 Republicans, 4 Democrats)

Notable First

Arkansas became the first state to be represented by two women concurrently when **Effigene Wingo** (D) won a special election and joined **Pearl Peden Oldfield** (D) in the state's U.S. House delegation.

70th Congress (1927–1929)

State	District	Name	Party Affiliation
Arkansas	2	Pearl Peden Oldfield[87]	Democrat
California	4	Florence P. Kahn	Republican
Kentucky	10	Katherine Langley[88]	Republican

---

[84]Wingo was selected in a special election to complete the term of her deceased husband.

[85]Owen was the daughter of famed orator and three-time presidential candidate William Jennings Bryan.

[86]McCormick was the widow of Sen. Medill McCormick, (R) Illinois, and the daughter of famed Republican political boss Mark Hanna.

[87]Oldfield was selected in a special election to complete the term of her deceased husband.

[88]Langley's husband had preceded her in Congress. After he was jailed for bootlegging, she contested his seat in the general election.

Massachusetts	5	Edith Nourse Rogers	Republican
New Jersey	12	Mary T. Norton	Democrat

69th Congress (1925–1927)

State	District	Name	Party Affiliation
California	4	Florence P. Kahn[89]	Republican
Massachusetts	5	Edith Nourse Rogers[90]	Republican
New Jersey	12	Mary T. Norton	Democrat

Notable First

Mary T. Norton, (D) New Jersey–12th, became the first Democratic woman elected to the U.S. House. She was preceded there by four Republican women.

Incumbent Not Returning from the 68th Congress

Mae E. Nolan, (R) California–5th, did not seek reelection.

68th Congress (1923–1925)

State	District	Name	Party Affiliation
California	5	Mae E. Nolan	Republican

Achieving Power

Mae E. Nolan, (R) California–5th, became chair of the House Committee on Expenditures in the Post Office Department; this was the first time a woman formally chaired a standing committee of the U.S. House.

Incumbents Not Returning from the 67th Congress

Alice Mary Robertson, (R) Oklahoma–2nd, was defeated in the general election.
Winnifred Mason Huck, (R) Illinois–AL, was defeated in the general election in her bid for another term from a different district.

Notable First: 1922

Adelina Otero-Warren, (R) New Mexico, became the first Hispanic woman to receive the congressional nomination of a major party. She was defeated in her bid to fill New Mexico's lone seat

---

[89]Kahn was selected in a special election to fill the seat of her deceased husband.

[90]Rogers was selected in a special June 1925 election to fill the seat of her deceased husband.

in the U.S. House of Representatives, receiving a respectable 45 percent of the vote. It would be sixty-seven years before a Hispanic woman was seated as a member of the U.S. House. (See 101st Congress, 1989–1991, for details.)

67th Congress (1921–1923)

State	District	Name	Party Affiliation
California	5	Mae E. Nolan[91]	Republican
Illinois	AL	Winnifred Mason Huck[92]	Republican
Oklahoma	2	Alice Mary Robertson	Republican

Notable Firsts

Alice Mary Robertson, (R) Oklahoma–2nd, became the second woman elected to the U.S. House of her own volition. She was not preceded in the chamber by a male relative, as were Mae E. Nolan and Winnifred Mason Huck.

Alice Mary Robertson (R) Oklahoma–2nd, also became the first woman to preside over a session of the U.S. House of Representatives on June 20, 1921.

66th Congress (1919–1921)

No women were elected to serve in the 66th Congress.

65th Congress (1917–1919)

State	District	Name	Party Affiliation
Montana	AL	Jeannette Rankin[93]	Republican

Notable First: 1866

Elizabeth Cady Stanton sought a seat in the U.S. House of Representatives (New York–8th) as an Independent, the first woman to run for a seat in that body. Even though Stanton was barred from voting for herself—women did not have the right to vote—she received twenty-four votes out of a total of more than 24,000 cast in the congressional election.

Notable First: 1864

Anna Elizabeth Dickinson, a noted speaker for abolition and women's rights, addressed a session of the U.S. House of Representatives at the invitation of a Republican representative for whom she

---

[91]Nolan was elected to complete the term of her deceased husband, John Nolan.

[92]Huck was elected November 1922 to complete the term of her father after he died in office.

[93]Rankin ran for the U.S. Senate in 1918 but was defeated, due in large part to her vote in the U.S. House against America's entry into World War I. Years later she was elected for one additional two-year term (77th Congress, 1941–1943) in the U.S. House.

had campaigned. When she made her speech, Pres. Abraham Lincoln was in the audience to hear it. Dickinson was the first woman to address the U.S. House.

Female Governors in Chronological Order of Service

1. Nellie Tayloe Ross	Democrat	Wyoming	01/05/25–01/03/27
2. Miriam Amanda Ferguson	Democrat	Texas	01/20/25–01/18/27, 01/17/33–01/15/35
3. Lurleen Burns Wallace	Democrat	Alabama	01/16/67–05/07/68
4. Ella Tambussi Grasso	Democrat	Connecticut	01/08/75–12/31/80
5. Dixy Lee Ray	Democrat	Washington	01/12/77–01/14/81
6. Martha Layne Collins	Democrat	Kentucky	12/13/83–12/08/87
7. Madeleine May Kunin	Democrat	Vermont	01/10/85–01/10/91
8. Kay Stark Orr	Republican	Nebraska	01/09/87–01/09/91
9. Rose Perica Mofford	Democrat	Arizona	04/04/88–03/06/91
10. Ann Willis Richards	Democrat	Texas	01/15/91–01/17/95
11. Barbara Hughey Roberts	Democrat	Oregon	01/14/91–01/09/95
12. Joan McInroy Finney	Democrat	Kansas	01/14/91–01/09/95
13. ***Christine Todd Whitman***	Republican	New Jersey	01/18/94–
14. ***Jeanne Bowers Shaheen***	Democrat	New Hampshire	01/15/97–
15. ***Jane Dee Hull***	Republican	Arizona	09/05/97–

Note: ***Bold italic*** denotes that governor is still serving.

How They Assumed Office

1. **Nellie Tayloe Ross,** (D) Wyoming (Born: 1876; Died: 1977). Politically prominent spouse: William B. Ross (D), governor 1923–1924
   Served: 01/05/25–01/03/27

   Elected on November 4, 1924, in a special election. Mrs. Ross, whose husband, Gov. William B. Ross (D), had died on October 2, 1924, and was temporarily succeeded by Wyoming's secretary of state, ran and won the right to complete the remaining two years of his term. She ran again in 1926 for a four-year term of her own but was defeated by Frank C. Emerson (R). In 1933 Pres. Franklin D. Roosevelt appointed Ross as the first female director of the U.S. Mint.

   Previous and subsequent elected political office: None

2. **Miriam Amanda Ferguson,** (D) Texas (Born: 1875; Died: 1961). Politically prominent spouse: James E. Ferguson (D), governor 1915–1917.
   Served: 01/20/25–01/18/27, 01/17/33–01/15/35

   Elected on November 4, 1924, to a two-year term. Midway into his second term, her husband, Gov. James "Pa" Ferguson (D), was impeached and then removed from office on August 25, 1917. Forbidden to contest the governor's office again and chafing to settle the score with his political enemies, he devised a plan to make his wife—nicknamed "Ma"—governor instead. With encouragement from her husband and the support of his political cronies, Mrs. Ferguson ran in 1924 using such campaign slogans as "Me for Ma" and "Two Governors for the Price of One." In 1926 she was defeated in the Democratic primary for renomination by Attorney General Dan Moody (D). The Democratic primary runoff of 1930 marked yet another defeat for her, but she recaptured the Democratic nomination in 1932, then won the governorship again for a two-year term on November 6, 1932, over Orville Bullington (R). Mrs. Ferguson sought renomination in 1934 but met another defeat in the Democratic primary, this time by James V. Allred (D). Prodded by her husband, she ran a final time in 1940, receiving a dismally low 8 percent of the vote. After that loss she retired from the election arena, living quietly until her death almost twenty-eight years later.

Previous and subsequent elected political office: None

3. **Lurleen Burns Wallace,** (D) Alabama (Born: 1926; Died: 1968). Politically prominent spouse: George C. Wallace (D), governor 1963–1967, 1971–1979, 1983–1987.
   Served: 01/16/67–05/07/68

Elected on November 8, 1966, to a four year-term. After her husband, Gov. George C. Wallace (D), was unsuccessful in convincing the state legislature to remove the restriction that prohibited him from a second consecutive term, he ran wife Lurleen Wallace in his stead. She won the Democratic primary without a runoff, then triumphed in November against James D. Martin (R), one of the leaders of a newly growing Republican Party. During the campaigns the Wallaces never concealed who would actually be the power in the office if she was elected. Mrs. Wallace made only short campaign speeches, usually promising to appoint her husband as her "number-one, one-dollar-a-year adviser" before turning the podium over to her husband for a lengthier spiel. Less than two years after assuming office she was stricken with cancer and died. George C. Wallace remarried, then returned to the governorship for three more terms.

Previous elected political office: None

4. **Ella Tambussi Grasso**, (D) Connecticut (Born: 1919; Died: 1981)
   Served: 01/08/75–12/31/80

Elected on November 5, 1974, to a four-year term. Grasso won reelection in 1978 to a second term but failed to complete it. Ill with cancer, she resigned the governorship on December 31, 1980, and died shortly thereafter.

Previous elected political office:
   Connecticut House of Representatives, 1953–1959
   Connecticut Secretary of State, 1959–1970
   U.S. House of Representatives, 1971–1974

5. **Dixy Lee Ray**, (D) Washington (Born: 1914; Died: 1994)
   Served: 01/12/77–01/14/81

Elected on November 2, 1976, to a four-year term. A former head of the Atomic Energy Commission under Pres. Jimmy Carter, Ms. Ray had a rocky term as governor yet announced her candidacy for reelection. Her attempt for a second term ended in the Democratic primary, when she lost the nomination to a state senator, James McDermott (D), by less than 10,000 votes.

Previous and subsequent elected political office: None

6. **Martha Layne Collins,** (D) Kentucky (Born: 1936)
   Served: 12/13/83–12/08/87

Elected on November 8, 1983, to a four-year term. Since Kentucky law did not permit governors to succeed themselves at that time, Mrs. Collins was ineligible to run for a second term.

Previous elected political office:
   Lieutenant Governor, 1979–1983
Subsequent elected political office: None

7. **Madeleine May Kunin**, (D) Vermont (Born: 1933)
   Served: 01/10/85–01/10/91

Elected on November 2, 1984, to a two-year term. She won reelection in 1986 and 1988, then declined to seek a fourth term. President Clinton later appointed her undersecretary in the education department, then ambassador to Switzerland, the land of her birth. Prior to her victory in 1984, Kunin had made one earlier unsuccessful attempt—in 1982—to win the governorship, but she was defeated in the general election.

Previous elected political office:
   Vermont House of Representatives, 1973–1979
   Lieutenant Governor, 1979–1983
Subsequent elected political office: None

8. **Kay Stark Orr**, (R) Nebraska (Born: 1939)
   Served: 01/09/87–01/09/91

Elected on November 4, 1986, to a four-year term. Mrs. Orr sought reelection to a second term in 1990 but went down in a narrow defeat—4,030 votes—in the general election to Ben Nelson (D). Many blamed her defeat on her choice for an appointment to the U.S. Senate; she was simply unable to satisfy all the factions seeking the appointment and lost much of their political support when her reelection rolled around.

Previous elected political office:
   Nebraska State Treasurer, 1981–1986
Subsequent elected political office: None

9. **Rose Perica Mofford**, (D) Arizona (Born: 1922)
   Served: 04/04/88–03/06/91

Succeeded to the office on April 4, 1988, when Gov. Evan Mecham (R) was impeached and removed from office by the Arizona legislature. Since Arizona did not have a lieutenant governor, Mofford, as secretary of state, was next in line to succeed to the governorship. She did not seek election in 1990 for a full four-year term of her own. Even then, Mofford's term of office had to be extended two months (until March 1991) to accommodate a special runoff, which was required when no candidate received a majority in the 1990 general election.

Previous elected political office:
   Arizona Secretary of State, 1977–1988
Subsequent elected political office: None

10. **Ann Willis Richards,** (D) Texas (Born: 1933)
    Served: 01/15/91–01/17/95

Elected on November 5, 1990, to a four-year term. She sought reelection to a second term in 1994 but was defeated by George W. Bush (R), eldest son of the former president.

Previous elected political office:
   Travis County, Texas, Commissioner, 1976–1982
   Texas State Treasurer, 1983–1991
Subsequent elected political office: None

11. **Barbara Hughey Roberts,** (D) Oregon (Born: 1936)
    Served: 01/14/91–01/09/95

Elected on November 5, 1990, to a four-year term. She did not seek reelection in 1994 to a second term. Previously, in 1974, Roberts had placed second in the Democratic primary for the gubernatorial nomination. Later that same year, after the winner of the Democratic nomination for U.S. Senate died unexpectedly, she was substituted in his place, but she lost to Sen. Robert Packwood (R) in the general election.

Previous elected political office:
   Parkrose, Oregon, School Board, 1973–1983
   Multnomah, Oregon, County Commission, 1978
   Oregon House of Representatives, 1981–1985
   Oregon Secretary of State, 1985–1991

12. **Joan McInroy Finney,** (D) Kansas (Born: 1925)
    Served: 01/14/91–01/09/95

Elected on November 5, 1990, to a four-year term. She did not seek reelection in 1994 to a second term. In 1996 Finney was an unsuccessful candidate in the special Democratic primary to fill the remainder—two years—of Sen. Bob Dole's (R) seat, after he retired to seek the presidency as the Republican nominee. She placed second in that race, losing to another woman, stockbroker Jill Docking (D).
Previous elected political office:
   Kansas State Treasurer, 1975–1991

13. **Christine Todd Whitman,** (R) New Jersey (Born: 1946)
    Served: 01/18/94–present

Elected on November 2, 1993, to a four-year term. For Whitman, it was a sweet victory. It removed the sting of her narrow defeat—by 58,936 votes out of almost 3 million cast, despite being outspent almost thirteen-to-one—in November 1990 as the Republican nominee against Sen. Bill Bradley (D). She won another four-year term in 1997 by an unexpectedly narrow margin.

Previous elected political office: None

14. **Jeanne Bowers Shaheen,** (D) New Hampshire (Born: 1947)
    Served: 01/15/97–present

Elected on November 5, 1996, to a two-year term. She was reelected in 1998 for an additional two-year term.

Previous elected political office:
    New Hampshire State Senate, 1991–1997

15. **Jane Dee Hull,** (R) Arizona (Born: 1935)
    Served: 09/05/97–present

Succeeded to the office on September 5, 1997, when Gov. Fife Symington (R) resigned. Hull was Arizona's second secretary of state in ten years to move up to the governorship—since the state has no lieutenant governor—after the incumbent left office under adverse circumstances. The previous time the governor was impeached; this time the incumbent resigned after he was convicted on several felony counts that he had lied to commercial lenders in order to save his tottering real estate empire. She was elected in 1998 to a full four-year term.

Previous elected political office:
    Arizona House of Representatives, 1979–1993
    Speaker of the House, 1989–1993
    Arizona Secretary of State, 1995–1997

Acting Governors

Many women, by virtue of their state constitutional or legislative leadership offices, have served temporarily as "acting" governors. Former Rep. **Barbara Jordan**, (D) Texas, is an excellent example. During her tenure in the Texas senate, she "acted" as the governor of Texas for two days when both the incumbent and the lieutenant governor were out of the state. No attempt has been made in this almanac to list all women who have served as acting governors, but one case should be mentioned due to the unusual circumstances involved in the situation.

Vesta M. Roy, (R) New Hampshire
Served: December 29, 1982–January 6, 1983

In November 1982 Gov. Hugh Gallen (D) was hospitalized with a blood infection. Under the New Hampshire constitution, the president of the state senate became acting governor. Due to the election that had just been held, the state senate dissolved at the end of November. The secretary of state then assumed the governor's duties until the newly elected state senate was sworn in and could elect new officers. Once the body met, senate members elected Vesta M. Roy as presiding officer, which also immediately made her the new "acting" governor.

On December 28, 1982, one week before the newly elected governor, John H. Sununu (R), was due to take office, Gov. Gallen died. Mrs. Roy was then faced with an unusual choice. She could formally take the oath of office as governor, but she would have to immediately resign from her senate seat, plus vacate her new office at the end of the week. After consultation with legal and constitutional authorities, she chose to remain in her "acting" capacity. When her unusual gubernatorial term was over, Mrs. Roy returned to serve several more years in the senate.

Female Gubernatorial Statistics

First Female to Seek the Nomination of a Major Party for Governor

Elizabeth Upham Yates, (D) Rhode Island, in 1920 for the Democratic nomination

Shortest Tenure of a Female Governor

Lurleen B. Wallace, (D) Alabama, who served from January 16, 1967, until May 7, 1968, when she died of cancer.

Longest Tenure of a Female Governor

Six years is the maximum that any woman has served as governor. **Madeleine Kunin**, (D) Vermont, holds this distinction: She served three full two-year terms (January 10, 1985–January 10, 1991). **Ella T. Grasso**, (D) Connecticut, (January 8, 1975–December 31, 1980) came very close to matching Kunin's tenure. Had she not fallen ill with cancer and resigned midway into her second term, Grasso probably would have served a full eight years. With her reelection to a second four-year term in 1997, **Christine T. Whitman**, (R) New Jersey, is now the likeliest woman to set a new record, if she serves all four years of her second term.

First State to Have More Than One Female Governor

Texas
1925–1927 and 1933–1935	Miriam A. Ferguson (D)
1991–1995	Ann W. Richards (D)

Other State to Have More Than One Female Governor

Arizona
1988–1991	Rose P. Mofford (D)
1997–	Jane D. Hull (R)

The Most Female Governors in the U.S. at One Time

The milestone of four concurrent female governors holding office was reached on January 15, 1991, with the inauguration of **Ann W. Richards**, (D) Texas. The members of the quartet were **Joan M. Finney**, (D) Kansas, **Rose P. Mofford**, (D) Arizona, and **Barbara H. Roberts**, (D) Oregon. Mofford was the only "unelected" member of the group, since she had become governor when the incumbent was removed from office. Due to leave office in January 1991, Mofford's term was extended due to the necessity of a runoff election, because the November 1990 gubernatorial ballot had been inconclusive.

First Race in Which Both Major-Party Candidates Were Female

There has been only one gubernatorial race in which the candidates of both major political parties were female. That was in Nebraska in 1986, when **Kay S. Orr** (R), state treasurer, and **Helen Boosalis** (D), mayor of Lincoln, faced off. Republican Orr won the contest, 53–47 percent.

First Succession of One Female Governor by Another

This has not occurred yet.

First Woman Elected Governor Whose Husband Had Preceded Her in the Statehouse

Nellie T. Ross, (D) Wyoming, was elected November 4, 1924, to succeed her husband, William B. Ross (D), who had died in office, to complete the remaining two years of his four-year term.

Other Women Whose Husbands Preceded Them in the Statehouse

Miriam A. Ferguson, (D) Texas, was preceded by her husband, James Ferguson (D), who had been elected for two terms (in 1914 and in 1916). He was impeached midway into his second term.

Lurleen B. Wallace, (D) Alabama, was preceded by her husband, George C. Wallace (D), who had served as governor for one term (1963–1967). After her tenure, he returned to the statehouse to serve three additional four-year terms (1971–1979, 1983–1987).

First Woman Elected Whose Husband Had Not Preceded Her in the Statehouse

Ella T. Grasso, (D) Connecticut, elected on November 5, 1974, for a four-year term.

Women Who Tried to Succeed Their Husbands in the Statehouse but Failed

Lydia Langer, (R) North Dakota, wife of William B. Langer, former governor (1932–1934) and future senator (January 1, 1941–November 8, 1959), was the Republican nominee for governor of North Dakota in 1934 (after her husband had been removed from office by the state supreme court). She lost her race against Thomas H. Moodie (D) by 17,479 votes, a 53.4–46.6 percent margin.

Mrs. Johnston Murray, (D) Oklahoma, wife of Gov. Johnston Murray (1951–1955), attempted to succeed her husband, who was constitutionally barred from a second term in office. She placed third in the 1954 Democratic primary.

Betty Hearnes, (D) Missouri, wife of former Gov. Warren Hearnes (1965–1973), was the Democratic candidate for governor in 1988 against incumbent John Ashcroft (R). She lost 64–36 percent.

Colleen Engler, (R) Michigan, former wife of Gov. John Engler (1990–), actually ran for governor *before* he did. In 1986, while they were married and both members of the state legislature, Colleen Engler ran in the Republican primary for the gubernatorial nomination, where she placed third. The winner of the primary then selected her as his running mate for the lieutenant governor slot, but they lost the November general election. Four years and one divorce later, her former husband, John Engler (R), won his first term as governor.

Barbara Snelling, (R) Vermont, wife of former Gov. Richard Snelling (1977–1985, 1991), encountered an unusual obstacle in her path to follow her husband as governor after he died in 1991. She was elected lieutenant governor in 1992 and was reelected in 1994. When the 1996 campaign season opened, Snelling led the race for the Republican gubernatorial nomination, then tragedy struck. She suffered a stroke, withdrew from the race, yet recovered in time to file for a state senate seat, which she won. In 1998 the nearly seventy-year-old Snelling was back on the campaign trail running for lieutenant governor again, undoubtedly planning another race for governor sometime in the future.

One woman whose husband was governor didn't try to succeed him. Instead, she made an unsuccessful run for a higher political office.

Lenore Romney, (R) Michigan, wife of former Gov. George Romney (1963–1969), was the unsuccessful Republican candidate for U.S. Senate from Michigan in 1970 against Sen. Phillip Hart (D). In 1994 her son, W. Mitt Romney (R), unsuccessfully opposed Sen. Edward Kennedy, (D) Massachusetts. The Romney family's quest for a U.S. Senate seat stretched a little farther in 1996, when a former daughter-in-law, Ronna Romney, was the unsuccessful Republican candidate in Michigan against Sen. Carl Levin (D).

Women Who Tried to Succeed Other Close Relatives in the Statehouse but Failed

Kathleen Brown, (D) California, state treasurer and the Democratic nominee for governor in 1994, was the daughter of former Gov. Pat Brown (1959–1967) and sister of former Gov. Jerry Brown (1975–1983). She was unsuccessful in her attempt to unseat Gov. Pete Wilson (R).

Mary Mead, (D) Wyoming, the Republican nominee for governor in 1990, was the daughter of a former governor (1963–1967) and senator (1967–1979), Clifford Hansen. She was unsuccessful in her attempt to unseat Gov. Mike Sullivan (D).

Anna Belle Clement O'Brien, (D) Tennessee, the sister of former Gov. Frank G. Clement (1953–1959, 1963–1967), was even less successful in her 1982 bid to be governor. She failed to get her party's nomination but did place second in the primary.

Female Governors Who Won Reelection

After winning one election for governor, five women have been successful in being elected to another term.

Miriam A. Ferguson, (D) Texas, won reelection in 1932 to a second two-year, nonconsecutive term; her first term was 1925–1927. After winning her two nonconsecutive terms, she never sought a third term.

Ella T. Grasso, (D) Connecticut, won reelection in 1978 to a second consecutive four-year term; her first term was 1975–1979. She died shortly after resigning almost midway through her second term.

Madeleine M. Kunin, (D) Vermont, won reelection in 1986 and 1988 to consecutive second and third two-year terms; her first term was 1985–1987. She did not seek a fourth term.

Christine T. Whitman, (R) New Jersey, won reelection in 1997 to a consecutive four-year term. Her first term was 1994–1998. She is constitutionally prohibited from a third successive term.

Jeanne B. Shaheen, (D) New Hampshire, won reelection in 1998 to a consecutive two-year term. Her first term was 1997–1999.

First Female Candidate to Defeat an Incumbent Male Governor

When **Joan M. Finney**, (D) Kansas, defeated one-term incumbent Gov. Mike Hayden (R) on November 6, 1990, she became the first female to oust an incumbent male governor. **Christine T. Whitman**, (R) New Jersey, became the second woman to do so when she dumped Gov. James Florio (D) on November 2, 1993.

Female Governors Who Were Defeated

After having served at least one term, the following five women were defeated in their reelection bids. Two defeats were in primaries, three in November general elections.

Nellie T. Ross, (D) Wyoming, was defeated on November 2, 1926, when she sought a four-year term of her own. She lost by fewer than 1,400 votes.

Miriam A. Ferguson, (D) Texas, was defeated in the Democratic primary in 1926, when she sought renomination as the party's candidate for a second two-year term.

Dixy L. Ray, (D) Washington, was defeated in the 1980 Democratic primary, when she sought renomination as the party's candidate for a second four-year term.

Kay S. Orr, (R) Nebraska, was defeated on November 6, 1990, when she sought reelection to a second four-year term. She lost by fewer than 4,100 votes.

Ann W. Richards, (D) Texas, was defeated on November 3, 1992, when she sought reelection to a second four-year term.

Female Gubernatorial Election Statistics

The following section provides voting statistics on those female governors who have contested elections, including primaries, primary runoffs, and general elections. Names in this section appear in chronological order of gubernatorial service, from earliest to most recent.

Nellie Tayloe Ross, (D) Wyoming

Year	Type	Candidate	Votes	%
1926	General	Frank C. Emerson (R)	35,651	50.9%
		Nellie T. Ross (D)	34,286	49.1%
1924	Special Election	Nellie T. Ross (D)	43,323	55.1%
		E. J. Sullivan (R)	25,275	44.9%

Miriam Amanda Ferguson, (D) Texas

Year	Type	Candidate	Votes	%
1932	General	Miriam A. Ferguson (D)	521,395	61.6%
		Orville Bullington (R)	322,589	38.1%
1932	Primary Runoff	Miriam A. Ferguson	477,644	50.2%
		Ross Sterling	473,846	49.6%
1932	Democratic Primary	Miriam A. Ferguson	402,238	41.8%
		Ross Sterling	296,383	30.8%
		Tom F. Hunter	220,391	22.9%
1930	Primary Runoff	Ross Sterling	473,371	55.2%
		Miriam A. Ferguson	384,402	44.8%
1930	Democratic Primary	Miriam A. Ferguson	242,959	29.2%
		Ross Sterling	170,754	20.5%
		Clint Small	138,934	16.7%
		Four others		34.0%
1926	Primary Runoff	Dan Moody	495,729	64.7%
		Miriam A. Ferguson	270,595	35.3%
1926	Democratic Primary	Dan Moody	409,732	49.9%
		Miriam A. Ferguson	283,482	34.5%
		Lynch Davidson	122,449	14.9%
1924	General	Miriam A. Ferguson (D)	422,563	58.9%
		George C. Butte (R)	294,920	41.1%
1924	Primary Runoff	Miriam A. Ferguson	413,751	56.7%
		F. D. Robertson	316,019	43.3%
1924	Democratic Primary	F. D. Robertson	193,508	27.5%
		Miriam A. Ferguson	146,424	20.8%
		Lynch Davidson	141,208	20.1%

Lurleen Burns Wallace, (D) Alabama

Year	Type	Candidate	Votes	%
1966	General	Lurleen B. Wallace (D)	537,505	63.4%
		James D. Martin (R)	262,943	31.0%
1966	Democratic Primary	Lurleen B. Wallace	480,841	54.1%
		Richmond Flowers	172,386	19.4%

		Carl Elliott	71,972	8.1%
		Bob Gilchrist	49,502	5.6%

Ella Tambussi Grasso, (D) Connecticut

1978	General	Ella T. Grasso (D)	613,109	59.0%
		Ronald A. Sarasin (R)	422,316	41.0%
1978	Democratic Primary	Ella T. Grasso	137,904	67.0%
		Robert K. Killian	66,924	33.0%
1974	General	Ella T. Grasso (D)	643,490	58.4%
		Robert H. Steele (R)	440,169	39.9%

Dixy Lee Ray, (D) Washington

1980	Democratic Primary	James McDermott	162,426	41.0%
		Dixy L. Ray	154,724	39.0%
1976	General	Dixy L. Ray (D)	821,797	53.1%
		John Spellman (R)	687,039	44.4%

Martha Layne Collins, (D) Kentucky

1983	General	Martha L. Collins (D)	561,674	54.0%
		Jim Bunning (R)	454,650	44.0%
1983	Democratic Primary	Martha L. Collins	223,692	34.0%
		Harvey Sloane	219,160	33.0%
		Grady Stumbo	199,795	30.0%

Madeleine May Kunin, (D) Vermont

1986	General	Madeleine M. Kunin (D)	92,379	47.0%
		Peter Smith (R)	75,162	38.0%
		Bernard Sanders (I)	28,430	14.0%
1984	General	Madeleine M. Kunin (D)	116,938	50.0%
		John J. Easton (R)	113,264	48.0%
1982	General	Richard Snelling (R)	92,588	55.0%
		Madeleine M. Kunin (D)	74,304	44.0%

Kay Stark Orr, (R) Nebraska

1990	General	E. Benjamin Nelson (D)	292,771	50.0%
		Kay S. Orr (R)	288,741	49.0%
1986	General	Kay S. Orr (R)	298,325	53.0%
		Helen Boosalis (D)	265,156	47.0%

Ann Willis Richards, (D) Texas

1994	General	George W. Bush Jr. (R)	2,350,493	54.0%
		Ann W. Richards (D)	2,014,399	46.0%
1990	General	Ann W. Richards (D)	1,911,620	51.0%
		Clayton Williams (R)	1,815,084	49.0%

1990	Democratic Runoff	Ann W. Richards	640,995	57.0%
		Jim Mattox	481,739	43.0%
1990	Democratic Primary	Ann W. Richards	580,191	39.0%
		Jim Mattox	546,103	37.0%
		Mark W. White	286,161	19.0%
		Four others	74,805	4.0%

Barbara Hughey Roberts, (D) Oregon

1990	General	Barbara H. Roberts (D)	508,749	43.0%
		Dave Frohnmayer (R)	444,646	40.0%
		Al Mobley (I)	144,062	13.0%

Joan McInroy Finney, (D) Kansas

1990	General	Joan M. Finney (D)	380,608	49.0%
		Mike Hayden (R)	333,589	43.0%
1990	Democratic Primary	Joan M. Finney	81,250	47.0%
		John Carlin	79,406	46.0%
		Fred Phelps	11,572	7.0%

Christine Todd Whitman, (R) New Jersey

1997	General	Christine T. Whitman (R)	1,123,534	47.0%
		James McGreevey (D)	1,096,581	46.0%
		Murray Sabrin (L)	113,648	5.0%
		Others	65,099	2.0%
1993	General	Christine T. Whitman (R)	1,236,124	49.0%
		James Florio (D)	1,210,031	48.0%
1993	Republican Primary	Christine T. Whitman	159,765	40.0%
		Cary Edwards	131,678	33.0%
		Jim Wallwork	96,034	24.0%
		Others	12,448	3.0%

Jeanne Bowers Shaheen, (D) New Hampshire

1998	General	Jeanne Shaheen (D)	210,720	66.0%
		Jay Lucas (R)	98,408	31.0%
		Others		3.0%
1998	Democratic Primary	Jeanne Shaheen	unopposed	
1996	General	Jeanne B. Shaheen (D)	284,131	57.0%
		Ovide Lamontagne (R)	196,278	40.0%
		Others	16,514	3.0%
1996	Democratic Primary	Jeanne B. Shaheen	52,293	86.0%
		Sid Lovett	4,289	7.0%
		Brian Woodworth	2,613	4.0%
		Others	1,849	3.0%

Jane D. Hull, (R) Arizona

1998	General	Jane D. Hull (R)	554,353	61.0%
		Paul Johnson (D)	328,268	36.0%
		Others		1.0%
1998	Republican Primary	Jane D. Hull	177,324	76.5%
		Jim Howl	30,699	13.2%
		Charles Brown	23,710	10.2%

Chronology of All Female Candidates for Governor (denotes winner)*

1912	Anna A. Maley	Socialist	Washington
1922	Alice L. Daly	Non-Partisan League	South Dakota
1924	*Miriam A. Ferguson	Democrat	Texas
	*Nellie T. Ross	Democrat	Wyoming
1926	Nellie T. Ross	Democrat	Wyoming
1932	*Miriam A. Ferguson	Democrat	Texas
1934	Lydia Langer	Non-Partisan League	North Dakota
	Josephine Roche	Democrat	Colorado
1950	Anastasia Frohmiller	Democrat	Arizona
1966	*Lurleen B. Wallace	Democrat	Alabama
1974	Shirley Crumpler	Republican	Nevada
	Louise Gore	Republican	Maryland
	*Ella T. Grasso[94]	Democrat	Connecticut
1976	Stella B. Hackel	Democrat	Vermont
	*Dixy L. Ray	Democrat	Washington
1978	*Ella T. Grasso	Democrat	Connecticut
1982	Roxanne Conlin	Democrat	Iowa
	Madeleine M. Kunin	Democrat	Vermont
1983	*Martha L. Collins	Democrat	Kentucky
1984	*Madeleine M. Kunin	Democrat	Vermont
1986	Julie Belaga	Republican	Connecticut
	Helen Boosalis	Democrat	Nebraska
	Patricia Cafferata[95]	Republican	Nevada
	*Madeleine M. Kunin	Democrat	Vermont
	Arliss Sturgulewski	Republican	Alaska
	*Kay S. Orr	Republican	Nebraska
	Norma Paulus	Republican	Oregon
	Carolyn Warner	Democrat	Arizona

---

[94]Grasso previously served two terms (1971–1975) in the U.S. House.

[95]Cafferata is the daughter of U.S. Rep. Barbara Vucanovich (R) of Nevada.

1988	Betty Hearnes	Democrat	Missouri
1990	Barbara Hafer	Republican	Pennsylvania
	Dianne G. Feinstein[96]	Democrat	California
	*Joan M. Finney	Democrat	Kansas
	Mary Mead	Republican	Wyoming
	Kay S. Orr	Republican	Nebraska
	*Ann W. Richards	Democrat	Texas
	*Barbara H. Roberts[97]	Democrat	Oregon
	Arliss Sturgulewski	Republican	Alaska
1992	Deborah Arnesen	Democrat	New Hampshire
	Dorothy Bradley	Democrat	Montana
	Elizabeth Leonard	Republican	Rhode Island
1993	*Christine T. Whitman[98]	Republican	New Jersey
	Mary Sue Terry	Democrat	Virginia
1994	Bonnie Campbell	Democrat	Iowa
	Susan M. Collins[99]	Republican	Maine
	Kathy Karpan	Democrat	Wyoming
	Dawn Clark Netsch	Democrat	Illinois
	Patricia F. Saiki[100]	Republican	Hawaii
	Ellen Sauerbrey	Republican	Maryland
	Ann W. Richards	Democrat	Texas
	Myrth York	Democrat	Rhode Island
1996	Ellen Craswell	Republican	Washington
	Judy Jacobson[101]	Democrat	Montana
	Margaret Kelly	Republican	Missouri
	Charlotte Pritt	Democrat	West Virginia
	Janet Rzewnicki	Republican	Delaware
	*Jeanne B. Shaheen	Democract	New Hampshire
1997	*Christine T. Whitman	Republican	New Jersey
1998	Laura Boyd	Democrat	Oklahoma
	Ruth Dwyer	Republican	Vermont
	*Jane Dee Hull	Republican	Arizona
	Jan Laverty Jones	Democrat	Nevada

---

[96]Feinstein was elected to the U.S. Senate in 1992.

[97]Roberts was unsuccessful in 1974 as the Democratic nominee for the U.S. Senate.

[98]Whitman was unsuccessful as the 1990 Republican nominee for the U.S. Senate.

[99]Collins was successful in 1996 as the Republican nominee for the U.S. Senate.

[100]Saiki had previously served two terms (1987–1991) in the U.S. House; she was unsuccessful in 1990 as Republican nominee for U.S. Senate.

[101]Jacobson, originally the nominee for lieutenant governor, became the last-minute replacement when the Democratic gubernatorial candidate died one week before the general election; as such she bore the distinction of having her name appear on the ballot for both offices.

Barbara Bailey Kennelly[102]	Democrat	Connecticut
Linda Crockett Lingle	Republican	Hawaii
Ellen Sauerbrey	Republican	Maryland
*Jeanne B. Shaheen	Democrat	New Hampshire
Gail Schoettler	Democrat	Colorado
Myrth York	Democrat	Rhode Island

Women Who Have Held Other State Executive Offices[103]

Alabama

Auditor
Susan Parker (D), 1999–
Patsy Duncan (R), 1995–1999
Jan Cook (D), 1983–1991
Agnes Baggett (D), 1975–1983
Melba Till Allen (D), 1967–1975
Bettye Frink (D), 1963–1967
Mary Texas Hurt Gardner (D), 1959–1963
Agnes Baggett (D), 1955–1959

Secretary of State
Mabel Amos (D), 1967–1975
Agnes Baggett (D), 1963–1967
Bettye Frink (D), 1959–1963
Mary Texas Hurt Garner (D), 1955–1959
Agnes Baggett (D), 1951–1955
Sybil Poole (D), 1944–1951

Treasurer
Lucille Baxley (D), 1995–
Annie Laurie Gunter (D), 1979–1987
Melba Till Allen (D), 1975–1979
Mary Texas Hurt Garner (D), 1963–1967
Agnes Baggett (D), 1959–1963, 1967–1975
Sybil Poole (D), 1951–1955

Alaska

Lieutenant Governor
Fran Ulmer (D), 1995–

Attorney General
Grace Schaible (D), 1987–1988

Arizona

Attorney General
Grace Napolitano (D), 1999–

Auditor
Jewel W. Jordan (D), 1951–1969
Anastasia Frohmiller (D), 1927–1951[104]

Secretary of State
Betsey Bayless (R), 1997–
Jane Dee Hull (R), 1995–1997[105]
Rose P. Mofford (D), 1977–1988[106]

---

[102]Kennelly previously served eight terms (1983–1999) in the U.S. House.

[103]These offices are a combination of election by popular vote, election by the state legislature, and appointment by the governor.

[104]Frohmiller was unsuccessful in 1950 as the Democratic candidate for governor.

[105]Hull became governor in 1997 upon the resignation of Gov. Fife Symington (R).

[106]Mofford became governor in 1988 upon the impeachment of Gov. Evan Mecham (R).

Superintendent of Public Instruction
   Lisa Graham Keegan (R), 1995–
   C. Diane Bishop (D), 1987–1995
   Carolyn Warner (D), 1975–1987[107]
   Sarah Folsom (R), 1965–1969
   Elsie Toles, 1921–1922

Treasurer
   Carol Springer (R), 1999–

Arkansas

Attorney General
   Mary Stallcup (D), 1991

Auditor
   Julia Hughes Jones (R), 1981–1995[108]

Secretary of State
   Sharon Priest (D), 1995–
   Nancy J. Hall (D), 1961–1963

Treasurer
   Jimmie Lou Fisher Lumpkin (D), 1981–
   Nancy J. Hall (D), 1963–1981

California

Controller
   Kathleen Connell (D), 1995–

Secretary of State
   March Fong Eu (D), 1975–1994

Superintendent of Public Instruction
   Delaine Eastin (D), 1995–

Treasurer
   Kathleen Brown (D), 1991–1995[109]
   Ivy Baker Priest (R), 1967–1975

Colorado

Lieutenant Governor
   Gail Schoettler (D), 1995–1999
   Nancy Dick (D), 1979–1987[110]

Attorney General
   Gale Norton (R), 1991–1999

Secretary of State
   Victoria "Vikki" Buckley (R), 1995–[111]
   Natalie Meyer (R), 1983–1995
   Mary Estill Buchanan (R), 1972–1983[112]

Superintendent of Public Instruction
   Nettie S. Freed (R), 1947–1951
   Inez J. Lewis (D), 1931–1947
   Mary C. C. Bradford, 1913–1921,
     1923–1927
   Helen M. Wixson, 1911–1913
   Katherine M. Cook, 1909–1911
   Katherine L. Craig (R), 1905–1909,
     1921–1923, 1927–1931
   Helen Grenfell, 1899–1905

---

[107]Warner was unsuccessful in 1986 as the Democratic nominee for governor and as a candidate in the 1976 Democratic primary for the U.S. Senate.

[108]Originally elected as a Democrat, Jones in 1992 made an unsuccessful bid in the Democratic primary to deny the senatorial nomination to Sen. Dale Bumpers, who was seeking his fourth term. By October of the following year she had switched to the Republican party.

[109]Brown was unsuccessful in 1994 as Democratic nominee for governor.

[110]Dick was unsuccessful in 1984 as Democratic nominee for the U.S. Senate.

[111]Buckley was the first Republican African American woman elected to a statewide executive office.

[112]Buchanan was unsuccessful in 1980 as Republican nominee for the U.S. Senate.

Treasurer
  Gail Schoettler (D), 1987–1995
  Virginia Blue (R), 1967–1971

Connecticut

Lieutenant Governor
  M. Jodi Rell (R), 1995–
  Eunice S. Groak (I), 1991–1995[113]

Attorney General
  Clarine N. Riddle (D), 1988–1991

Comptroller
  Nancy Wyman (D), 1995–

Secretary of State
  Susan Bysiewicz (D), 1999–
  Pauline Kezer (R), 1991–1995[114]
  Julia H. Tashjian (D), 1983–1991
  Maura Melley (D), 1982
  Barbara Bailey Kennelly (D), 1979–1982[115]
  Gloria Schaffer (D), 1971–1979[116]
  Ella T. Grasso (D), 1959–1971[117]
  Mildred P. Allen (R), 1955–1959
  Alice K. Leopold (R), 1951–1953
  Winifred McDonald (D), 1949–1951
  Francis Burke Redick, 1943–1945,
    1947–1949
  Chase Going Woodhouse (D), 1941–1943[118]
  Sara B. Crawford, 1939–1941

Treasurer
  Denise Nappier (D), 1999–

Delaware

Lieutenant Governor
  Ruth Ann Minner (D), 1985–1989, 1993–

Attorney General
  M. Jane Brady (R), 1995–[119]

Secretary of State
  Fannie Harrington, 1925–1927

Treasurer
  Janet C. Rzewnicki (R), 1983–1999[120]
  Mary D. Jornlin (R), 1973–1977
  Emily H. Womach (D), 1971–1973
  Annabelle Smith Everett (D), 1959–1967
  Vera G. Davis (R), 1957–1959

Florida

Secretary of State
  Katherine Harris (R), 1999–
  Sandy B. Mortham (R), 1995–1999

Georgia

Secretary of State
  Cathy Cox (D), 1999–

Superintendent of Education
  Linda Shrenko (R), 1995–

Hawaii

Lieutenant Governor
  Mazie K. Hirono (D), 1994–[121]
  Jean Sadako King (D), 1978–1982[122]

---

[113]Groak was the candidate for governor in 1994 of the A Connecticut Party, but she lost the general election.

[114]Kezer was unsuccessful in her bid for the 1994 Republican gubernatorial nomination.

[115]Kennelly was selected in a special 1982 election to fill the seat in the U.S. House of an incumbent who had died.

[116]Schaffer was unsuccessful in 1976 as the Democratic nominee for the U.S. Senate.

[117]Grasso served two terms in the U.S. House (1971–1975) and was also the governor (January 8, 1975–December 31, 1980).

[118]Woodhouse also severed two terms in the U.S. House (1945–1947, 1949–1951).

[119]Brady was unsuccessful as the 1990 Republican nominee for the U.S. Senate.

[120]Rzewnicki was unsuccessful as the 1996 Republican nominee for governor.

Attorney General
    Margery Bronster (D), 1994–

Idaho

Superintendent of Public Instruction
    Marilyn Howard (D), 1999–
    Anne C. Fox (R), 1995–1999
    Myrtle R. Davis (R), 1929–1933
    Mabelle M. Lyman (R), 1927–1929
    Elizabeth Russum (R), 1923–1927
    Ethel E. Redfield (R), 1917–1923
    Bernice McCoy (R), 1915–1917
    Grace M. Shephard (R), 1911–1915
    S. Belle Chamberlain (R), 1907–1911
    Mae L. Scott (R), 1903–1907
    Permeal French (D), 1899–1903

Treasurer
    Lydia Justice Edwards (R), 1987–1999
    Marjorie Ruth Moon (D), 1963–1987
    Margaret Gilbert (R), 1953–1955
    Lela D. Painter (R), 1947–1953
    Ruth G. Moon (D), 1945–1947, 1955–1959
    Myrtle Enking (D), 1933–1945

Illinois

Lieutenant Governor
        Corinne Wood (R), 1999–

Comptroller
    Loleta A. Didrickson (R), 1995–1999
    Dawn Clark Netsch (D), 1991–1995[123]

Treasurer
    Judy Baar Topinka (R), 1995–

Indiana

Attorney General
    Pamela F. Carter (D), 1993–1997

Auditor
    Connie Nass (R), 1999–
    Ann G. DeVore (R), 1987–1995
    Mary Aikins Currie (D), 1971–1979
    Trudy S. Etherton (R), 1969–1971
    Dorothy Gardner (R), 1961–1965

Secretary of State
    Sue Anne Gilroy (R), 1994–

Superintendent of Public Instruction
    Suellen Reed (R), 1993–

Treasurer
    Joyce Brinkman (R), 1995–1999
    Marjorie H. O'Laughlin (R), 1985–1995
    Grace B. Urbahns (R), 1927–1931

Iowa

Lieutenant Governor
    Sally Pederson (D), 1999–
    Joy Corning (R), 1991–1999
    Jo Ann Zimmerman (D), 1987–1991

Attorney General
    Bonnie Campbell (D), 1991–1995[124]

Secretary of State
    Elaine Baxter (D), 1987–1995[125]
    Mary Jane Odell (R), 1980–1987
    Ola Miller (D), 1933–1937

---

[121]Hirono and her predecessor, Jean Sadako King (1978–1982), hold the record for being the only Asian American women who have been elected to the highest statewide executive positions in the U.S.

[122]In 1982 King challenged the incumbent governor, George Ariyoshi, in the Democratic primary, but she lost.

[123]Netsch was unsuccessful in 1994 as the Democratic nominee for governor.

[124]Campbell was unsuccessful in 1994 as the Democratic nominee for governor.

[125]Baxter was unsuccessful in two races—in 1992 and again in 1994—for a seat in the U.S. House of Representatives from Iowa's 3rd District.

Superintendent of Public Instruction
  Jessie M. Parker, 1939–1955
  Agnes Samuelson, 1927–1939
  May E. Francis (R), 1923–1927

Kansas

Lieutenant Governor
  Sheila Frahm (R), 1995–1996[126]

Attorney General
  Carla Stovall (R), 1995–

Secretary of State
  Elwill M. Shanahan (R), 1966–1979

Superintendent of Public Instruction
  Elizabeth Wooster, 1921–1923

Treasurer
  Sally Thompson (D), 1991–1997[127]
  Joan M. Finney (D), 1975–1991[128]

Kentucky

Lieutenant Governor
  Martha L. Collins (D), 1979–1983[129]
  Thelma Stovall (D), 1975–1979[130]

Auditor
  Mary Ann Tobin (D), 1983–1987
  Mary Louise Foust (D), 1955–1959,
    1971–1975[131]

Secretary of State
  Frances Jones Mills (D), 1979–1983
  Thelma Stovall (D), 1955–1959, 1963–1967,
    1971–1975
  Sara W. Mahon (D), 1933–1936
  Ella Lewis (D), 1929–1933
  Emma Guy Cromwell (D), 1925–1929

Superintendent of Public Instruction
  Alice McDonald (D), 1983–1987

Treasurer
  Frances Jones Mills (D), 1979–1983,
    1991–1995
  Thelma Stovall (D), 1959–1963, 1967–1971
  Pearl Runyon (D), 1951–1956
  Emma Guy Cromwell (D), 1930–1933

Louisiana

Lieutenant Governor
  Kathleen B. Blanco (D), 1996–
  Melinda Schwegmann (D), 1992–1996[132]

Secretary of State
  Alice Lee Grosjean (D), 1930

Treasurer
  Mary Loretta Landrieu (D), 1987–1996[133]
  Mary Evelyn Parker (D), 1969–1987

---

[126]Frahm was appointed to the U.S. Senate on May 24, 1996.

[127]Thompson was unsuccessful in 1996 as the Democratic nominee for the U.S. Senate.

[128]Finney later served as governor (1991–1995).

[129]Collins later served as governor (1983–1987).

[130]Stovall was an unsuccessful candidate in the 1979 Democratic primary for governor.

[131]Foust was unsuccessful in 1980 as the Republican nominee for the U.S. Senate after she had switched parties.

[132]Schwegmann was unsuccessful in the 1995 "jungle" primary for the governorship.

[133]Landrieu was unsuccessful in the 1995 "jungle" primary for the governorship, but she did win a seat in the U.S. Senate in the 1996 election.

Maine

Maine is one of only two states (West Virginia is the other) that has never elected by popular vote a woman to a statewide executive position.

Treasurer
Dale McCormick (D), 1996–

Maryland

Lieutenant Governor
Kathleen Kennedy Townsend (D), 1995–[134]

Secretary of State
Lorraine Sheehan (D), 1983–1987
Vivian V. Simpson (D), 1949–1951

Treasurer
Lucille Maurer (D), 1987–

Massachusetts

Lieutenant Governor
Jane M. Swift (R), 1999–
Evelyn F. Murphy (D), 1987–1991[135]

Treasurer
Shannon P. O'Brien (D), 1999–

Michigan

Lieutenant Governor
Connie Binsfeld (R), 1991–1999
Martha W. Griffiths (D), 1983–1991[136]

Matilda R. Wilson (R), 1940[137]

Attorney General
Jennifer Grandholm (D), 1999–

Secretary of State
Candice S. Miller (R), 1995–

Minnesota

Lieutenant Governor
Mae Schunk (Reform), 1999–
Joanne Benson (R), 1995–1999
Joanell Dyrstad (R), 1991–1995[138]
Marlene Johnson (D), 1983–1991

Auditor
Judith Dutcher (R), 1995–

Secretary of State
Mary Kiffmeyer (R), 1999–
Joan Anderson Growe (D), 1975–1999[139]
Virginia Holm (R), 1953–1955

Treasurer
Carol Johnson (D), 1999–

Mississippi

Lieutenant Governor
Evelyn Gandy (D), 1975–1979[140]

Treasurer
Evelyn Gandy (D), 1959–1963, 1967–1971

---

[134]Townsend is the daughter of Robert F. Kennedy, the former U.S. attorney general, U.S. senator, and Democratic presidential candidate.

[135]In 1990 Murphy was an unsuccessful candidate in the Democratic primary for the gubernatorial nomination.

[136]Griffiths had previously served in the U.S. House (1955–1975) for ten terms.

[137]Wilson was the first woman (appointed) to hold the office of lieutenant governor in the U.S.

[138]Dyrstad was unsuccessful in the 1994 Republican primary when she sought the nomination for the U.S. Senate.

[139]Growe was unsuccessful in 1984 as the Democratic nominee for the U.S. Senate.

[140]Gandy was unsuccessful in both 1971 and 1979 in her quest for the Democratic nomination for governor. Both times she was the leader in the primary but lost the runoff.

Missouri

Lieutenant Governor
    Harriet Woods (D), 1985–1989[141]
    Hilary A. Bush (D), 1961–1965

Auditor
    Claire McCaskill (D), 1999–
    Margaret Kelly (R), 1985–1999[142]

Secretary of State
    Rebecca McDowell Cook (D), 1994–
    Judith Moriarty (D), 1993–1994[143]

Montana

Auditor
    Andrea "Andy" Hempsted Bennett (R),
    1985–1993[144]

Superintendent of Public Instruction
    Nancy Keenan (D), 1989–
    Georgia Ruth Rice (D), 1977–1981
    Dolores Colberg (D), 1969–1977
    Harriet Miller (R), 1957–1965, then (D)
    1965–1969
    Mary M. Condon (D), 1949–1957
    Elizabeth Ireland (R), 1941–1949
    Ruth Reardon, 1937–1941
    May Trumper, 1921–1923

Treasurer
    Hollis G. Connors (R), 1969–1977
    Edna Hinman (R), 1955–1957, 1961–1965
    Alta E. Fisher, 1949–1953

Nebraska

Lieutenant Governor
    Kim Robak (D), 1993–1999
    Maxine Moul (D), 1991–1993

Auditor
    Kate Witek (R), 1999–

Treasurer
    Dawn Rockey (D), 1991–1995
    Kay S. Orr (R), 1983–1987[145]
    Bertha I. Hill (R), 1958–1959

Nevada

Lieutenant Governor
    Lorraine Hunt (R), 1999–
    Sue Wagner (R), 1991–1995
    Maude Frazier (D), 1962

Attorney General
    Frankie Sue Del Papa (D), 1991–

Controller
    Kathy Augustine (R), 1999–

Secretary of State
    Cheryl Lau (R), 1991–1995[146]
    Frankie Sue Del Papa (D), 1987–1991

Superintendent of Public Instruction
    Mildred Bray (D), 1937–1951

---

[141]Woods was unsuccessful in 1986 as the Democratic nominee for the U.S. Senate.

[142]Kelly was unsuccessful in 1996 as the Republican nominee for governor.

[143] Moriarty was removed from office on December 12, 1994, by Missouri's supreme court after she was found guilty of having backdated qualification papers to permit her son to run for the U.S. House of Representatives.

[144]Bennett was unsuccessful in 1992 as a candidate in the Republican primary for the gubernatorial nomination.

[145]Orr later served as governor (1987–1991); she was defeated for reelection in 1991.

[146]In 1994 Lau was an unsuccessful contestant in the primary for the Republican gubernatorial nomination.

Treasurer
  Patty Cafferata (R), 1983–1987[147]

New Hampshire

Treasurer
  Georgie A. Thomas (R), 1988–

New Jersey

Attorney General
  Deborah T. Poritz (R), 1993–1996[148]

Secretary of State
  Lonna R. Hooks (R), 1993–
  Joan Haberle (D), 1989–1993
  Jane Burgio (R), 1983–1989

Treasurer
  Feather O'Connor (D), 1985–1989
  Katherine E. White (D), 1962

New Mexico

Attorney General
  Patricia Madrid (D), 1999–

Secretary of State
  Stephanie Gonzales (D), 1991–1999
  Rebecca Vigil-Giron (D), 1987–1991, 1999–
  Clara Padilla Jones (D), 1983–1987
  Shirley Hooper (D), 1979–1983
  Ernestine D. Evans (D), 1967–1971,
    1975–1979
  Alberta Miller (D), 1963–1967
  Betty Fiorina (D), 1959–1963, 1971–1975

  Natalie Smith Buck (D), 1955–1959
  Beatrice Bassett Roach Gottlieb (D),
    1951–1955
  Alicia M. Romero (D), 1947–1951
  Cecilia T. Cleveland (D), 1943–1947
  Jessie M. Gonzales (D), 1939–1943
  Elizabeth F. Gonzales (D), 1935–1939
  Marguerite P. Baca (D), 1931–1935
  Jesusita Perrault (R), 1929–1931
  Jennie Fortune (D), 1927–1929
  Soledad C. Chacon (D), 1923–1927

Superintendent of Public Education
  Grace J. Corrigan (D), 1939–1943
  Georgia L. Lusk (D), 1931–1935,
    1943–1947, 1955–59[149]
  Isabel Eckles, 1923–1927

New York

Lieutenant Governor
  Mary Donohue (R), 1999–
  Elizabeth McCaughey Ross (R, D),
    1995–1999
  Mary Ann Krupsak (D), 1975–1979[150]

Secretary of State
  Gail S. Shaffer (D), 1983–1995
  Caroline K. Simon (R), 1959–1963
  Florence M. S. Knapp (R), 1925–1927

North Carolina

Secretary of State
  Elaine Marshall (D), 1997–
  Janice Faulkner (D), 1996–1997

---

[147]Cafferata was unsuccessful in 1986 as Republican nominee for governor; her mother is U.S. Rep. Barbara Vucanovich (R) of Nevada.

[148]Poritz resigned in 1996 when she was appointed to the state supreme court.

[149]Lusk served one term (1947–1949) in the U.S. House.

[150]In 1978 Krupsak challenged the incumbent governor, Hugh Carey, in the Democratic primary for the gubernatorial nomination, but she lost.

North Dakota

Lieutenant Governor
  Rosemarie Myrdal (R), 1993–
  Ruth Meiers (D), 1985–1987

Attorney General
  Heidi Heitkamp (D), 1993–

Auditor
  Berta E. Baker (R), 1933–1957

Superintendent of Public Instruction
  Bertha R. Palmer (R), 1927–1933
  Minnie J. Nielson (NP), 1919–1927
  Emma B. Bates (D), 1895–1897
  Laura J. Eisenhuth (D-Independent),
    1893–1895[151]

Treasurer
  Kathi Gilmore (D), 1993–
  Bernice Ashridge (R), 1969–1973
  Berta E. Baker (R), 1929–1933

Ohio

Lieutenant Governor
      Maureen O'Connor (R), 1999–
  Nancy A. Hollister (R), 1995–1999

Attorney General
  Betty D. Montgomery (R), 1995–

Treasurer
  Mary Ellen Withrow (D), 1983–1994[152]
  Gertrude Donahey (D), 1971–1983

Oklahoma

Lieutenant Governor
  Mary Fallin (R), 1995–

Attorney General
  Susan Loving (D), 1991–1995

Auditor
  Imogene E. Holmes (D), 1963–1965

Secretary of State
  Hannah Diggs Atkins (D), 1987–1991
  Jeannette Edmondson (D), 1979–1987

Superintendent of Public Instruction
  Sandy Garrett (D), 1991–

Treasurer
  Claudette Henry (R), 1991–1995

Oregon

Secretary of State
  Barbara H. Roberts (D), 1983–1991[153]
  Norma Paulus (R), 1975–1983[154]

Superintendent of Public Instruction
  Norma Paulus (NP), 1989–1999

Pennsylvania

Attorney General
  Anne X. Alpern (D), 1959–1961[155]

Auditor General
  Barbara Hafer (R), 1988–1997[156]
  Grace McCalmont Sloan (D), 1965–1969

---

[151]Eisenhuth was the first woman elected to a statewide executive post in the U.S.

[152]Withrow resigned in 1994 after she was appointed treasurer of the United States by Pres. Bill Clinton.

[153]Roberts later served as governor (1991–1995); she was unsuccessful in the 1974 election as the Democratic nominee for the U.S. Senate.

[154]Paulus was unsuccessful in 1986 as the Republican nominee for governor.

[155]Alpern was the first woman appointed state attorney general in the U.S.

[156]Hafer was unsuccessful in 1990 as the Republican nominee for governor.

Secretary of the Commonwealth
   Yvette Kane (R), 1995–
   Brenda K. Mitchell (D), 1991–1995
   Ethel D. Allen (R), 1979–1983
   C. Delores Tucker (D), 1971–1977[157]
   Sophia M. R. O'Hara (R), 1939–1943

Secretary of Internal Affairs
   Genevieve Blatt (D), 1955–1967[158]

Treasurer
   Barbara Hafer (R), 1997–
   Catherine Baker Knoll (D), 1988–1997
   Grace McCalmont Sloan (D), 1961–1965,
   1969–1977

Rhode Island

Attorney General
   Arlene Violet (R), 1985–1987[159]

Secretary of State
   Barbara M. Leonard (R), 1993–1995
   Kathleen S. Connell (D), 1987–1993
   Susan L. Farmer (R), 1983–1987

Treasurer
   Nancy J. Mayer (R), 1993–1999

South Carolina

Lieutenant Governor
   Nancy Stevenson (D), 1979–1983

Superintendent of Education

   Inez Tenenbaum (D), 1999–
   Barbara Nielsen (R), 1991–1999

South Dakota

Lieutenant Governor
   Carole Hillard (R), 1995–

Auditor
   Alice Kundert (R), 1969–1977
   Betty Lou Casey (R), 1961–1963
   Essie Wiedenman (R), 1961
   Harriet Horning (D), 1959–1961
   Fay Albee (R), 1957–1959

Secretary of State
   Joyce Hazeltine (R), 1987–
   Alice Kundert (R), 1977–1987
   Lorna B. Herseth (D), 1973–1977
   Alma Larson (R), 1965–1973
   Essie Wiedenman (R), 1961–1965
   Selma Sandness (D), 1959–1961
   Clara Halls (D), 1957–1959
   Geraldine Ostroot (R), 1951–1957
   Annamae Riiff (R), 1949–1951
   L. M. Larson (R) 1943–1947
   Olive Ringsrud, 1939–1943[160]
   Goldie Wells (D), 1937–1939
   Myrtle Morrison (D), 1935–1937
   Elizabeth Coyne (R), 1931–1935
   Gladys Pyle (R), 1927–1931[161]

---

[157]Tucker was an unsuccessful candidate in the 1980 Democratic primary for the U.S. Senate nomination.

[158]Blatt was unsuccessful in 1964 as the Democratic nominee for the U.S. Senate.

[159]Violet, who was a Roman Catholic nun when she sought the position, was the first woman elected state attorney general in the U.S.

[160]Ringsrud was a candidate in the 1940 Republican primary for the senatorial nomination, but she lost to then Gov. Harlan Bushfield.

[161]After leading in the 1930 Republican primary for the gubernatorial nomination, Pyle failed to win the 35 percent required to ensure the nomination. At the state convention to choose the nominee, she was denied the prize when two other candidates joined forces to defeat her. Pyle was later elected to serve an interim term in the U.S. Senate (November 9, 1938–January 3, 1939).

Treasurer
   Hazel Dean (R), 1945–1947

Tennessee

Comptroller
   Jeanne S. Bodfish (D), 1954

Secretary of State
   Mary H. Carr (D), 1944–1947

Texas

Comptroller
      Carolyn K. Rylander (R), 1999–

Secretary of State
   Myra A. McDaniel (D), 1984–1987
   Jane Y. McCallum (D), 1927–1933
   Emma Grigsby Meharg (D), 1925–1927

Superintendent of Public Instruction
   Annie Webb Blanton (D), 1919–1923

Treasurer
   Martha Whitehead (D), 1993–1996
   Kay B. Hutchison (R), 1991–1993[162]
   Ann W. Richards (D), 1983–1991[163]

Utah

Lieutenant Governor
   Olene S. Walker (R), 1993–

Attorney General
   Jan Graham (D), 1993–

Vermont

Lieutenant Governor
   Barbara W. Snelling (R), 1993–1997
   Madeleine M. Kunin (D), 1979–1983
   Consuelo Northrop Bailey (R), 1955–1957[164]

Auditor
   Anne Powers (R), 1941–1943

Secretary of State
   Deborah Markowitz (D), 1999–

Treasurer
   Stella B. Hackel (D), 1975–1977[165]

Virginia

Attorney General
   Mary Sue Terry (D), 1985–1993[166]

Secretary of the Commonwealth
   Elizabeth Beamer (R), 1993–
   Pamela Womack (D), 1989–1993
   Sandy Bowen (D), 1985–1989
   Laurie Naismith (D), 1981–1985
   Patricia R. Perkinson (I), 1977–1978
   Cynthia S. Newman (R), 1973–1977
   Martha Bell Conway (D), 1953–1973
   Thelma Y. Gordon (D), 1949–1953

Treasurer
   Alice W. Handy (D), 1985–1989

Washington

Attorney General
   Christine Gregoire (D), 1993–

---

[162]Hutchison was elected to the U.S. Senate on June 7, 1993.

[163]Richards later served as governor (1991–1995) but was defeated in 1994 reelection bid.

[164]Bailey was the first woman elected lieutenant governor in the U.S.

[165]Hackel was unsuccessful in 1976 as the Democratic nominee for governor.

[166]Terry was unsuccessful in 1993 as the Democratic nominee for governor.

Secretary of State
  Belle C. Reeves (D), 1938–1948

Superintendent of Public Instruction
  Teresa Terry Bergeson (NP), 1997–
  Judith Billings (NP), 1989–1997
  Pearl A. Wanamaker (NP), 1941–1957
  Josephine C. Preston (R), 1913–1929

West Virginia

West Virginia is one of only two states (Maine is the other) that has never elected by popular vote a woman to a statewide executive position.

Secretary of State
  Helen Holt (R), 1957–1959[167]

Wisconsin

Secretary of State
  Vel Phillips (D), 1979–1983[168]
  Glenn M. Wise (R), 1955–1957

Superintendent of Public Instruction
  Barbara Thompson (NP), 1973–1981

Treasurer
  Cathy S. Zeuske (R), 1991–1995

Dena Smith (R), 1957–1959, 1961–1969

Wyoming

Auditor
  Minnie A. Mitchell (R), 1955–1967

Secretary of State
  Diana Ohman (R), 1995–1999
  Kathy Karpan (D), 1987–1995[169]
  Thyra Thomson (R), 1963–1987[170]

Superintendent of Public Instruction
  Judy Catchpole (R), 1995–
  Diana Ohman (R), 1991–1995
  Lynn Simons (D), 1979–1991
  Velma Linford (D), 1955–1963
  Edna Stolt (R), 1947–1955
  Esther Anderson (R), 1939–1947
  Katharine A. Morton (R), 1919–1935
  Edith K. O. Clark (R), 1915–1919
  Rose A. Bird Maley (D), 1911–1915
  Estelle Reel (R), 1895–1899

Treasurer
  Cynthia Lummis (R), 1999–
  Shirley Wittler (R), 1975–1983
  Minnie A. Mitchell (R), 1952–1955,
    1967–1971

Women in State Legislatures

Statistics

In 1998 women held 19 percent of the seats in the upper houses of the state legislatures and 23 percent in the lower houses. Every state has at least one woman legislator in both the upper and lower chambers of their state legislatures, but women are underrepresented according to their percentage of the overall population of each state.

---

[167]Holt, the widow of former U.S. Sen. Rush Holt (R), was appointed to her position.

[168]Phillips was the first African American woman elected to a statewide executive position in the U.S.

[169]Karpan was unsuccessful in 1994 as the Democratic nominee for governor and again in 1996 as the Democratic nominee for the U.S. Senate.

[170]Thomson's husband, Keith, a U.S. representative, was elected to the U.S. Senate in November 1960. He died later that month before his scheduled swearing-in as a senator in January 1961.

In both the combined upper and lower chambers, women are best represented in Washington, where they hold 38 percent of the seats. Their worst representation in the combined upper and lower chambers occurs in Alabama, where they hold only 4.3 percent of the seats.

Longest Continuous Service

Brynhild Haugland, (R) North Dakota, was first elected in 1938 to North Dakota's state house of representatives and served until 1990.

E. C. "Polly" Rosenbaum, (D) Arizona, was appointed in 1949 to fill the seat of her deceased husband in the Arizona house of representatives. A teacher by profession, Mrs. Rosenbaum served until 1994, when she was past ninety years old.

Notable Firsts: 1994

In Alaska women were sworn in as the presiding officers in both houses of the state legislature—**Gail Phillips** (R) as speaker of the state house and **Drue Pearce** (R) as state senate president pro tem—making this the first time that females concurrently chaired both houses of a state's legislature.

Nimi McConigley, (R) Wyoming, was elected to that state's house of representatives, the first female Asian Indian–American elected to a state legislature in the U.S.

Notable First: 1992

Georgianna Lincoln, (D) Alaska, an Athabascan, was elected to the state senate, the first Native American woman to sit in a state senate.

Notable First: 1991

Diane E. Bajoie, (D) Louisiana, was elected to the state senate on March 23, 1991, the first time that all ninety-nine state legislative houses had female members concurrently.

Notable First: 1974

Thelma Garcia Buchholdt, (D) Alaska, and **Velma M. Santos**, (R) Hawaii, became the first Filipino American women elected to a state legislature in the U.S.

Notable First: 1972

Barbara Jordan, (D) Texas, first elected in 1966, became president pro tem of the Texas state senate. She was the first African American woman to preside over a state legislative body, which on several occasions allowed her to "act" as governor when both the governor and lieutenant governor of Texas were absent from the state.

Notable First: 1966

Moni Minn (D), elected to the Hawaii house of representatives, became the first Korean American woman elected to a state legislature in the U.S. Minn had been appointed earlier in the year to fill the seat of her deceased husband.

Notable First: 1956

Patsy T. Mink, (D) Hawaii, became the first Japanese American woman elected to a state/territorial legislature when she was elected to Hawaii's house of representatives. When Hawaii achieved statehood in 1959, she moved into the state senate. In 1964 she was elected to the U.S. House of Representatives.

Notable First: 1952

Cora M. Brown, (R) Michigan, became the first African American woman elected to a state senate seat.

Notable First: 1938

Crystal Bird Fauset, (D) Pennsylvania, became the first African American woman elected to a state legislature.

Notable First: 1933

Minnie D. Craig, (Non-Partisan League) North Dakota, was elected speaker of the North Dakota house of representatives and became the first woman in the U.S. to hold that position in a permanent capacity (see **Notable First: 1923**). She served from January 3, 1933, until March 31, 1933.

Notable First: 1931

Louise H. Coe, (D) New Mexico, elected president pro tem of the New Mexico state senate, was the first woman in the U.S. to hold that position.

Notable Firsts: 1930

Fedelina Lucero Gallegos (R) and **Porfirria H. Saiz** (D), both of New Mexico, became the first Hispanic women elected to a state legislature.

Dolly Smith Cusker (Akers), (D) Montana, became the second—although many say the first—Native American woman elected to a state legislature.

Notable First: 1927

Minnie Buckingham-Harper, (R) West Virginia, became the first African American woman to sit in a state legislature when she was appointed to the seat of her deceased husband in her state's house of delegates.

Notable First: 1925

Rosalie Enos Lyons Keliinoi, (R) Hawaii, was elected to a seat in the Hawaii territorial house, the first female native Hawaiian elected to a state/territorial legislature.

Notable First: 1924

Cora Belle Reynolds Anderson, (R) Michigan, of Chippewa descent, became the first Native American woman elected to a state legislature when she was elected to Michigan's state house of representatives.

Notable First: 1923

Sarah Lucille Turner, (D) Missouri, served as "acting" speaker of the Missouri house of representatives, the first woman to preside over a state legislative body.

Notable First: 1916

Maggie Smith Hathaway, (D) Montana, was elected Democratic floor leader and became the first woman to hold a leadership position in a state legislature.

Notable First: 1896

Martha Hughes, (D) Utah, was the first woman elected to a state senate seat.

Notable First: 1884

Clara Cressingham, **Carrie C. Holly,** and **Frances Klock**, all Republicans, became the first women elected to a state legislature when they won election to the Colorado state house of representatives.

Female Speakers of State Lower Legislative Chambers

Moira K. Lyons, (D) Connecticut, 1999–
Donna Sytek, (R) New Hampshire, 1997–
Elizabeth H. Mitchell, (D) Maine, 1996–
Doris Allen, (R) California, 1995
Bev Clarno, (R) Oregon, 1995–1996
Jo Ann Davidson, (R) Ohio, 1995–
Gail Phillips, (R) Alaska, 1995–
Ramona Barnes, (R) Alaska, 1993–1994
Dee Long, (DFL) Minnesota, 1992–1993
Jane Dee Hull, (R) Arizona, 1989–1992
Debra Andress, (R) South Dakota, 1987–1988

Vera Katz, (D) Oregon, 1985–1991
Verda I. Jones, (R) Wyoming, 1969
Edness Kimball Wilkins, (D) Wyoming, 1966
Consuelo Northrop Bailey, (R) Vermont, 1953–1955
Minnie D. Craig, (Non-Partisan League) North Dakota, 1933
Sarah Lucille Turner, (D) Missouri, 1923, (acting speaker)

Women in the Judiciary

U.S. Supreme Court Justices

1981– **Sandra Day O'Connor**, (R) Arizona, nominated by Pres. Ronald Reagan
1993– **Ruth Bader Ginsburg**, (D) District of Columbia, nominated by Pres. Bill Clinton

A Missed Notable Moment

Pres. Harry S. Truman was supposedly dissuaded from naming **Florence Ellinwood Allen**, (D) Ohio—first woman to sit on a state supreme court and first female federal judge—to a seat on the U.S. Supreme Court in the late 1940s. The other justices—all male—are supposed to have complained that they would not be able to sit around with their shoes off discussing the merits of cases if a woman was a member of their group.

Notable First: 1995

U.S. Supreme Court associate justice **Sandra Day O'Connor**, third in seniority on the court, presided over a session of the Supreme Court. This was the first time that a woman had so presided over a session of the Court.

Notable First: 1992

Leah Sears-Collins, (D) Georgia, who had been appointed in March 1992 to the Georgia Supreme Court by Gov. Zell Miller, became the first African American female elected to a seat on any state's supreme court when she won a full term on that same court in the November general election.

Notable First: 1991

Sandra Gardebring was appointed to Minnesota's state supreme court and joined justices **Rosalie E. Wahl**, **M. Jeanne Coyne**, and **Esther Moellering Tomljanovich** on the seven-member court, making Minnesota's the first state supreme court in the nation with a majority of female justices.

Notable First: 1989

Joyce Kennard, (R) California, partly of Indonesian descent, was named by Gov. George Deukmejian (R) to the California Supreme Court. She became the first Asian American female to sit on a state supreme court. The second was **Joyce Nakayama**, a Japanese American, who was appointed to the Hawaii Supreme Court in 1993.

Notable First: 1988

Juanita Kidd Stout, (D) Pennsylvania, was appointed by Gov. Robert Casey to a seat on Pennsylvania's supreme court, the first African American woman to hold a state supreme court seat.

Notable First: 1987

Dorothy Comstock Riley, Michigan, became the first Hispanic female chief justice of a state supreme court.

Notable First: 1966

Constance Baker Motley, (D) New York, became the first female African American federal judge.[171]

Notable First: 1965

Lorna Lockwood, (R) Arizona, who in 1960 was the second woman popularly elected as a justice of a state supreme court, became the first woman to be elected chief justice of a state supreme court. She was following in the footsteps of her father, Alfred C. Lockwood, who had also once been Arizona's chief justice.

Notable First: 1963

Sarah T. Hughes, federal district court judge of Texas, swore in Lyndon B. Johnson as the 36th president, the first woman to administer the presidential oath of office.

Notable First: 1949

Burnita S. Matthews, (D) District of Columbia, became the first female federal district court judge when she was appointed to the U.S. District Court for the District of Washington, D.C., by Pres. Harry S. Truman.

Notable First: 1939

Jane M. Brolin became the first African American female to hold a judgeship in the U.S. when Mayor Fiorello La Guardia appointed her to New York City's Court of Domestic Relations.

---

[171]Pres. John Kennedy had earlier appointed Marjorie M. Lawson as a juvenile court judge in Washington, D.C., at that time a "federal" appointment, but she did not hold a federal judgeship.

Notable First: 1934

Florence Ellinwood Allen (D), a justice on the Ohio Supreme Court, was named by Pres. Franklin D. Roosevelt to the Sixth Circuit court of appeals and became the first woman appointed to a U.S. circuit court of appeals.

Notable First: 1928

Genevieve Cline, (R) Ohio, became the first woman appointed to the federal bench when Pres. Calvin Coolidge appointed her to the U.S. Customs Court. She served twenty-five years until her retirement in 1953.

Notable First: 1925

Hortense Ward of Texas became the first woman to serve as a state supreme court chief justice when she headed a special all-female supreme court hearing a case; the sitting supreme court justices, all of them male, had recused themselves.

Notable First: 1922

Florence Ellinwood Allen, (D) Ohio, won a statewide election and gained a seat on that state's supreme court. In doing so, she became the first woman elected to a state supreme court. She won reelection to the position in 1928. In 1926 Allen tried for the Democratic nomination for the U.S. Senate, but she was defeated in the primary.

Notable First: 1918

Kathryn Sellers was named a judge in the juvenile court of Washington, D.C., the first woman in the U.S. to hold a judgeship. Previously Ms. Sellers had also been the first female district attorney in the U.S.

Women at the Local Level

Notable First: 1991

Jacquelyn Barrett (D) was elected sheriff of Fulton County, Georgia, the first African American female popularly elected county sheriff in the U.S.

Notable Firsts: 1983

Penny Harrington, of Portland, Oregon, became the first female police chief of a major American city.
Lily Chen (D) was elected mayor of Monterey Park, California, the first Chinese American woman in the U.S. to hold that position.

Notable First: 1982

Loretta Glickman was elected mayor of Pasadena, California, the first female African American elected mayor of a large American city.

Notable First: 1980

Carol Kawanami was elected mayor of Villa Park, California, the first female Japanese American mayor in the U.S.

Notable First: 1974

Lelia Smith was elected mayor of Taft, Oklahoma, the first female African American mayor in the U.S.

Notable First: 1926

Bertha Knight Landes was elected mayor in Seattle, Washington, after having previously served on the city council, the first female mayor of a large American city.

Notable First: 1920

Mrs. Jane Johnson was elected sheriff of Roscommon County, Michigan, the first woman elected county sheriff in the U.S.

Notable First: 1910

Kanab, Utah, elected a five-member—all female—city council, the first all-female local government in the U.S.

Notable First: 1887

Susanna M. Salter was elected mayor of Orgonia, Kansas, the first woman to hold the position of mayor in the U.S.

Notable First: 1792

Mrs. Sarah De Crow was appointed postmaster of Hartford, North Carolina, the first woman appointed to a federal position after the adoption of the U.S. Constitution.

Notable First: 1775

Mary K. Goddard of Baltimore, Maryland, was the first woman to hold the position of postmaster in the U.S., a post she held from 1775 until 1789.

African Americans in American Politics

A Brief Chronology

1802 **First state to grant the right to vote to African Americans**

Ohio adopted a new constitution in 1802, one provision of which extended the right to vote to free African Americans.

1855 **First African American elected to public office**

John M. Langston, representing the Liberty Party, was elected town clerk of Brownheim Township, Ohio, in 1855. He was probably the first African American elected to public office in the U.S. Later, during Reconstruction, Langston was also elected to the U.S. House of Representatives as a Republican from Virginia.

First African American nominated for statewide office

Frederick Douglass, who ran for New York secretary of state on the ticket of the New York Liberty Party in 1855, was the first African American nominated for a statewide office. Despite its large African American population, New York did not elect an African American to a statewide office until almost 140 years later, in 1994.

1866 **First African Americans elected to a state legislature**

Edwin G. Walker and **Charles L. Mitchell**, both Republicans, were elected to the Massachusetts legislature in 1866. Within a few years African Americans were serving in several state legislatures, especially in the southern states after Reconstruction laws were passed.

1867 **First African American elected mayor**

Monroe Baker, elected mayor of St. Martin, a small town in Louisiana, in 1867 was probably the first African American popularly elected mayor in the U.S.

First popularly elected body in the U.S. to have an African American majority

The Louisiana Constitutional Convention of 1867—elected to write a new constitution for the state after its seizure by Union troops during the Civil War—was the first popularly elected body in the U.S. to have an African American majority.

1868 First African American elected to the U.S. House of Representatives

John W. Menard, a Republican of Louisiana, was elected to the U.S. House of Representatives. Menard, however, never served. His election credentials were challenged, and the House refused to seat him.

First African American majority in a state legislative house

The state house of representatives that convened in **South Carolina** in 1868 had eighty-seven African Americans out of a total membership of 127. This was the first (and only) time that African Americans have held a majority of the seats in a state legislative house.

First African American delegates to a major political party's national convention

Pinckney B. S. Pinchback and **James J. Harris**, both from Louisiana, attended the 1868 Republican National Convention as official voting delegates.

1869 First African American sworn into the U.S. Senate

Hiram Revels, a Republican, was sworn in as the first African American member of the U.S. Senate in 1869. Ironically, the seat from Mississippi that Revels held had last been occupied by Jefferson Davis before the Civil War; Davis had left the U.S. Senate to assume the presidency of the Confederacy.

1870 First constitutional guarantee to African Americans of their right to vote

The 15th Amendment to the U.S. Constitution, adopted in 1870, removed race, color, and prior condition of servitude as barriers to the right to vote. It did not, as is commonly thought, extend the vote to all African Americans. A variety of legal and often illegal means such as "grandfather" clauses and poll taxes continued for a number of years, denying many African Americans their voting rights.

First African American sworn into the U.S. House of Representatives

Joseph H. Rainey, (R) South Carolina, was sworn in and seated in the U.S. House of Representatives in 1870.

First African American to serve on a state supreme court

Jonathan Jasper Wright was appointed in 1870 as an associate justice of the South Carolina Supreme Court.

1872 First African American governor

Pinckney B. S. Pinchback, Republican, succeeded to the office of governor of Louisiana and held it for slightly more than thirty days at the end of 1872 after the incumbent resigned.

1904 First African American candidate for the presidency

George Edwin Taylor, the presidential candidate of the **National Liberal Party**, was the first African American candidate to run for the presidency on a minor party ticket.

1911 **First African American in a federal subcabinet–level position**

William H. Lewis was appointed as an assistant attorney general by Pres. William H. Taft.

1915 **First African American elected to the city council of a large American city**

Oscar DePriest, Republican, was elected to the city council of Chicago, Illinois, in 1915.

1927 **First African American woman to serve in a state legislature**

Minnie Buckingham-Harper, Republican, was appointed by the governor to the seat of her deceased husband in West Virginia's legislature.

1937 **First African American federal judge**

William Hastie, Democrat, was appointed by Pres. Franklin D. Roosevelt as a United States district judge in the Virgin Islands.

1938 **First African American woman elected to a state legislative seat**

Crystal Bird Fauset, (D) Pennsylvania, was elected to a seat in that state's house of representatives.

1939 **First African American woman to hold a judgeship**

Jane Brolin was appointed a municipal judge in New York City by Mayor Fiorello F. La Guardia.

1940 **First African American to bear the diplomatic rank of U.S. ambassador**

Edward F. Dunbar was appointed as U.S. ambassador to Liberia.

1951 **First African American to chair a standing committee in the U.S. House of Representatives**

William Dawson, (D) Illinois, became chair of the House Expenditures Committee.

1952 **First African American woman to appear on the ballot as a vice presidential candidate**

Carlotta A. Bass, of New York, appeared on the ticket of the Progressive Party as their nominee for vice president.

1961 **First African American to head a federal agency**

Robert C. Weaver was appointed head of the Federal Housing Authority by Pres. John F. Kennedy.

1962 **First African Americans elected to statewide office since Reconstruction**

Edward Brooke, (R) Massachusetts, was elected state attorney general, and Gerald Lamb, (D) Connecticut, was elected state treasurer in the November 1962 elections.

1965 **First African American woman to bear the title of U.S. ambassador**

Patricia Roberts Harris was appointed U.S. ambassador to Luxembourg by Pres. Lyndon B. Johnson.

1966 First African American woman to become a federal judge[1]

Constance Baker Motley, (D) New York, was appointed to a federal judgeship by Pres. Lyndon B. Johnson.

First African American to serve in a federal cabinet post

Robert C. Weaver became the first African American U.S. cabinet officer when he was sworn in as secretary of housing and urban development.

First African American elected to the U.S. Senate by popular vote

Edward Brooke, Republican, was elected to the U.S. Senate by the voters of Massachusetts.

1967 First African American U.S. Supreme Court justice

Thurgood Marshall was appointed as an associate justice of the U.S. Supreme Court by Pres. Lyndon B. Johnson.

First African American elected mayor of a large U.S. city

Carl Stokes, Democrat, was elected mayor of Cleveland, Ohio.

1969 First African American woman sworn into the U.S. House of Representatives

Shirley B. Chisholm, (D) New York, was sworn into the U.S. House of Representatives as its first African American female member.

1971 Black Congressional Caucus is formed

After meeting informally for several years, the African American members of the U.S. House of Representatives, ten in 1971, joined together and formed the Black Congressional Caucus.

1972 First African American to have her name placed in nomination for president by a major political party

Shirley B. Chisholm, (D) New York, had her name formally placed in nomination for president at the Democratic National Convention.

1974 First African American woman elected mayor

Lelia Smith was elected mayor of Taft, Oklahoma.

1977 First African American woman to serve in a federal cabinet position

Patricia Roberts Harris was sworn in as secretary of housing and urban development to serve in the cabinet of Pres. Jimmy Carter.

---

[1]Pres. John F. Kennedy had earlier appointed Marjorie M. Lawson as a juvenile court judge in Washington, D.C., at that time a "federal" appointment, but she did not hold a federal judgeship.

1982 **First African American woman elected mayor of a large city**

Loretta Glickman was elected mayor of Pasadena, California.

1984 **First African American state supreme court chief justice**

Robert N. C. Nix Jr., (D) Pennsylvania, was appointed chief justice of that state's supreme court.

1988 **First African American to place second in balloting for the presidential nomination at the convention of a major political party**

Rev. Jesse Jackson of Illinois, after a strong run in the Democratic presidential primaries and caucuses, received 1,218 $^1/_2$ delegate votes—the second highest total—on the first ballot at the Democratic National Convention.

First African American woman to appear on the presidential ballots min all fifty states

Lenora Fulani, of New York, appeared on the ballot in all fifty states as the presidential nominee of the National Alliance Party.

First African American woman to serve as a justice on a state supreme court

Juanita Kidd Stout, (D) Pennsylvania, was appointed as an associate justice of that state's supreme court.

1989 **First African American popularly elected governor**

L. Douglas Wilder, Democrat, was elected governor of Virginia after a tightly fought campaign.

First African American to head a major national political party

Ron Brown was chosen as chair of the National Democratic Party.

1993 **First African American woman sworn into the U.S. Senate**

Carol Moseley-Braun, Democrat, was sworn in as the junior senator from the state of Illinois.

African Americans and Political Power

The following chart (by state) details the total number of African Americans who have served their states in three of the most powerful positions in U.S. politics: governor, U.S. Senate (both appointed and elected), and U.S. House of Representatives.

State	Governor	U.S. Senate	U.S. House
Alabama	-	-	4
Alaska	-	-	-
Arizona	-	-	-

Arkansas	-	-	-
California	-	-	9
Colorado	-	-	-
Connecticut	-	-	1
Delaware	-	-	-
Florida	-	-	4
Georgia	-	-	5
Hawaii	-	-	-
Idaho	-	-	-
Illinois	-	1	14
Indiana	-	-	2
Iowa	-	-	-
Kansas	-	-	-
Kentucky	-	-	-
Louisiana	1	-	3
Maine	-	-	-
Maryland	-	-	4
Massachusetts	-	1	-
Michigan	-	-	5
Minnesota	-	-	-
Mississippi	-	2	3
Missouri	-	-	2
Montana	-	-	-
Nebraska	-	-	-
Nevada	-	-	-
New Hampshire	-	-	-
New Jersey	-	-	1
New Mexico	-	-	-
New York	-	-	8
North Carolina	-	-	6
North Dakota	-	-	-
Ohio	-	-	2
Oklahoma	-	-	1
Oregon	-	-	-
Pennsylvania	-	-	4
Rhode Island	-	-	-
South Carolina	-	-	9
South Dakota	-	-	-
Tennessee	-	-	2
Texas	-	-	5
Utah	-	-	-
Vermont	-	-	-
Virginia	1	-	2
Washington	-	-	-
West Virginia	-	-	-

| Wisconsin | - | - | - |
| Wyoming | - | - | - |

| Total African Americans Who Have Served | 2 | 4 | 96 |

Best and Worst States for African Americans Achieving Power

The most salient fact is that African Americans are underrepresented in almost every state based on their overall population. It is almost impossible to determine which state could be considered the "best" in terms of African Americans achieving power. At present in **Maryland**, where African Americans constitute about 30 percent of the population, they come closest to achieving a fair share of power in at least one area. They currently hold two seats (out of eight total)—or 25 percent—in the state's U.S. House delegation.

The worst states would undoubtedly have to be several of the southern ones. There, African Americans make up anywhere from 25 percent to 40-plus percent of the population yet hold nowhere near that percentage of congressional seats.

African Americans in the U.S. Cabinet

The President's Cabinet

The first African American member of a U.S. presidential cabinet was **Robert Weaver** (see below), appointed in 1966. He might actually have entered the cabinet several years earlier had the situation been different. In 1962 Pres. John F. Kennedy proposed to upgrade the Federal Housing Authority, headed at that time by Weaver, to a full cabinet position, but he met stiff resistance when conservative members of Congress realized that if the plan was implemented the likely choice to head the new branch would be Weaver, an African American.

Secretary of Agriculture

Mike Espy, 1993–1995, appointed by Bill Clinton

Secretary of Commerce

Ronald H. Brown, 1993–1996, appointed by Bill Clinton

Secretary of Housing and Urban Development

Robert C. Weaver, 1966–1969, appointed by Lyndon B. Johnson
Patricia Roberts Harris,[2] 1977–1979, appointed by Jimmy Carter
Samuel R. Pierce Jr., 1981–1989, appointed by Ronald Reagan

---

[2]Harris was the first African American woman to serve as a U.S. cabinet official. In 1965, when Pres. Lyndon B. Johnson appointed her ambassador to Luxembourg, she became the first African American woman to hold that diplomatic rank in the U.S. Foreign Service.

Secretary of Transportation

William T. Coleman Jr.,[3] 1975–1977, appointed by Gerald Ford
Rodney Slater, 1997– , appointed by Bill Clinton

Secretary of Energy

Hazel R. O'Leary, 1993–1996, appointed by Bill Clinton

Secretary of Health, Education, and Welfare

Patricia Roberts Harris, 1979–1979, appointed by Jimmy Carter

Secretary of Health and Human Services

Patricia Roberts Harris, 1979–1981, appointed by Jimmy Carter
Louis W. Sullivan, 1989–1993, appointed by George Bush

Secretary of Labor

Alexis Herman, 1997– , appointed by Bill Clinton

Secretary of Veterans Affairs

Jesse Brown, 1993–1997, appointed by Bill Clinton
Togo D. West Jr., 1997– , appointed by Bill Clinton

African Americans in the Executive Branch

Notable First: 1993

Jocelyn Elders, (D) Arkansas, appointed by Pres. Bill Clinton as surgeon general, the first African American to hold that position.

Notable Firsts: 1989

Audrey Forbes Manley, appointed by Pres. George Bush, the first African American female assistant secretary of health and human services.
Clifton Wharton Jr., appointed by Pres. George Bush, the first African American deputy secretary of state.

---

[3]In 1949, when he became a clerk for Supreme Court Justice Felix Frankfurter, Coleman set another record: He was the first African American to be a law clerk in the U.S. Supreme Court.

Notable First: 1984

Aulana Louise Peters, appointed by Pres. Ronald Reagan, the first African American female to sit on the Securities and Exchange Commission.

Notable First: 1980

Carlos Cardozo Campbell, appointed by Pres. Jimmy Carter, the first African American assistant secretary of commerce.

Notable First: 1978

Carolyn Robertson Payton, appointed by Pres. Jimmy Carter, the first African American (and female) to head the Peace Corps.

Notable Firsts: 1977

Clifford Alexander Jr., appointed by Pres. Jimmy Carter, the first African American to hold the position of secretary of the army.

Azie Taylor Morton, appointed by Pres. Jimmy Carter, the first African American treasurer of the United States.

Eleanor Holmes Norton, (D) District of Columbia, appointed by Pres. Jimmy Carter, the first African American (and first female) to head the Equal Employment Opportunity Commission.

Notable First: 1972

Benjamin Hooks, (D) Tennessee, appointed by Pres. Richard Nixon, the first African American to hold the chair of the Federal Communications Commission.

Notable First: 1968

Barbara Watson, appointed by Pres. Lyndon B. Johnson, the first African American (and the first female) to become assistant secretary of state.

Notable First: 1966

Andrew F. Brimmer, appointed by Pres. Lyndon B. Johnson, the first African American appointed as a governor of the Federal Reserve Board.

Notable First: 1961

Robert C. Weaver, (D) New York, appointed as administrator of the Housing and Home Finance Agency by Pres. John F. Kennedy, the first African American to head a federal agency.

Notable First: 1954

J. Ernest Wilkins, appointed by Pres. Dwight Eisenhower as assistant secretary of labor, the second African American appointed to a federal subcabinet–level position.

Notable First: 1936

Mary McLeod Bethune, named director of Negro Affairs in the National Youth Administration, the first African American woman to receive a major federal appointment.

Notable First: 1911

William H. Lewis, appointed by Pres. William H. Taft as assistant attorney general, the first African American to reach subcabinet-level rank in the executive branch.

Notable First: 1881

The signature of **Blanche K. Bruce**, registrar of the Treasury, appeared on U.S. currency. The former one-term U.S. senator, (R) Mississippi, was appointed to his post by Pres. James A. Garfield.

Notable First: 1869

Ebenezer Don Carlos Bassett, appointed minister to Haiti by Pres. Ulysses S. Grant, the first African American to hold that diplomatic rank.

African Americans at the National Party Level

Notable First: 1992

Ronald Brown became the first African American chair to preside over the national convention of a major political party when he wielded the gavel during the Democratic National Convention.

Notable First: 1989

Ronald Brown became chair of the National Democratic Party, the first African American to head a major political party.

Notable Firsts: 1988

Lenora Fulani, (National Alliance Party) New York, became the first African American woman to appear on the presidential ballot in all fifty states.

Rev. Jesse Jackson of Illinois, after a strong run in the Democratic presidential primaries, received 1,218 $^{1}/_{2}$ delegate votes—the second highest total—on the first ballot at the Democratic National Convention.

Notable First: 1976

Barbara Jordan of Texas, a two-term member of the U.S. House of Representatives, became the first African American and the first woman to deliver the keynote speech at a Democratic National Convention.

Notable First: 1972

Shirley B. Chisholm of New York, a two-term member of the U.S. House of Representatives and a contender during the Democratic primary season in twelve states, had her name formally placed in nomination for president at the Democratic National Convention. In doing so, she became the first African American woman accorded that honor. She received 152 delegate votes on the first (and only) convention ballot.

Notable Firsts: 1968

Rev. Channing E. Phillips of Washington, D.C., became the first African American formally nominated for president at the convention of a major political party. He received 67 $\frac{1}{2}$ votes on the first (and only) ballot at the Democratic National Convention.

Julian Bond of Georgia became the first African American to be nominated from the convention floor for vice president at any Democratic National Convention. After questions arose during the balloting as to whether he was old enough to accept the nomination should he win it, Bond withdrew his name.

Notable First: 1952

Carlotta A. Bass of New York became the first African American woman to appear on the national presidential ballot as a vice presidential candidate when she ran on the Progressive ticket.

Notable First: 1924

A. P. Collins of New York became the first African American to participate as a full delegate to any Democratic National Convention.

Notable First: 1904

George Edwin Taylor ran as the presidential candidate of the National Liberal Party, the first African American candidate to seek the presidency on a minor party ticket.

Notable First: 1884

John R. Lynch of Mississippi, who wielded the gavel during a session at the 1884 Republican National Convention, became the first African American to preside temporarily over the national convention of a major political party.

Notable First: 1878

Blanche K. Bruce, U.S. senator from Mississippi, received several votes from the floor for president at the National Republican Convention, the first African American to do so at the national convention of a major party.

Notable First: 1872

Frederick Douglass became the first African American to be nominated as a vice presidential candidate. He ran on the Equal Rights Party ticket headed by feminist Victoria Claflin Woodhull.

Notable First: 1868

Pinckney B. S. Pinchback and **James J. Harris**, both from Louisiana, attended the 1868 Republican National Convention as official voting delegates, the first African American delegates to a major political party's national convention.

Notable First: 1866

Frederick Douglass became the first African American delegate to a national political convention, when he attended the convention held by the National Loyalists Union Party.

Notable First: 1843

Henry H. Garnet, **Samuel R. Ward**, and **Charles B. Ray** became the first African American delegates to a political convention when they attended the Liberty Party's New York state convention.

African American U.S. Senators in Chronological Order of Service

Senator	Party	State	Dates Served
1. Hiram Rhodes Revels	Republican	Mississippi	02/25/1870–03/03/1871
2. Blanche Kelso Bruce	Republican	Mississippi	03/04/1875–03/03/1881
3. Edward William Brooke III	Republican	Massachusetts	01/03/67–01/01/79
4. Carol Moseley-Braun	Democrat	Illinois	01/05/93–01/05/99

How They Assumed Office

1. **Hiram Rhodes Revels,** (R) Mississippi (Born: 1822; Died: 1901)
   Served: 02/25/1870–03/03/1871

   Elected by the Mississippi state legislature in 1870 as one of the two men sent back to the U.S. Senate when the state was readmitted to the Union after the Civil War. After serving a little less than a year, Revels was replaced in another election by the Mississippi legislature with a white

Republican. He had been born free, of African American and reputed Native American (Lumbee/Croatan) descent, and was a banker before entering politics in 1868, when he was appointed as an alderman in Natchez, Mississippi. After his senatorial term, Revels served as president of Alcorn College in Mississippi for two different periods. By the time he died the public had almost forgotten the record he had set as the country's first African American U.S. senator.

Previous elected public office:
   Mississippi State Senate, 1869–1870
Subsequent public office:
   Mississippi Secretary of State, 1873 (appointed to serve a short period of time)

2. **Blanche Kelso Bruce,** (R) Mississippi (Born: 1841; Died: 1898)
   Served: 03/04/1875–03/03/1881

Elected by the Mississippi legislature in 1874 to a full six-year term. Bruce, a former slave, assumed the seat held by Jefferson Davis before he left to become president of the Confederacy. By the end of Bruce's term Democrats had reclaimed control of Mississippi's legislature, replacing the alliance of African Americans and "carpetbagger" Republicans that had controlled the state after its readmission to the Union in 1870. The new legislature refused to reelect Bruce to a second term, replacing him with James Z. George, a white Democrat. After completing his term, Bruce continued to live in Washington, D.C., and remained involved in Mississippi Republican politics. In 1881 he refused an appointment as ambassador to Brazil because that country still had legalized slavery. Instead, he accepted an appointment as registrar of the Treasury, a post he held 1881–1889.

Previous elected public office:
   Bolivar County, Mississippi, Sheriff and Superintendent of Schools
Subsequent elected public office: None

3. **Edward William Brooke III,** (R) Massachusetts (Born: 1919)
   Served: 01/03/67–01/01/79

Elected on November 8, 1966, to a full six-year term. Brooke was the first African American popularly elected to the U.S. Senate. He had begun his political career by filing for office in both the Democratic and Republican primaries a few years earlier. After he won the Republican nod for an office, he continued to seek office under the GOP banner, culminating in his victory for the U.S. Senate. He won a second term in 1972. When he sought a third term in 1978, his recent divorce and sundry family troubles hampered his campaign, and he was defeated by U.S. Rep. Paul E. Tsongas (D).

Previous elected public office:
   Massachusetts Attorney General, 1963–1966
Subsequent elected public office: None

4. **Carol Moseley-Braun,** (D) Illinois (Born: 1947)
   Served: 01/05/93–01/05/99

Elected on November 3, 1992, to a full six-year term. Moseley-Braun, Cook County's recorder of deeds and a former member of the state's house of representatives, entered the Democratic primary for senator a distinct underdog—or so many thought. Her two opponents were incumbent Sen. Alan Dixon, heavily favored to win renomination for a third term, and businessman Albert J. Hofeld. As the campaign wore on, Hofeld spent heavily on media attacks against Dixon, who launched counterattacks on him. Meanwhile, Moseley-Braun kept campaigning away and began to look like a viable candidate to an electorate rapidly becoming disenchanted with her two male opponents. On primary night, she squeezed out a slim victory.

Moseley-Braun was one of ten women to win Democratic senatorial nominations in 1992. The confirmation hearings of Clarence Thomas for the Supreme Court focused the spotlight on the underrepresentation of women in the U.S. Senate. Democrats, at their 1992 Democratic presidential convention, made much of that fact, which gave an added boost to all campaigns of female candidates, including that of Moseley-Braun. Women's rights and African American groups coalesced around her candidacy, and she surged past Richard Williamson (R), a former aide to President Reagan, to win her Senate seat by a 53–43 percent margin. In doing so, she established two important milestones: she became the first African American woman elected to the U.S. Senate, and she became the first woman to defeat an elected, incumbent U.S. senator.

Defeated for reelection in 1998.

Previous elected public office:
    Illinois House of Representatives, 1978–1988
    Cook County, Illinois, Recorder of Deeds, 1989–1992

African American U.S. Senatorial Statistics

Longest Tenure of an African American Senator

Edward W. Brooke III, (R) Massachusetts, who served for twelve years during two full six-year terms, from January 3, 1967, through January 1, 1979.

First State Represented by More Than One African American U.S. Senator

Mississippi
    02/25/1870–03/03/1871   Hiram R. Revels (R)
    03/04/1875–03/03/1881   Blanche K. Bruce (R)

First Vote Cast in U.S. Senate by an African American

Hiram R. Revels, (R) Mississippi, cast a vote in March 1870 on a minor procedural matter.

First African American to Preside over the U.S. Senate

Blanche K. Bruce, (R) Mississippi, during a session in 1878.

First African American Chair of a U.S. Senate Committee

Blanche K. Bruce, (R) Mississippi, chair of the Levees and Dikes of the Mississippi River Committee.

First African American Senator Defeated in a Popular Vote

Edward W. Brooke III, (R) Massachusetts, who lost his bid for a third six-year term on November 7, 1978.

First African American to Defeat an Incumbent Senator

Carol Moseley-Braun, (D) Illinois, who defeated Sen. Alan Dixon in the 1992 Democratic primary.

African American U.S. Senatorial Election Statistics

The following section provides voting statistics on those African American senators who contested elections, including primaries, primary runoffs, and general elections. Since two of the four African Americans who have held U.S. Senate seats were appointed by state legislatures, they did not face elections for their seats. Names in this section appear in chronological order of senatorial service, from earliest to most recent.

Edward William Brooke, (R) Massachusetts

1978	General	Paul E. Tsongas (D)	1,093,283	55.0%
		Edward W. Brooke III (R)	890,584	45.0%
1972	General	Edward W. Brooke III (R)	1,505,932	65.0%
		John J. Droney (D)	823,278	35.0%
1966	General	Edward W. Brooke III (R)	1,213,473	61.0%
		Endicott Peabody (D)	774,761	39.0%

Carol Moseley-Braun, (D) Illinois

1998	General	Peter Fitzgerald (R)	1,691,994	51.0%
		Carol Moseley-Braun (D)	1,565,265	47.0%
		Other		3.0%
1998	Democratic Primary	Carol Moseley-Braun	unopposed	
1992	General	Carol Moseley-Braun (D)	2,631,229	53.0%
		Richard S. Williamson (R)	2,126,833	43.0%
1992	Democratic Primary	Carol Moseley-Braun	557,694	38.0%
		Alan J. Dixon	504,077	35.0%
		Albert F. Hofeld	394,497	27.0%

Chronology of All African American Candidates for U.S. Senate[4]
(* denotes winner)

1966	*Edward W. Brooke III	Republican	Massachusetts
1972	*Edward W. Brooke III	Republican	Massachusetts
	John L. Leflore	National Democratic	Alabama

---

[4]This chronology does not include the African American U.S. senators who served during Reconstruction after the Civil War, as they were elected by their state legislatures rather than by popular vote.

1974	James H. Brannen III	Republican	Connecticut
1978	Edward W. Brooke III	Republican	Massachusetts
	Charles Evers	Independent	Mississippi
1988	Alan Keyes	Republican	Maryland
	Maurice Dawkins	Republican	Virginia
1990	Harvey Gantt	Democrat	North Carolina
1992	*Carol Moseley-Braun	Democrat	Illinois
	Alan Keyes	Republican	Maryland
1994	Ron Sims	Democrat	Washington
	Alan Wheat[5]	Democrat	Missouri
	L. Douglas Wilder[6]	Independent	Virginia
1996	Harvey Gantt	Democrat	North Carolina
1998	Gary A. Franks[7]	Republican	Connecticut
	Carol Moseley-Braun	Democrat	Illinois

African Americans Serving in the U.S. House of Representatives[8]

106th Congress (1999–2001)

State	District	Name	Party Affiliation
Alabama	7	Earl Hilliard	Democrat
California	9	Barbara Lee	Democrat
California	32	Julian Dixon	Democrat
California	35	Maxine Waters	Democrat
California	37	Juanita Millender-McDonald	Democrat
Florida	3	Corrine Brown	Democrat
Florida	17	Carrie P. Meek	Democrat
Florida	23	Alcee Hastings	Democrat
Georgia	2	Sanford D. Bishop Jr.	Democrat
Georgia	5	John Lewis	Democrat
Georgia	4	Cynthia McKinney	Democrat
Illinois	1	Bobby Rush	Democrat
Illinois	2	Jesse Jackson Jr.	Democrat
Illinois	7	Danny Davis	Democrat
Indiana	10	Julia M. Carson	Democrat

[5]Wheat had previously served six terms (1983–1995) in the U.S. House.

[6]Wilder, a former governor and Democrat running as an Independent, withdrew from the race in mid-September, then announced his support for his opponent and longtime political antagonist, incumbent Sen. Chuck Robb (D), who was locked in a tight battle for reelection. The move was seen as a maneuver to deny an election victory to their ultraconservative opponent, Oliver North (R), who had been leading the race because of a split Democratic vote.

[7]Franks had previously served three terms (1991–1997) in the U.S. House.

[8]Several African Americans have been elected to the U.S. House of Representatives from both the District of Columbia and the Virgin Islands. Since these people are considered "nonvoting" delegates and not representatives, they have not been included in this section.

Louisiana	2	William J. Jefferson	Democrat
Maryland	4	Albert R. Wynn	Democrat
Maryland	7	Elijah Cummings	Democrat
Michigan	14	John Conyers Jr.	Democrat
Michigan	15	Carolyn C. Kilpatrick	Democrat
Mississippi	2	Bennie G. Thompson	Democrat
Missouri	1	William Clay	Democrat
New Jersey	10	Donald M. Payne	Democrat
New York	6	Gregory W. Meeks	Democrat
New York	10	Edolphus Towns	Democrat
New York	11	Major R. Owens	Democrat
New York	15	Charles B. Rangel	Democrat
North Carolina	1	Eva M. Clayton	Democrat
North Carolina	12	Melvin L. Watt	Democrat
Ohio	11	Stephanie Tubbs-Jones	Democrat
Oklahoma	4	J.C. Watts	Republican
Pennsylvania	2	Chaka Fattah	Democrat
South Carolina	6	James E. Clyburn	Democrat
Tennessee	9	Harold E. Ford Jr.	Democrat
Texas	18	Sheila Jackson-Lee	Democrat
Texas	30	Eddie Bernice Johnson	Democrat
Virginia	3	Robert C. (Bobby) Scott	Democrat

Total African Americans Serving

37 (36 Democrats, 1 Republican)

Female African American Representation

12 Women

California	9	Barbara Lee	Democrat
California	35	Maxine Waters	Democrat
California	37	Juanita Millender-McDonald	Democrat
Florida	3	Corrine Brown	Democrat
Florida	17	Carrie P. Meek	Democrat
Georgia	4	Cynthia McKinney	Democrat
Indiana	10	Julia M. Carson	Democrat
Michigan	15	Carolyn C. Kilpatrick	Democrat
North Carolina	1	Eva Clayton	Democrat
Ohio	11	Stephanie Tubbs-Jones	Democrat
Texas	18	Sheila Jackson-Lee	Democrat
Texas	30	Eddie Bernice Johnson	Democrat

Senior African American Member

John Conyers Jr., (D) Michigan–14th, first elected in 1964.

Wielding Power

With the Republicans in majority control of the U.S. House of Representatives, there were no African American committee chairs in the 106th Congress; several African American Democratic members hold Ranking Minority Member status on their committees.

Losing African American Candidates

In addition to the thirty-seven African Americans elected in November 1998 to the 106th Congress, both parties fielded other African American candidates. The Republicans seemed less successful in their effort to recruit African American candidates this year than they had been in years past, plus their candidates were plagued by other problems. For example, one of their most highly touted candidates, **Dylan Glenn**, Georgia—2nd, was unable to even win his Republican primary.

African American Incumbents Not Returning from the 105th Congress

One African American incumbent retired and did not seek reelection:

Louis Stokes, (D) Ohio–11th

105th Congress (1997–1999)

State	District	Name	Party Affiliation
Alabama	7	Earl Hilliard	Democrat
California	9	Ronald V. Dellums[9]	Democrat
California	9	Barbara Lee[10]	Democrat
California	32	Julian Dixon	Democrat
California	35	Maxine Waters	Democrat
California	37	Juanita Millender-McDonald	Democrat
Florida	3	Corrine Brown	Democrat
Florida	17	Carrie P. Meek	Democrat
Florida	23	Alcee Hastings	Democrat
Georgia	2	Sanford D. Bishop Jr.	Democrat
Georgia	5	John Lewis	Democrat
Georgia	4	Cynthia McKinney	Democrat
Illinois	1	Bobby Rush	Democrat
Illinois	2	Jesse Jackson Jr.	Democrat

[9]Dellums resigned effective February 6, 1998.

[10]Lee was elected in a special April 7, 1998, election to replace Ronald Dellums, who had resigned.

Illinois	7	Danny Davis	Democrat
Indiana	10	Julia M. Carson	Democrat
Louisiana	2	William J. Jefferson	Democrat
Maryland	4	Albert R. Wynn	Democrat
Maryland	7	Elijah Cummings	Democrat
Michigan	14	John Conyers Jr.	Democrat
Michigan	15	Carolyn C. Kilpatrick	Democrat
Mississippi	2	Bennie G. Thompson	Democrat
Missouri	1	William Clay	Democrat
New Jersey	10	Donald M. Payne	Democrat
New York	6	Floyd H. Flake[11]	Democrat
New York	6	Gregory Meeks[12]	Democrat
New York	10	Edolphus Towns	Democrat
New York	11	Major R. Owens	Democrat
New York	15	Charles B. Rangel	Democrat
North Carolina	1	Eva M. Clayton	Democrat
North Carolina	12	Melvin L. Watt	Democrat
Ohio	11	Louis Stokes	Democrat
Oklahoma	4	J. C. Watts	Republican
Pennsylvania	2	Chaka Fattah	Democrat
South Carolina	6	James E. Clyburn	Democrat
Tennessee	9	Harold E. Ford Jr.	Democrat
Texas	18	Sheila Jackson-Lee	Democrat
Texas	30	Eddie Bernice Johnson	Democrat
Virginia	3	Robert C. "Bobby" Scott	Democrat

Total African Americans Serving

39 (38 Democrats, 1 Republican)

Female African American Representation

11 Women

California	9	Barbara Lee	Democrat
California	35	Maxine Waters	Democrat
California	37	Juanita Millender-McDonald	Democrat
Florida	3	Corrine Brown	Democrat
Florida	17	Carrie P. Meek	Democrat
Georgia	4	Cynthia McKinney	Democrat
Indiana	10	Julia M. Carson	Democrat
Michigan	15	Carolyn C. Kilpatrick	Democrat

[11]Flake resigned November 15, 1997, in order to devote more time to the church, where he served as minister.

[12]Meeks was elected in a special February 3, 1998, election to replace Flake, who had resigned.

North Carolina	1	Eva Clayton	Democrat
Texas	18	Sheila Jackson-Lee	Democrat
Texas	30	Eddie Bernice Johnson	Democrat

Senior African American Member

John Conyers, Jr., (D) Michigan–14th, first elected in 1964.

Wielding Power

With the Republicans in majority control of the U.S. House of Representatives, there were no African American committee chairs in the 105th Congress; four African American Democratic members held ranking minority member status on their committees.

Losing African American Candidates

In addition to the thirty-seven African Americans elected in November 1996 to the 105th Congress, both parties fielded other African American candidates, with the Republicans presenting twenty-four candidates themselves.

African American Incumbents Not Returning from the 104th Congress

Three African American incumbents retired and did not seek reelection:

Cardiss Collins, (D) Illinois–7th
Cleo Fields, (D) Louisiana–4th
Harold Ford, (D) Tennessee–9th

One was defeated in the primary for her district:

Barbara-Rose Collins, (D) Michigan–15th

One lost in the general election:

Gary A. Franks, (R) Connecticut–5th

104th Congress (1995–1997)

State	District	Name	Party Affiliation
Alabama	7	Earl Hilliard	Democrat
California	9	Ronald V. Dellums	Democrat
California	32	Julian Dixon	Democrat
California	35	Maxine Waters	Democrat
California	37	Walter R. Tucker III[13]	Democrat

---

[13]Tucker resigned on December 15, 1995, after his conviction for taking bribes while serving as mayor of Compton, California.

California	37	Juanita Millender-McDonald[14]	Democrat
Connecticut	5	Gary A. Franks	Republican
Florida	3	Corrine Brown	Democrat
Florida	19	Carrie P. Meek	Democrat
Florida	23	Alcee Hastings	Democrat
Georgia	2	Sanford D. Bishop Jr.	Democrat
Georgia	5	John Lewis	Democrat
Georgia	11	Cynthia McKinney	Democrat
Illinois	1	Bobby Rush	Democrat
Illinois	2	Mel Reynolds[15]	Democrat
Illinois	2	Jesse Jackson Jr.[16]	Democrat
Illinois	7	Cardiss Collins	Democrat
Louisiana	2	William J. Jefferson	Democrat
Louisiana	4	Cleo Fields[17]	Democrat
Maryland	4	Albert R. Wynn	Democrat
Maryland	7	Kweisi Mfume[18]	Democrat
Maryland	7	Elijah Cummings[19]	Democrat
Michigan	14	John Conyers Jr.	Democrat
Michigan	15	Barbara-Rose Collins	Democrat
Mississippi	2	Bennie G. Thompson	Democrat
Missouri	1	William Clay	Democrat
New Jersey	10	Donald M. Payne	Democrat
New York	6	Floyd H. Flake	Democrat
New York	10	Edolphus Towns	Democrat
New York	11	Major R. Owens	Democrat
New York	15	Charles B. Rangel	Democrat
North Carolina	1	Eva M. Clayton	Democrat
North Carolina	12	Melvin L. Watt	Democrat
Ohio	11	Louis Stokes	Democrat
Oklahoma	4	J. C. Watts[20]	Republican
Pennsylvania	2	Chaka Fattah	Democrat
South Carolina	6	James E. Clyburn	Democrat
Tennessee	9	Harold E. Ford	Democrat
Texas	18	Sheila Jackson-Lee	Democrat
Texas	30	Eddie Bernice Johnson	Democrat
Virginia	3	Robert C. "Bobby" Scott	Democrat

[14]Millender-McDonald was elected in a special March 19, 1996, election to replace Walter Tucker III, who had resigned.

[15]Reynolds resigned on October 1, 1995, after being convicted on sexual misconduct charges.

[16]Jackson won a December 12, 1995, special election to replace Mel Reynolds.

[17]Fields was unsuccessful as the Democratic nominee for governor in 1995.

[18]Mfume resigned on February 18, 1996, in order to assume the presidency of the NAACP.

[19]Cummings won an April 15, 1996, special election to replace Kweisi Mfume, who had resigned.

[20]Watts had previously served one term (1991–1995) as state corporation commissioner, an elected statewide position in Oklahoma.

Total African Americans Serving

41 (39 Democrats, 2 Republicans)

Female African American Representation

10 Women

California	35	Maxine Waters	Democrat
California	37	Juanita Millender-McDonald	Democrat
Florida	3	Corrine Brown	Democrat
Florida	17	Carrie P. Meek	Democrat
Georgia	11	Cynthia McKinney	Democrat
Illinois	7	Cardiss Collins	Democrat
Michigan	15	Barbara-Rose Collins	Democrat
North Carolina	1	Eva Clayton	Democrat
Texas	18	Sheila Jackson-Lee	Democrat
Texas	30	Eddie Bernice Johnson	Democrat

Senior African American Member

John Conyers Jr., (D) Michigan–14th, first elected in 1964.

Wielding Power

When the Republicans won majority control of the U.S. House of Representatives, the three African American committee chairs—all Democrats—from the 103rd Congress lost their leadership positions. They all assumed ranking minority member status on their committees.

Notable First

For the first time since 1891—nearly 104 years—two African American Republicans served together in the U.S. House.

Losing African American Candidates

In addition to the thirty-eight African Americans elected in November 1994 to the 104th Congress, the two major political parties also fielded a record number of other African American candidates. For instance, the Republicans fielded twenty-two other African American candidates—many running in primarily non–African American–majority districts—who failed to be elected. Besides the two African American Republicans who were elected, five others received more than 40 percent of the vote in their districts.

African American Incumbents Not Returning from the 103rd Congress

Three African American incumbents, all Democrats, did not return from the 103rd Congress. Two lost their seats to challengers in the Democratic primary in their district:

Lucien Blackwell, Pennsylvania–2nd
Craig Washington, Texas–18th

One incumbent, **Alan B. Wheat**, (D) Missouri–5th, was defeated as the Democratic nominee for the U.S. Senate.

103rd Congress (1993–1995)

State	District	Name	Party Affiliation
Alabama	7	Earl Hilliard	Democrat
California	9	Ronald V. Dellums	Democrat
California	32	Julian Dixon	Democrat
California	35	Maxine Waters	Democrat
California	37	Walter R. Tucker III	Democrat
Connecticut	5	Gary A. Franks	Republican
Florida	3	Corrine Brown	Democrat
Florida	19	Carrie P. Meek	Democrat
Florida	23	Alcee Hastings	Democrat
Georgia	2	Sanford D. Bishop Jr.	Democrat
Georgia	5	John Lewis	Democrat
Georgia	11	Cynthia McKinney	Democrat
Illinois	1	Bobby Rush	Democrat
Illinois	2	Mel Reynolds	Democrat
Illinois	7	Cardiss Collins	Democrat
Louisiana	2	William J. Jefferson	Democrat
Louisiana	4	Cleo Fields	Democrat
Maryland	4	Albert R. Wynn	Democrat
Maryland	7	Kweisi Mfume	Democrat
Michigan	14	John Conyers Jr.	Democrat
Michigan	15	Barbara-Rose Collins	Democrat
Mississippi	2	Mike Espy[21]	Democrat
Mississippi	2	Bennie G. Thompson	Democrat
Missouri	1	William Clay	Democrat
Missouri	5	Alan B. Wheat	Democrat
New Jersey	10	Donald M. Payne	Democrat
New York	6	Floyd H. Flake	Democrat
New York	10	Edolphus Towns	Democrat
New York	11	Major R. Owens	Democrat
New York	15	Charles B. Rangel	Democrat
North Carolina	1	Eva M. Clayton	Democrat
North Carolina	12	Melvin L. Watt	Democrat
Ohio	11	Louis Stokes	Democrat

[21]Mike Espy resigned during the 103rd Congress to become secretary of agriculture. In the special election to fill his seat, Bennie Thompson won and was sworn in during the 103rd Congress.

Pennsylvania	2	Lucien Blackwell	Democrat
South Carolina	6	James E. Clyburn	Democrat
Tennessee	9	Harold E. Ford	Democrat
Texas	18	Craig Washington	Democrat
Texas	30	Eddie Bernice Johnson	Democrat
Virginia	3	Robert C. "Bobby" Scott	Democrat

Total African Americans Serving

38 (37 Democrats, 1 Republican)

Female African American Representation

8 Women

California	35	Maxine Waters	Democrat
Florida	3	Corrine Brown	Democrat
Florida	17	Carrie P. Meek	Democrat
Georgia	11	Cynthia McKinney	Democrat
Illinois	7	Cardiss Collins	Democrat
Michigan	15	Barbara-Rose Collins	Democrat
North Carolina	1	Eva Clayton	Democrat
Texas	30	Eddie Bernice Johnson	Democrat

Senior African American Member

John Conyers Jr., (D) Michigan–14th, first elected in 1964.

Wielding Power

William Clay, (D) Missouri–1st, was chair of the House Committee on the Post Office.
John Conyers Jr. (D) Michigan–14th, was chair of the House Committee on Government Operations.

Achieving Power

Ronald Dellums, (D) California–9th, became chair of the House Armed Services Committee. In 1977, when he took his seat on that committee, he was the first African American ever to serve on it.

African American Incumbent Not Returning from the 102nd Congress

One incumbent chose to retire and not seek reelection:

Mervyn Dymally, California–37th

Two incumbents lost their seats to challengers in the Democratic primary in their district:

Charles Hayes, Illinois–1st
Gus Savage, Illinois–2nd

102nd Congress (1991–1993)

State	District	Name	Party Affiliation
California	8	Ronald V. Dellums	Democrat
California	28	Julian C. Dixon	Democrat
California	29	Maxine Waters	Democrat
California	37	Mervyn Dymally	Democrat
Connecticut	5	Gary Franks	Republican
Georgia	5	John Lewis	Democrat
Illinois	1	Charles Hayes	Democrat
Illinois	2	Gus Savage	Democrat
Illinois	7	Cardiss Collins	Democrat
Louisiana	2	William Jefferson	Democrat
Maryland	7	Kweisi Mfume	Democrat
Michigan	1	John Conyers Jr.	Democrat
Michigan	13	Barbara-Rose Collins	Democrat
Mississippi	2	Mike Espy	Democrat
Missouri	1	William L. Clay	Democrat
Missouri	5	Alan B. Wheat	Democrat
New Jersey	10	Donald Payne	Democrat
New York	6	Floyd Flake	Democrat
New York	11	Edolphus Towns	Democrat
New York	12	Major Owens	Democrat
New York	16	Charles B. Rangel	Democrat
Ohio	21	Louis Stokes	Democrat
Pennsylvania	2	William H. Gray III[22]	Democrat
Pennsylvania	2	Lucien Blackwell	Democrat
Tennessee	9	Harold Ford	Democrat
Texas	18	Craig Washington	Democrat

Total African Americans Serving

26 (25 Democrats, 1 Republican)

Female African American Representation

3 Women

California	29	Maxine Waters	Democrat
Illinois	7	Cardiss Collins	Democrat
Michigan	13	Barbara-Rose Collins	Democrat

Senior African American Member

John Conyers Jr., (D) Michigan–14th, first elected in 1964.

---

[22]William Gray III resigned during the 102nd Congress to become president of the United Negro College Fund. In the special election to fill his seat, Lucien Blackwell won and was sworn in during the 102nd Congress.

Wielding Power

John Conyers Jr., (D) Michigan–14th, was chair of the House Committee on Government Operations.
Ronald Dellums, (D) California–9th, was chair of the House District of Columbia Committee.

Achieving Power

William Clay, (D) Missouri–1st, became chair of the House Committee on the Post Office.

Notable First

Gary Franks, Connecticut–5th, became the first Republican African American elected to the U.S. House of Representatives in fifty-four years.

African American Incumbents Not Returning from the 101st Congress

Two incumbents chose not to seek reelection:

George W. Crockett, (D) Michigan–13th
Augustus F. Hawkins, (D) California–29th

101st Congress (1989–1991)

State	District	Name	Party Affiliation
California	8	Ronald V. Dellums	Democrat
California	28	Julian C. Dixon	Democrat
California	29	Augustus F. Hawkins	Democrat
California	31	Mervyn Dymally	Democrat
Georgia	5	John Lewis	Democrat
Illinois	1	Charles Hayes	Democrat
Illinois	2	Gus Savage	Democrat
Illinois	7	Cardiss Collins	Democrat
Maryland	7	Kweisi Mfume	Democrat
Michigan	1	John Conyers Jr.	Democrat
Michigan	13	George W. Crockett	Democrat
Mississippi	2	Mike Espy	Democrat
Missouri	1	William L. Clay	Democrat
Missouri	5	Alan B. Wheat	Democrat
New Jersey	10	Donald Payne	Democrat
New York	6	Floyd Flake	Democrat
New York	11	Edolphus Towns	Democrat
New York	12	Major Owens	Democrat
New York	16	Charles B. Rangel	Democrat

Ohio	21	Louis Stokes	Democrat
Pennsylvania	2	William H. Gray III	Democrat
Tennessee	9	Harold Ford	Democrat
Texas	18	Mickey Leland[23]	Democrat
Texas	18	Craig Washington	Democrat

Total African Americans Serving

23 (all Democrats)

Female African American Representation

1 Woman

| Illinois | 7 | Cardiss Collins | Democrat |

Senior African American Member

Augustus F. Hawkins, (D) California–29th, first elected in 1962.

Wielding Power

Ronald Dellums, (D) California–9th, was chair of the House District of Columbia Committee.
Augustus F. Hawkins, (D) California–29th, was chair of the House Committee on Education and Labor.

Achieving Power

John Conyers Jr., (D) Michigan–14th, became chair of the House Committee on Government Operations.

African American Incumbents Not Returning from the 100th Congress

All African American incumbents were returned to office.

100th Congress (1987–1989)

State	District	Name	Party Affiliation
California	8	Ronald V. Dellums	Democrat
California	28	Julian C. Dixon	Democrat
California	29	Augustus F. Hawkins	Democrat
California	31	Mervyn Dymally	Democrat

[23]Mickey Leland was killed in a plane crash in Africa. In the special election to fill his seat, Craig Washington won and was sworn in during the 101st Congress.

Georgia	5	John Lewis	Democrat
Illinois	1	Charles Hayes	Democrat
Illinois	2	Gus Savage	Democrat
Illinois	7	Cardiss Collins	Democrat
Maryland	7	Kweisi Mfume	Democrat
Michigan	1	John Conyers Jr.	Democrat
Michigan	13	George W. Crockett	Democrat
Mississippi	2	Mike Espy	Democrat
Missouri	1	William L. Clay	Democrat
Missouri	5	Alan Wheat	Democrat
New York	6	Floyd Flake	Democrat
New York	11	Edolphus Towns	Democrat
New York	12	Major Owens	Democrat
New York	16	Charles B. Rangel	Democrat
Ohio	21	Louis Stokes	Democrat
Pennsylvania	2	William H. Gray III	Democrat
Tennessee	9	Harold Ford	Democrat
Texas	18	Mickey Leland	Democrat

Total African Americans Serving

22 (all Democrats)

Female African American Representation

1 Woman

Illinois	7	Cardiss Collins	Democrat

Senior African American Member

Augustus F. Hawkins, (D) California–29th, first elected in 1962.

Wielding Power

Ronald Dellums, (D) California–9th, was chair of the House District of Columbia Committee.
William H. Gray III, (D) Pennsylvania–2nd, was chair of the House Budget Committee.
Augustus F. Hawkins, (D) California–29th, was chair of the House Committee on Education and Labor.

African American Incumbents Not Returning from the 99th Congress

One incumbent was beaten by a challenger in the Democratic primary in his district:

Alton R. Waldon, New York–6th

One incumbent, **Parren Mitchell**, (D) Maryland–7th, sought a state office—lieutenant governor—and was defeated in the Democratic primary for the nomination.

99th Congress (1985–1987)

State	*District*	*Name*	*Party Affiliation*
California	8	Ronald V. Dellums	Democrat
California	28	Julian C. Dixon	Democrat
California	29	Augustus F. Hawkins	Democrat
California	31	Mervyn Dymally	Democrat
Illinois	1	Charles Hayes	Democrat
Illinois	2	Gus Savage	Democrat
Illinois	7	Cardiss Collins	Democrat
Maryland	7	Parren H. Mitchell	Democrat
Michigan	1	John Conyers Jr.	Democrat
Michigan	13	George W. Crockett	Democrat
Missouri	1	William L. Clay	Democrat
Missouri	5	Alan B. Wheat	Democrat
New York	6	Alton R. Waldon[24]	Democrat
New York	11	Edolphus Towns	Democrat
New York	12	Major Owens	Democrat
New York	16	Charles B. Rangel	Democrat
Ohio	21	Louis Stokes	Democrat
Pennsylvania	2	William H. Gray III	Democrat
Tennessee	9	Harold Ford	Democrat
Texas	18	Mickey Leland	Democrat

Total African Americans Serving

20 (all Democrats)

Female African American Representation

1 Woman

Illinois	7	Cardiss Collins	Democrat

Senior African American Member

Augustus F. Hawkins, (D) California–29th, first elected in 1962.

Wielding Power

Ronald Dellums, (D) California–9th, was chair of the House District of Columbia Committee.

Achieving Power

William H. Gray III, (D) Pennsylvania–2nd, became chair of the House Budget Committee.

---

[24]Waldon was elected in a special election in June 1986 and seated in Congress. Three months later, in the September 1986 Democratic primary, he lost the nomination for the seat to another African American.

Augustus F. Hawkins, (D) California–29th, became chair of the House Committee on Education and Labor.

African American Incumbent Not Returning from the 98th Congress

One incumbent was beaten in the Democratic primary in her district by a non–African American: **Katie Hall**, Indiana–1st

98th Congress (1983–1985)

State	District	Name	Party Affiliation
California	8	Ronald V. Dellums	Democrat
California	28	Julian C. Dixon	Democrat
California	29	Augustus F. Hawkins	Democrat
California	31	Mervyn Dymally	Democrat
Illinois	1	Harold Washington[25]	Democrat
Illinois	1	Charles Hayes	Democrat
Illinois	2	Gus Savage	Democrat
Illinois	7	Cardiss Collins	Democrat
Indiana	1	Katie Hall	Democrat
Maryland	7	Parren H. Mitchell	Democrat
Michigan	1	John Conyers Jr.	Democrat
Michigan	13	George W. Crockett	Democrat
Missouri	1	William L. Clay	Democrat
Missouri	5	Alan B. Wheat	Democrat
New York	11	Edolphus Towns	Democrat
New York	12	Major Owens	Democrat
New York	16	Charles B. Rangel	Democrat
Ohio	21	Louis Stokes	Democrat
Pennsylvania	2	William H. Gray III	Democrat
Tennessee	9	Harold Ford	Democrat
Texas	18	Mickey Leland	Democrat

Total African Americans Serving

20 (all Democrats)

Female African American Representation

2 Women

Illinois	7	Cardiss Collins	Democrat
Indiana	1	Katie Hall	Democrat

---

[25]Harold Washington was elected mayor of Chicago in 1983. In the special election to replace him, his seat was won by Charles Hayes, who was sworn in during the 98th Congress.

Senior African American Member

Augustus F. Hawkins, (D) California–29th, first elected in 1962.

Wielding Power

Ronald Dellums, (D) California–9th, was chair of the District of Columbia Committee.
Augustus F. Hawkins, (D) California–29th, was chair of the House Administration Committee.

African American Incumbent Not Returning from the 97th Congress

One incumbent chose to retire and not seek reelection:

Shirley Chisholm, (D) New York–12th

97th Congress (1981–1983)

State	District	Name	Party Affiliation
California	8	Ronald V. Dellums	Democrat
California	28	Julian C. Dixon	Democrat
California	29	Augustus F. Hawkins	Democrat
California	31	Mervyn Dymally	Democrat
Illinois	1	Harold Washington	Democrat
Illinois	2	Gus Savage	Democrat
Illinois	7	Cardiss Collins	Democrat
Indiana	1	Katie Hall	Democrat
Maryland	7	Parren H. Mitchell	Democrat
Michigan	1	John Conyers Jr.	Democrat
Michigan	13	George W. Crockett	Democrat
Missouri	1	William L. Clay	Democrat
New York	12	Shirley Chisholm	Democrat
New York	19	Charles B. Rangel	Democrat
Ohio	21	Louis Stokes	Democrat
Pennsylvania	2	William H. Gray III	Democrat
Tennessee	8	Harold Ford	Democrat
Texas	18	Mickey Leland	Democrat

Total African Americans Serving

18 (all Democrats)

Female African American Representation

3 Women

Illinois	7	Cardiss Collins	Democrat
Indiana	1	Katie Hall	Democrat
New York	12	Shirley Chisholm	Democrat

Senior African American Member

Augustus F. Hawkins, (D) California–29th, first elected in 1962.

Wielding Power

Ronald Dellums, (D) California–9th, was chair of the District of Columbia Committee.

Achieving Power

Augustus F. Hawkins, (D) California–29th, became chair of the House Administration Committee.

African American Incumbents Not Returning from the 96th Congress

One incumbent chose to retire and not seek reelection:

Charles C. Diggs Jr., (D) Michigan–13th

One incumbent lost to a challenger in the Democratic primary in his district:

Bennett Stewart, Illinois–1st

96th Congress (1979–1981)

State	District	Name	Party Affiliation
California	8	Ronald V. Dellums	Democrat
California	28	Julian C. Dixon	Democrat
California	29	Augustus F. Hawkins	Democrat
Illinois	1	Bennett M. Stewart	Democrat
Illinois	7	Cardiss Collins	Democrat
Maryland	7	Parren H. Mitchell	Democrat
Michigan	1	John Conyers Jr.	Democrat
Michigan	13	Charles C. Diggs Jr.	Democrat
Missouri	1	William L. Clay	Democrat
New York	12	Shirley Chisholm	Democrat
New York	19	Charles B. Rangel	Democrat
Ohio	21	Louis Stokes	Democrat
Pennsylvania	2	William H. Gray III	Democrat
Tennessee	8	Harold Ford	Democrat
Texas	18	Mickey Leland	Democrat

Total African Americans Serving

15 (all Democrats)

Female African American Representation

2 Women

Illinois	7	Cardiss Collins	Democrat
New York	12	Shirley Chisholm	Democrat

Senior African American Member

Charles C. Diggs Jr., (D) Michigan–13th, first elected in 1954.

Achieving Power

Ronald Dellums, (D) California–9th, became chair of the District of Columbia Committee.

African American Incumbents Not Returning from the 95th Congress

Three incumbents chose to retire and not seek reelection:

Barbara Jordan, (D) Texas–18th
Ralph Metcalfe, (D) Illinois–1st
Robert C. Nix Sr., (D) Pennsylvania–2nd

One incumbent, **Yvonne B. Burke**, (D) California–28th, won the Democratic nomination for another office—state attorney general of California; she lost the general election by a 53–43 percent margin.

95th Congress (1977–1979)

State	District	Name	Party Affiliation
California	8	Ronald V. Dellums	Democrat
California	28	Yvonne B. Burke	Democrat
California	29	Augustus F. Hawkins	Democrat
Georgia	5	Andrew H. Young[26]	Democrat
Illinois	1	Ralph H. Metcalfe	Democrat
Illinois	7	Cardiss Collins	Democrat
Maryland	7	Parren H. Mitchell	Democrat
Michigan	1	John Conyers Jr.	Democrat
Michigan	13	Charles C. Diggs Jr.	Democrat
Missouri	1	William L. Clay	Democrat
New York	12	Shirley Chisholm	Democrat
New York	19	Charles B. Rangel	Democrat
Ohio	21	Louis Stokes	Democrat
Pennsylvania	2	Robert C. Nix Sr.	Democrat
Tennessee	8	Harold Ford	Democrat
Texas	18	Barbara Jordan	Democrat

Total African Americans Serving

16 (all Democrats)

---

[26]Andrew Young resigned his seat on January 29, 1977, to become U.S. ambassador to the United Nations. When the special election was held to replace him, it was not won by an African American.

Female African American Representation

4 Women

California	28	Yvonne B. Burke	Democrat
Illinois	7	Cardiss Collins	Democrat
New York	12	Shirley Chisholm	Democrat
Texas	18	Barbara Jordan	Democrat

Senior African American Member

Charles C. Diggs Jr., (D) Michigan–13th, first elected in 1954.

Wielding Power

Charles C. Diggs Jr., (D) Michigan–13th, was chair of the House District of Columbia Committee.

Achieving Power

Robert C. Nix Sr., (D) Pennsylvania–2nd, became chair of the House Committee on Post Office and Civil Service.

94th Congress (1975–1977)

State	District	Name	Party Affiliation
California	8	Ronald V. Dellums	Democrat
California	28	Yvonne B. Burke	Democrat
California	29	Augustus F. Hawkins	Democrat
Georgia	5	Andrew H. Young	Democrat
Illinois	1	Ralph H. Metcalfe	Democrat
Illinois	7	Cardiss Collins	Democrat
Maryland	7	Parren H. Mitchell	Democrat
Michigan	1	John Conyers Jr.	Democrat
Michigan	13	Charles C. Diggs Jr.	Democrat
Missouri	1	William L. Clay	Democrat
New York	12	Shirley Chisholm	Democrat
New York	19	Charles B. Rangel	Democrat
Ohio	21	Louis Stokes	Democrat
Pennsylvania	2	Robert C. Nix Sr.	Democrat
Tennessee	8	Harold Ford	Democrat
Texas	18	Barbara Jordan	Democrat

Total African Americans Serving

16 (all Democrats)

Female African American Representation

4 Women

State	District	Name	Party
California	28	Yvonne B. Burke	Democrat
Illinois	7	Cardiss Collins	Democrat
New York	12	Shirley Chisholm	Democrat
Texas	18	Barbara Jordan	Democrat

Senior African American Member

Charles C. Diggs Jr., (D) Michigan–13th, first elected in 1954.

Wielding Power

Charles C. Diggs Jr., (D) Michigan–13th, was chair of the House District of Columbia Committee.

93rd Congress (1973–1975)

State	District	Name	Party Affiliation
California	8	Ronald V. Dellums	Democrat
California	28	Yvonne B. Burke	Democrat
California	29	Augustus F. Hawkins	Democrat
Georgia	5	Andrew H. Young	Democrat
Illinois	1	Ralph H. Metcalfe	Democrat
Illinois	7	Cardiss Collins	Democrat
Maryland	7	Parren H. Mitchell	Democrat
Michigan	1	John Conyers Jr.	Democrat
Michigan	13	Charles C. Diggs Jr.	Democrat
Missouri	1	William L. Clay	Democrat
New York	12	Shirley Chisholm	Democrat
New York	19	Charles B. Rangel	Democrat
Ohio	21	Louis Stokes	Democrat
Pennsylvania	2	Robert C. Nix Sr.	Democrat
Texas	18	Barbara Jordan	Democrat

Total African Americans Serving

15 (all Democrats)

Notable First

Barbara Jordan, (D) Texas–18th, became the first African American woman elected to Congress from the old states of the Confederacy.

Female African American Representation

4 Women

California	28	Yvonne B. Burke	Democrat
Illinois	7	Cardiss Collins	Democrat
New York	12	Shirley Chisholm	Democrat
Texas	18	Barbara Jordan	Democrat

Senior African American Member

Charles C. Diggs Jr., (D) Michigan–13th, first elected in 1954.

Achieving Power

Charles C. Diggs Jr., (D) Michigan–13th, became chair of the House District of Columbia Committee.

92nd Congress (1971–1973)

State	District	Name	Party Affiliation
California	7	Ronald V. Dellums	Democrat
California	21	Augustus F. Hawkins	Democrat
Illinois	1	Ralph H. Metcalfe	Democrat
Illinois	6	George W. Collins[27]	Democrat
Illinois	6	Cardiss Collins	Democrat
Maryland	7	Parren H. Mitchell	Democrat
Michigan	1	John Conyers Jr.	Democrat
Michigan	13	Charles C. Diggs Jr.	Democrat
Missouri	1	William L. Clay	Democrat
New York	12	Shirley Chisholm	Democrat
New York	18	Charles B. Rangel	Democrat
Ohio	21	Louis Stokes	Democrat
Pennsylvania	2	Robert C. Nix Sr.	Democrat

Total African Americans Serving

13 (all Democrats)

Female African American Representation

2 Women

Illinois	7	Cardiss Collins	Democrat
New York	12	Shirley Chisholm	Democrat

---

[27]Midway into his term, Collins was killed in an air crash. In a special election to replace him, the seat was won by his wife, Cardiss Collins (D).

Senior African American Member

Charles C. Diggs Jr., (D) Michigan–13th, first elected in 1954.

African American Incumbents Not Returning from the 95th Congress

One incumbent chose to retire and not seek reelection:

William Dawson, (D) Illinois–1st

One incumbent was defeated by a challenger in the Democratic primary in his district:

Adam Clayton Powell Jr., New York–18th

91st Congress (1969–1971)

State	District	Name	Party Affiliation
California	21	Augustus F. Hawkins	Democrat
Illinois	1	William Dawson	Democrat
Illinois	6	George W. Collins	Democrat
Michigan	1	John Conyers Jr.	Democrat
Michigan	13	Charles C. Diggs Jr.	Democrat
Missouri	1	William L. Clay	Democrat
New York	12	Shirley Chisholm	Democrat
New York	18	Adam Clayton Powell Jr.	Democrat
Ohio	21	Louis Stokes	Democrat
Pennsylvania	2	Robert C. Nix Sr.	Democrat

Total African Americans Serving

10 (all Democrats)

Notable First

Shirley Chisholm, (D) New York–12th, became the first African American woman elected to the U.S. House of Representatives.

Notable First

The total number of African Americans—ten—in this Congress surpassed the previous high total for any one Congress. The 43rd Congress (1873–1875) had convened eighty-five years earlier with seven African American members.

Senior African American Member

William Dawson, (D) Illinois–1st, first elected in 1942.

Wielding Power

William Dawson, (D) Illinois–1st, was chair of the House Committee on Government Operations.

90th Congress (1967–1969)

State	District	Name	Party Affiliation
California	21	Augustus F. Hawkins	Democrat
Illinois	1	William Dawson	Democrat
Michigan	1	John Conyers Jr.	Democrat
Michigan	13	Charles C. Diggs Jr.	Democrat
New York	18	Adam Clayton Powell Jr.[28]	Democrat
Pennsylvania	2	Robert C. Nix Sr.	Democrat

Wielding Power

William Dawson, (D) Illinois–1st, was chair of the House Committee on Government Operations.

89th Congress (1965–1967)

State	District	Name	Party Affiliation
California	21	Augustus F. Hawkins	Democrat
Illinois	1	William Dawson	Democrat
Michigan	1	John Conyers Jr.	Democrat
Michigan	13	Charles C. Diggs Jr.	Democrat
New York	18	Adam Clayton Powell Jr.	Democrat
Pennsylvania	2	Robert C. Nix Sr.	Democrat

Wielding Power

William Dawson, (D) Illinois–1st, was chair of the House Committee on Government Operations.
Adam Clayton Powell Jr., (D) New York–18th, was chair of the House Committee on Education and Labor.

88th Congress (1963–1965)

State	District	Name	Party Affiliation
California	21	Augustus F. Hawkins	Democrat
Illinois	1	William Dawson	Democrat
Michigan	13	Charles C. Diggs Jr.	Democrat
New York	18	Adam Clayton Powell Jr.	Democrat
Pennsylvania	2	Robert C. Nix Sr.	Democrat

---

[28]The 90th Congress refused to seat Adam Clayton Powell due to legal problems.

Wielding Power

William Dawson, (D) Illinois–1st, was chair of the House Committee on Government Operations.
Adam Clayton Powell Jr., (D) New York–18th, was chair of the House Committee on Education and Labor.

Notable First

When **Augustus F. Hawkins**, (D) California–21st, won his seat in the November 1962 elections, he became the first African American elected to Congress from west of the Mississippi River (excluding Louisiana).

87th Congress (1961–1963)

State	District	Name	Party Affiliation
Illinois	1	William Dawson	Democrat
Michigan	13	Charles C. Diggs Jr.	Democrat
New York	16	Adam Clayton Powell Jr.	Democrat
Pennsylvania	4	Robert C. Nix Sr.	Democrat

Wielding Power

William Dawson, (D) Illinois–1st, was chair of the House Committee on Government Operations.

Achieving Power

Adam Clayton Powell Jr., (D) New York–18th, became chair of the House Committee on Education and Labor.

86th Congress (1959–1961)

State	District	Name	Party Affiliation
Illinois	1	William Dawson	Democrat
Michigan	13	Charles C. Diggs Jr.	Democrat
New York	16	Adam Clayton Powell Jr.	Democrat
Pennsylvania	4	Robert C. Nix Sr.	Democrat

Wielding Power

William Dawson, (D) Illinois–1st, was chair of the House Committee on Government Operations.

85th Congress (1957–1959)

State	District	Name	Party Affiliation
Illinois	1	William Dawson	Democrat
Michigan	13	Charles C. Diggs Jr.	Democrat

| New York | 16 | Adam Clayton Powell Jr. | Democrat |
| Pennsylvania | 4 | Robert C. Nix Sr. | Democrat |

Wielding Power

William Dawson, (D) Illinois–1st, was chair of the House Committee on Government Operations.

84th Congress (1955–1957)

State	District	Name	Party Affiliation
Illinois	1	William Dawson	Democrat
Michigan	13	Charles C. Diggs Jr.	Democrat
New York	16	Adam Clayton Powell Jr.	Democrat

Wielding Power

William Dawson, (D) Illinois–1st, was chair of the House Committee on Government Operations.

83rd Congress (1953–1955)

State	District	Name	Party Affiliation
Illinois	1	William Dawson	Democrat
New York	16	Adam Clayton Powell Jr.	Democrat

Wielding Power

William Dawson, (D) Illinois–1st, was chair of the House Committee on Government Operations.

82nd Congress (1951–1953)

State	District	Name	Party Affiliation
Illinois	1	William Dawson	Democrat
New York	22	Adam Clayton Powell Jr.	Democrat

Achieving Power

William Dawson, (D) Illinois–1st, became the first African American to head a standing committee of the U.S. House of Representatives—the Committee on Government Operations.

81st Congress (1949–1951)

State	District	Name	Party Affiliation
Illinois	1	William Dawson	Democrat
New York	22	Adam Clayton Powell Jr.	Democrat

80th Congress (1947–1949)

State	District	Name	Party Affiliation
Illinois	1	William Dawson	Democrat
New York	22	Adam Clayton Powell Jr.	Democrat

79th Congress (1945–1947)

State	District	Name	Party Affiliation
Illinois	1	William Dawson	Democrat
New York	22	Adam Clayton Powell Jr.	Democrat

78th Congress (1943–1945)

State	District	Name	Party Affiliation
Illinois	1	William Dawson	Democrat

77th Congress (1941–1943)

State	District	Name	Party Affiliation
Illinois	1	Arthur Mitchell	Democrat

76th Congress (1939–1941)

State	District	Name	Party Affiliation
Illinois	1	Arthur Mitchell	Democrat

75th Congress (1937–1939)

State	District	Name	Party Affiliation
Illinois	1	Arthur Mitchell	Democrat

74th Congress (1935–1937)

State	District	Name	Party Affiliation
Illinois	1	Arthur Mitchell	Democrat

Notable First

Arthur Mitchell became the first Democratic African American to serve in the House of Representatives. He had been preceded in that chamber by twenty-one Republican African Americans.

73rd Congress (1933–1935)

State	District	Name	Party Affiliation
Illinois	1	Oscar DePriest	Republican

72nd Congress (1931–1933)

State	District	Name	Party Affiliation
Illinois	1	Oscar DePriest	Republican

71st Congress (1929–1931)

State	District	Name	Party Affiliation
Illinois	1	Oscar DePriest	Republican

Notable First

Joseph L. McLemore became the first Democratic African American nominee for the U.S. House when he ran in Missouri's 12th Congressional District. He lost the election to a popular Republican incumbent, 41.6–58.4 percent.

57th Congress (1901–1903)
through 70th Congress (1927–1929)

For thirteen Congresses (the 57th Congress through the 70th Congress), a period of twenty-six years, no African Americans served in the U.S. House of Representatives.

56th Congress (1899–1901)

State	District	Name	Party Affiliation
North Carolina	2	George White	Republican

55th Congress (1897–1899)

State	District	Name	Party Affiliation
North Carolina	2	George White	Republican

54th Congress (1895–1897)

State	District	Name	Party Affiliation
South Carolina	1	George W. Murray	Republican

53rd Congress (1893–1895)

State	District	Name	Party Affiliation
South Carolina	7	George W. Murray	Republican

52nd Congress (1891–1893)

State	District	Name	Party Affiliation
North Carolina	2	Henry P. Cheatham	Republican

51st Congress (1889–1891)

State	*District*	*Name*	*Party Affiliation*
North Carolina	2	Henry P. Cheatham	Republican
South Carolina	7	Thomas E. Miller	Republican
Virginia	4	John M. Langston[29]	Republican

50th Congress (1887–1889)

The 50th Congress had no African Americans serving in the U.S. House of Representatives.

49th Congress (1885–1887)

State	*District*	*Name*	*Party Affiliation*
North Carolina	2	James E. O'Hara	Republican
South Carolina	7	Robert Smalls	Republican

48th Congress (1883–1885)

State	*District*	*Name*	*Party Affiliation*
North Carolina	2	James E. O'Hara	Republican

47th Congress (1881–1883)

State	*District*	*Name*	*Party Affiliation*
Mississippi	6	John R. Lynch	Republican
South Carolina	7	Robert Smalls	Republican

46th Congress (1879–1881)

The 46th Congress had no African Americans serving in the U.S. House of Representatives.

45th Congress (1877–1879)

State	*District*	*Name*	*Party Affiliation*
South Carolina	2	Richard H. Cain	Republican
South Carolina	1	Joseph H. Rainey	Republican
South Carolina	5	Robert Smalls	Republican

---

[29]Langston's Democratic opponent was first declared the victor then unseated, and Langston did not take the seat until September 1890. In 1855, when he was elected town clerk of Brownheim Township, Ohio, Langston became the first African American known to have been elected to public office in the U.S. After his congressional term ended he also served as minister-resident to Haiti and chargé d'affaires to Santo Domingo.

44th Congress (1875–1877)

State	District	Name	Party Affiliation
Alabama	1	Jeremiah Haralson[30]	Republican
Florida	2	Josiah T. Walls[31]	Republican
Louisiana	6	Charles E. Nash	Republican
Mississippi	6	John R. Lynch	Republican
North Carolina	2	John A. Hyman	Republican
South Carolina	1	Joseph H. Rainey	Republican
South Carolina	5	Robert Smalls	Republican

43rd Congress (1873–1875)

State	District	Name	Party Affiliation
Alabama	2	James T. Rapier	Republican
Florida	AL	Josiah T. Walls	Republican
Mississippi	6	John R. Lynch	Republican
South Carolina	1	Joseph H. Rainey	Republican
South Carolina	2	Alonzo J. Ransier	Republican
South Carolina	3	Robert B. Elliot	Republican
South Carolina	AL	Richard H. Cain	Republican

Notable First: 1874

Joseph H. Rainey, (R) South Carolina, became the first African American to preside over a session of the U.S. House of Representatives.

42nd Congress (1871–1873)

State	District	Name	Party Affiliation
Alabama	1	Benjamin Turner	Republican
Florida	AL	Josiah T. Walls[32]	Republican
South Carolina	1	Joseph H. Rainey	Republican
South Carolina	2	Robert C. DeLarge	Republican
South Carolina	3	Robert B. Elliot	Republican

41st Congress (1869–1871)

State	District	Name	Party Affiliation
Georgia	AL	Jefferson F. Long[33]	Republican
South Carolina	1	Joseph H. Rainey[34]	Republican

---

[30]Haralson, who was born a slave but was also a friend of Confederate Pres. Jefferson Davis, has a unique distinction among all the people who have served in Congress. Some years after his term he was working as a coal miner in Colorado when he mysteriously disappeared. It was later determined that he had been killed and eaten by wild animals. Haralson is thus the only member of Congress to ever have suffered that type of demise.

[31]Walls was refused his seat in an electoral dispute over the alleged intimidation of voters.

[32]Walls served until January 1873, when he was unseated in a dispute about his election.

[33]Long was elected in a special election to serve an abbreviated term from December 1870 through March 1871.

[34]Rainey, winner of a special election to replace a white incumbent who had resigned, was sworn in on December 12, 1870, as the first African American member of the U.S. House.

Notable First: 1871

Jefferson F. Long, (R) Georgia, became the first African American to deliver a speech as a member on the floor of the U.S. House of Representatives on February 1, 1871, speaking on opposing the removal of political restrictions on former Confederates.

Notable First: 1868

John Willis Menard, (R) Louisiana, became the first African American elected to the U.S. House of Representatives, but the chamber refused to seat him, claiming election irregularities. Menard was allowed to speak from the floor of the House on February 27, 1869, becoming the first African American to address the chamber.

African American Governors[35]
in Chronological Order of Service

1. Pinckney Benton Stewart Pinchback	Republican	Louisiana	2/08/1872–01/13/1873
2. Lawrence Douglas Wilder	Democrat	Virginia	01/15/90–01/13/94

How They Assumed Office

1. **Pinckney Benton Stewart Pinchback**, (R) Louisiana (Born: 1837; Died: 1921)
   Served: 12/08/1872–01/13/1873

Succeeded on December 8, 1872, to the office after the impeachment of the incumbent. Pinchback, the eighth child of a white Mississippi planter and a free black mother, spent most of his life in Ohio. In 1862, after the Union forces had captured New Orleans, he made his way south and served in several special U.S. Army units. After leaving the army, he entered politics and was elected to the Louisiana legislature, where he rose to a leadership position. After Gov. Henry Clay Warmoth (R) was impeached and removed from office during the final three weeks of his term in 1872, Pinchback, as president of the state senate—and de facto lieutenant governor due to the death of the elected lieutenant governor the previous year—was next in line for the governorship. He served until William P. Kellogg (R), who had been elected in the November 1872 election, was sworn in.

   Later in 1873, after his short gubernatorial term ended, Pinchback was elected by the state legislature first to the U.S. House of Representatives and then, before he could take his seat there, to the U.S. Senate, becoming the only person in American history to lay claims to seats in both houses of Congress simultaneously. Both legislative chambers denied him a seat, citing charges of election irregularity and bribery. In later years he was surveyor of customs (1882–1885), and he was a U.S. marshal in New York City during the 1890s.

---

[35]Since the Virgin Islands was authorized to elect its own governor by popular vote beginning in 1970, several African Americans have been elected to the office. They are not included in this section because the Virgin Islands is a U.S. territory, not a state.

Previous elected public office:
  Louisiana State Senate, 1868–1871
  Louisiana Lieutenant Governor, 1871–1872 (as president pro tem of the state senate, he suc-
    ceeded to this position when the incumbent, another African American, died in office)
Subsequent elected public office: See above

2. **Lawrence Douglas Wilder**, (D) Virginia (Born: 1931)
   Served: 01/15/90–01/13/94

Elected on November 7, 1989, to a four-year term. Wilder won a hard-fought, close (6,741
votes) victory over a Republican opponent to become the first popularly elected African American governor in U.S. history. Midway through his term, he made a somewhat feeble entry into
the race for the 1992 Democratic presidential nomination. Critics said he had his eye on the vice
presidential nomination, but he withdrew shortly after entering the race, then completed the balance of his term quietly. Since Virginia doesn't permit governors to run for succeeding terms,
Wilder was unable to seek another term in 1993.

When the 1994 U.S. Senate race began to shape up in Virginia as a contentious battle between
incumbent Sen. Charles Robb (D), a former governor and political foe of Wilder's, and Irangate
figure Oliver North, Wilder muttered about jumping into the fray. Once North secured the Republican nomination, a dissident Republican filed as an Independent, making the contest a three-
man race. After that development, Wilder formally tossed his hat into the ring, but both he and
Marshall Coleman, the dissident Republican, lagged far behind Robb and North in the polls. In
October 1994 Wilder withdrew from the Senate race, giving Robb a lukewarm endorsement,
which may have provided the slim margin for his reelection victory the following month. By
1997 Wilder was again making political news in Virginia by refusing to endorse the Democratic
candidate for governor and making noise about tossing his support to the Republicans.

Previous elected public office:
  Virginia State Senate, 1969–1985
  Virginia Lieutenant Governor, 1985–1989
Subsequent Elected Public Office: None

African American Gubernatorial Statistics

Longest Term Served by an African American Governor

L. Douglas Wilder, (D) Virginia, who served four years—January 15, 1990–January 13, 1994.

African American Gubernatorial Election Statistics

The following section provides voting statistics on those African American governors who contested elections, including primaries, primary runoffs, and general elections. Names in this section
appear in chronological order by gubernatorial service, from earliest to most recent.

Lawrence Douglas Wilder, (D) Virginia

1989	General	L. Douglas Wilder (D)	896,936	50.0%
		J. Marshall Coleman (R)	890,195	50.0%
1989	Democratic Primary	L. Douglas Wilder nominated by convention		

Chronology of All African American Candidates for Governor (denotes winner)*

1971	Charles Evers	Independent	Mississippi
1982	Thomas Bradley[36]	Democrat	California
1986	Thomas Bradley	Democrat	California
	William Lucas[37]	Republican	Michigan
1989	*L. Douglas Wilder[38]	Democrat	Virginia
1990	Theo Mitchell[39]	Democrat	South Carolina
1995	Cleo Fields[40]	Democrat	Louisiana

African Americans Who Have Held Other State Executive Offices[41]

Arkansas

Superintendent of Education
Joseph C. Corbin (R), 1873–1875

Commissioner of Public Works
James T. White (R), 1873–1874

California

Lieutenant Governor
Mervyn Dymally (D), 1975–1979[42]

Superintendent of Public Instruction
Wilson Riles (D), 1971–1983

Colorado

Lieutenant Governor
Joe Rogers (R), 1999–
George L. Brown (D), 1975–1979[43]

Secretary of State
Victoria "Vikki" Buckley (R), 1995–[44]

---

[36]Bradley was serving as mayor of Los Angeles both times when he won the Democratic nomination in the California gubernatorial races.

[37]Lucas was serving as sheriff of Wayne County and had only recently switched from the Democratic Party to the Republican Party when he won the nomination for the Michigan gubernatorial race.

[38]Wilder was the incumbent lieutenant governor when he made his winning race for governor.

[39]Mitchell was serving as a state senator when he made his unsuccessful gubernatorial run.

[40]Fields was serving in the U.S. House when he made his unsuccessful gubernatorial run.

[41]These offices are a combination of election by popular vote, election by the state legislature, and appointment by the governor.

[42]Dymally later served five terms (1981–1991) in the U.S. House.

[43]In 1956 Brown set a record: He became the first African American ever elected to any state senate west of the Mississippi River.

[44]Buckley was the first African American female Republican elected to statewide office.

Connecticut

Treasurer
   Denise Nappier (D), 1999–
   Joseph Suggs (D), 1993–1995
   Francisco L. Borges (D), 1987–1993
   Henry E. Parker (D), 1979–1987
   Gerald A. Lamb (D), 1963–1971[45]

Florida

Secretary of State
   Jonathan C. Gibbs (R), 1868–1871

Superintendent/Commissioner of Education
   Doug Jamerson (D), 1993–1995
   Jonathan C. Gibbs (R), 1872–1874

Georgia

Attorney General
   Thurbet E. Baker, 1997–

Illinois

Attorney General
   Roland W. Burris (D), 1991–1995[46]

Comptroller
   Roland W. Burris (D), 1979–1991[47]

Secretary of State
   Jesse White (D), 1999–

Indiana

Attorney General

Pamela F. Carter (D), 1993–1997

Clerk of the Supreme and Appellate Courts
   Dwayne Brown, 1991–1995

Kansas

Auditor
   Edward "Edwin" P. McCabe (R),
      1882–1884[48]

Louisiana

Lieutenant Governor
   Ceasar C. Antoine (R), 1872–1877
   P. B. S. Pinchback (R), 1871–1872[49]
   Oscar J. Dunn (R), 1868–1871[50]

Secretary of State
   Pierre G. Deslonde (R), 1872–1876

Superintendent of Education
   William G. Brown (R), 1873–1876

Treasurer
   Antoine Dubuclet (R), 1868–1874

Massachusetts

Attorney General
   Edward W. Brooke (R), 1963–1966[51]

Michigan

Auditor General
   Otis M. Smith (D), 1959–1961

---

[45]Lamb, in a rare case of minority-versus-minority politics, defeated another African American, Republican nominee William Graham, to win his first term as treasurer. He and Edward Brooke (R), elected attorney general of Massachusetts, were the first African Americans since Reconstruction elected to statewide office in the U.S.

[46]Burris gave up this post for an unsuccessful bid for the 1994 Democratic gubernatorial nomination; after that defeat he then ran an unsuccessful campaign as an Independent for mayor of Chicago in 1995.

[47]Midway into his second term in 1984, Burris unsuccessfully sought the Democratic nomination for U.S. Senate.

[48]McCabe was the first African American elected to a statewide office outside the South.

[49]Pinchback was acting governor for thirty-six days during 1872–1873.

[50]Dunn was the first African American elected lieutenant governor in the U.S.

[51]Brooke and Gerald A. Lamb (D), elected treasurer of Connecticut the same year, were the first African Americans since Reconstruction elected to statewide office in the U.S. Brooke had previously lost a statewide race in 1960 as the Republican nominee for secretary of state. He was later elected to the U.S. Senate, where he served two terms (1967–1979).

Secretary of State
Richard H. Austin (D), 1971–1995[52]

Treasurer
Loren Eugene Monroe (D), 1979–1983

Mississippi

Lieutenant Governor
Alexander K. Davis (R), 1873–1876

Secretary of State
James Hill (R), 1874–1878
Hannibal C. Carter (R), 1873
M. M. McLeod (R), 1983
Hiram R. Revels (R), 1872–1873[53]
James Lynch (R), 1870–1872

Superintendent of Education
T. W. Cardozo (R), 1874–1876

New Jersey

Secretary of State
Lonna R. Hooks (R), 1993–

New Mexico

Treasurer
James B. Lewis (D), 1987–1991

New York

Comptroller
H. Carl McCall (D), 1995–

North Carolina

Auditor
Ralph Campbell (D), 1993–

Ohio

Secretary of State

J. Kenneth Blackwell (R), 1999–

Treasurer
J. Kenneth Blackwell (R), 1993–1999

Oklahoma

Secretary of State
Hannah Diggs Atkins (D), 1987–1991

State Corporation Commissioner
J. C. Watts (R), 1991–1995[54]

Oregon

Treasurer
Jim Hill (D), 1991–[55]

Pennsylvania

Secretary of the Commonwealth
Ethel D. Allen (R), 1979–1983
C. Delores Tucker (D), 1973–1977[56]

South Carolina

Lieutenant Governor
Richard H. Gleaves (R), 1872–1877
Alonzo J. Ransier (R), 1870–1872[57]

Attorney General
Robert B. Elliott (R), 1876–1877[58]

Secretary of State
Henry E. Hayne (R), 1872–1877
Francis L. Cardoso (R), 1868–1872[59]

Secretary of Treasury
Francis L. Cardoso (R), 1872–1877

Texas

Secretary of State
Ron Kirk (D), 1994

---

[52]Austin unsuccessfully sought the Democratic nomination for U.S. Senate in 1976.

[53]Revels also served in th U.S. Senate (1870–1871).

[54]Watts was elected to the U.S. House in 1994 from Oklahoma's 4th District.

[55]Hill, in a rare example of a minority-versus-minority campaign, won his treasurer's post by defeating David Chen (R), a Chinese American, in the general election.

[56]Tucker was an unsuccessful candidate in the 1980 Democratic primary for the U.S. Senate nomination.

[57]Ransier also served one term (1873–1875) in the U.S. House.

[58]Elliott also served two terms (1871–1875) in the U.S. House.

[59]Cardoso was the first African American state cabinet officer in the U.S.

Virginia

Lieutenant Governor
　　L. Douglas Wilder (D), 1985–1989[60]

Wisconsin

Secretary of State
　　Vel Phillips (D), 1979–1983[61]

African Americans in State Legislatures

Notable First: 1972

Barbara Jordan, (D) Texas, first elected in 1966, became president pro tem of the Texas senate. As such, she was the first African American woman to preside over a state legislative body, which on several occasions allowed her to "act" as governor when both the governor and lieutenant governor of Texas were absent from the state.

Notable First: 1971

Cecil A. Partee, (D) Illinois, became the president pro tem of the state senate, the first African American to head a branch of a state legislature since Reconstruction.

Notable First: 1952

Cora M. Brown, (R) Michigan, became the first African American woman elected to a state senate seat.

Notable First: 1938

Crystal Bird Fauset, (D) Pennsylvania, became the first African American woman elected to a state legislature.

Notable First: 1927

Minnie Buckingham-Harper, (R) West Virginia, became the first African American woman to sit in a state legislature. She was appointed to her husband's seat after his death.

Notable First: 1922

Henry W. Shields, (D) New York, was elected to the state house of representatives, the first African American Democrat elected to public office.

Notable First: 1872

Samuel J. Lee, (R) South Carolina, was the first African American elected speaker of a state's house of representatives. The South Carolina legislature that convened two years later, in 1874, was

---

[60]Wilder also served as governor (1989–1993).
[61]Phillips was the first African American woman elected to statewide office.

also the first state legislature in which the presiding offices in both houses were held by African Americans, with Stephen A. Swails (R) as president pro tem of the state senate.

Notable First: 1868

The South Carolina legislature convened and its lower house (the general assembly) had eighty-seven African American members—all Republican—out of a total membership of 127. This was the first state legislative body controlled by African Americans. Whites became a majority in the body again in 1874.

Notable First: 1866

Edwin G. Walker (R) and **Charles L. Mitchell** (R), both of Massachusetts, became the first African Americans elected to a state legislature. Years later Walker changed his party affiliation to the Democratic Party.

African American Speakers of State Lower Legislative Chambers

Daniel T. Blue, (D) of North Carolina, 1990–1994
Willie Lewis Brown Jr., (D) of California, 1980–1995
K. Leroy Irvis, (D) of Pennsylvania, 1977–1979, 1982–1988
S. Howard Woodson Jr., (D) of New Jersey, 1974–1975
Robert B. Elliott,[62] (R) of South Carolina, 1874–1877
Isaac D. Shadd, (R) of Mississippi, 1874–1875
John R. Lynch,[63] (R) of Mississippi, 1872–1873
Samuel J. Lee, (R) of South Carolina, 1872–1874

African Americans in the Judiciary

U.S. Supreme Court Justices

1967–1991   **Thurgood Marshall**, (D) New York, appointed by Pres. Lyndon B. Johnson
1991–   **Clarence Thomas**, (R) Virginia, appointed by Pres. George Bush

---

[62]Elliott had served in the U.S. House of Representatives since 1871 and resigned his congressional seat to assume the speakership.

[63]Lynch also served as Mississippi secretary of state (1870–1872) and in the U.S. House of Representatives (1873–1877, 1881–1883).

Notable First: 1996

Adolpho A. Birch Jr., a justice on the Tennessee Supreme Court, ascended to the position of chief justice, the first time an African American had held that position on a state supreme court in a southern state since Reconstruction.

Notable First: 1992

Leah Sears-Collins, (D) Georgia, who was appointed in March 1992 to the Georgia Supreme Court by Gov. Zell Miller, became the first African American woman to win an election to a seat on any state's supreme court when she was elected to a full term in the November general election.

Notable First: 1988

Juanita Kidd Stout, (D) Pennsylvania, appointed by Gov. Robert Casey to Pennsylvania's supreme court, was the first African American woman to hold a seat on any state's supreme court.

Notable First: 1984

Robert N. C. Nix Jr., (D) Pennsylvania, elected chief justice of Pennsylvania's supreme court, was the first African American to hold the chief justice position in any state supreme court.

Notable First: 1975

Joseph Hatchett, (D) Florida, became the first African American state supreme court justice in the south since Reconstruction.

Notable First: 1966

Constance Baker Motley, (D) New York, was the first African American woman to hold a federal judgeship. She was appointed by Pres. Lyndon B. Johnson to the U.S. District Court for the Southern District of New York.

Notable First: 1961

James B. Parsons became the first African American appointed to a federal district court. He was elevated to Illinois's northern district seat by Pres. John F. Kennedy.

Notable First: 1939

Jane M. Brolin became the first African American female to be appointed to a judgeship in the United States when Mayor Fiorello La Guardia appointed her to the New York City Court of Domestic Relations.

Notable First: 1937

William Hastie became the first African American appointed to the federal bench when Pres. Franklin D. Roosevelt appointed him to the U.S. District Court of the Virgin Islands. In 1946 Pres. Harry S. Truman appointed him to the position of governor of the Virgin Islands, making him the first African American governor (even though unelected) to hold office in the U.S. since Reconstruction. President Truman also appointed him to the U.S. circuit court of appeals in 1949.

Notable First: 1873

Mifflin W. Gibbs, (R) Arkansas, was elected a city judge in Little Rock, Arkansas, the first African American popularly elected to a judgeship in the U.S.

Notable First: 1870

Jonathan J. Wright, (R) South Carolina, was elected by the state legislature to one of three seats on the state supreme court. Wright, the first African American to sit as a justice on a state supreme court, served until his resignation in 1877.

African Americans at the Local Level

Notable First: 1991

Jacquelyn Barrett, (D) Georgia, elected sheriff of Fulton County, Georgia, was the first African American female popularly elected a county sheriff in the U.S.

Notable Firsts: 1982

Loretta Glickman elected mayor of Pasadena, California, was the first female African American elected mayor of a large American city.
Mary Hall, (D) of Pagedale, Missouri, presides as mayor over an all-female, all–African American city administration.

Notable First: 1974

Lelia Smith elected mayor of Taft, Oklahoma, was the first female African American mayor in the U.S.

Notable First: 1967

Carl Stokes (D) elected mayor of Cleveland, Ohio, was the first African American mayor of a large American city.

Notable First: 1966

Lucius Amberson (D), elected sheriff of Macon County, Alabama, was the first African American popularly elected sheriff in the U.S. since Reconstruction.

Notable First: 1915

Oscar DePriest (R) elected to the city council of Chicago, Illinois, was the first African American to serve on the governing body of a large American city.

Notable First: 1870

Robert H. Wood, elected mayor of Natchez, Mississippi, in 1870, was probably the first African American elected mayor of an American city.

Notable First: 1867

Monroe Baker, elected mayor of St. Martin, a small town in Louisiana, in 1867, was probably the first African American elected mayor in the U.S.

Notable First: 1855

John M. Langston, elected town clerk of Brownheim Township, Ohio, in 1855, was probably the first African American elected to public office in the U.S. Later, during Reconstruction, Langston was also elected to the U.S. House of Representatives from Virginia.

Hispanics in American Politics

A Brief Chronology

1822 First Hispanic to serve in the U.S. Congress

Joseph Marion Hernández, elected on the Whig ticket as the territorial delegate from the new territory of Florida, was seated in the U.S. House of Representatives.

1875 First Hispanic governor

Romualdo Pacheco, Republican, assumed office as governor of California following the incumbent's resignation.

1878 First Hispanic elected governor

Alonzo Garcelon, Democrat, was elected for a one-year term as governor of Maine.

1912 First Hispanic speaker of a state's house of representatives

Roman L. Baca, Republican, was elected speaker of the state house of representatives shortly after New Mexico was admitted to the Union.

1928 First Hispanic elected to the U.S. Senate

Octaviano A. Larrazolo, (R) New Mexico, was elected to the U.S. Senate in a special election to fill the seat of a deceased incumbent.

1930 First Hispanic woman elected to a state legislature

Fedelina Lucero Gallegos, Republican, was elected to the Mew Mexico house of representatives.

1932 First Hispanic appointed to the U.S. Supreme Court

Benjamin N. Cardozo, New York, was appointed associate justice of the U.S. Supreme Court by Pres. Herbert Hoover.

1976 Hispanic Congressional Caucus formed

Consisting of five members, all serving in the U.S. House of Representatives, the Hispanic Congressional Caucus was formed in 1976.

This section makes only minor mention of persons of Hispanic descent elected prior to a state's admission to the Union or those elected in Puerto Rico and the Virgin Islands, since they are territories, not states.

1977 First female Hispanic to hold rank of U.S. ambassador

Mari-Luci Jaramillo, (D) New Mexico, was appointed by Pres. Jimmy Carter U.S. ambassador to Honduras.

**1981 First Hispanic to chair a standing committee of the
U.S. House of Representatives**

Henry B. Gonzalez, (D) Texas, assumed the chair of the House Committee on Agriculture.

1987 First Hispanic female chief justice of a state supreme court

Dorothy Comstock Riley, Michigan, assumed the position of chief justice of that state's supreme court.

1988 First Hispanic to serve in a federal cabinet position

Lauro F. Cavazos of Texas was appointed secretary of education by Pres. Ronald Reagan.

1989 First Hispanic female member of the U.S. House of Representatives

Ileana Ros-Lehtinen, (R) Florida, was sworn in as the first female Hispanic member of the U.S. House of Representatives.

Hispanics and Political Power

The following chart (by state) details the total number of Hispanics who have served their states in three of the most powerful positions in U.S. politics: governor, U.S. Senate (both appointed and elected), and U.S. House of Representatives.

State	Governor	U.S. Senate	U.S. House
Arizona	1	-	1
California	1	-	10
Florida	1	-	2
Illinois	-	-	1
Louisiana	-	-	2
Maine	1	-	-
New Jersey	-	-	1
New Mexico	4	3	7
New York	-	-	4
Texas	-	-	10
Total Hispanics Who Have Served	8	3	38

Best and Worst States for Hispanics Achieving Power

Even though Hispanics compose the second-largest minority in the U.S. and are expected to become the largest minority sometime early in the twenty-first century, the Hispanic population is concentrated in only a few states. Even in those places they have yet to assume a share of the political power in proportion to their overall population.

California presents a prime example of the political impotency of Hispanics. It was estimated in 1992 that Hispanics compose 25.8 percent of California's population; thus they could be expected to frequently contest statewide positions. Not true. California's one Hispanic governor succeeded to the office temporarily in the late 1800s. Only twice since 1900 has a Hispanic managed to win a nomination for statewide office, and both lost. In 1954 Edward H. Roybal, then a member of the Los Angeles city council (and later elected to the U.S. House of Representatives), won the Democratic nomination for lieutenant governor. Hank Lopez won the Democratic nomination for secretary of state in 1954, but he was the only member of the Democratic ticket that lost statewide election during a Democratic landslide in which his party swept all other statewide offices. California, which should be fertile political ground indeed for Hispanics considering their numbers, should be considered the worst state politically for the ethnic group. Due to increased voter participation by Hispanics in the late 1990s, however, this is expected to drastically change during the next decade.

New Mexico, admitted to the Union in 1912, undoubtedly has to be considered the "best" state for Hispanics overall in exercising their political power.

Hispanics in the U.S. Cabinet

The President's Cabinet

The first Hispanic member of a U.S. presidential cabinet was **Lauro F. Cavazos** (see below), appointed in 1988.

Secretary of Energy

Bill Richardson, 1998– , appointed by Bill Clinton
Federico Peña, 1997–1998, appointed by Bill Clinton

Secretary of the Interior

Manual Lujan Jr., 1989–1993, appointed by George Bush

Secretary of Housing and Urban Development

Henry Cisneros, 1993–1997, appointed by Bill Clinton

Secretary of Transportation

Federico Peña, 1993–1997, appointed by Bill Clinton

Secretary of Education

Lauro F. Cavazos, 1988–1991, appointed by Ronald Reagan; reappointed by George Bush

Hispanics in the Executive Branch

Notable Firsts: 1990

Jimmy Gurulé, (R) Indiana, appointed by Pres. George Bush, was the first Hispanic assistant attorney-general.

Antonia C. Novello, the first Hispanic (Puerto Rican) and female surgeon general of the United States, appointed by Pres. George Bush.

Notable First: 1979

Edward Hidalgo, appointed by Pres. Jimmy Carter, was the first Hispanic appointed secretary of the U.S. Navy.

Notable First: 1977

Mari-Luci Jaramillo, appointed by Pres. Jimmy Carter, was the first Hispanic woman to hold the rank of U.S. ambassador.

Notable First: 1971

Romana Acosta Banuelos, (R) of California, appointed by Pres. Richard Nixon, was the first Hispanic (Mexican American) to hold the position of U.S. treasurer; she served until 1974.

Other Hispanic U.S. Treasurers

Catalina Vásques Villapondo, (R) Texas, 1989–1993
Katherine D. Ortega, (R) New Mexico, 1983–1989

Notable First: 1961

Arturo Morales Carrión, (D) Puerto Rico, appointed by Pres. John F. Kennedy, was the first Hispanic (Puerto Rican) to be appointed deputy assistant secretary of state.

Hispanics at the National Party Level

As can be shown by the sparse statistics below, the involvement of Hispanics on the national scene of American politics has thus far been dismal. This can be certain to change, however, since they are on the verge of replacing African Americans numerically as the largest U.S. minority group. Undoubtedly both major political parties will soon begin to feature Hispanic members in leading roles in hopes of enticing other Hispanics to the party.

Given the number of Hispanics of both sexes now serving as elected officials in the two major parties, their involvement in seeking the highest offices will soon change. Hispanics will soon become serious contenders for the presidential and vice presidential positions in the Democratic and Republican Parties.

Notable First: 1984

Katherine D. Ortega of New Mexico, treasurer of the United States, delivered the keynote address at the Republican National Convention, the first Hispanic to do so at the national convention of a major political party.

Notable First: 1972

Roberto Mondragon of New Mexico became the first Hispanic chair of the Democratic National Committee.

Notable First: 1970

La Raza Unida (The United Race), the first Hispanic third party in eighty years, was founded in Texas. After winning some local races in Texas and even a school board seat in Washington, D.C., in 1977, it lost much of its appeal as the Democratic and Republican Parties began to court Hispanic voters more assiduously.

Notable First: 1890

El Partido del Pueblo Unido (The United People's Party), the first truly Hispanic third party, was founded in New Mexico Territory. It won a few seats in local elections and a seat on the territorial council but soon faded away.

Hispanic U.S. Senators in Chronological Order of Service

1. Octaviano Ambrosio Larrazolo   Republican   New Mexico   12/07/28–03/03/29
2. Dennis Chavez   Democrat   New Mexico   05/11/35–11/18/62
3. Joseph Manuel Montoya   Democrat   New Mexico   11/04/64–01/03/77

How They Assumed Office

1. **Octaviano Ambrosio Larrazolo**, (R) New Mexico (Born: 1859; Died: 1930)
   Served: 12/07/28–03/03/29

   Elected on November 6, 1928, in a special election to serve the balance—three months—of deceased Sen. Andrieus Jones's (D) term. Another election held the same day filled the seat for a new full six-year term. Larrazolo did not run in the election for the full term.

   Previous elected public office:
   El Paso, Texas, District Attorney
   El Paso, Texas, School Board

New Mexico Governor, 1919–1921
New Mexico State Legislature, 1927–1928
Subsequent elected public office: None

2. **Dennis Chavez**, (D) New Mexico (Born: 1888; Died: 1962)
Served: 05/11/35–11/18/62

Received an interim appointment on May 11, 1935, from Gov. Clyde Tingley (D) to fill the seat of deceased Sen. Bronson Cutting (R) until a special election could be held to fill the remainder—almost five years—of his term. Ironically, Cutting had defeated Chavez for the same Senate seat nine months earlier. Chavez ran and won the special election of November 3, 1936, for the balance of the term. He also won full terms in 1940, 1946, 1952, and 1958, dying in office in late 1962.

Previous elected public office:
New Mexico House of Representatives, 1923–1931
U.S. House of Representatives, 1931–1935
Subsequent elected public office: None (died in office)

3. **Joseph M. Montoya**, (D) New Mexico (Born: 1915; Died: 1978)
Served: 11/04/64–01/03/77

Elected on November 3, 1964, to a full six-year term. He was sworn in immediately because the occupant of the seat (his election opponent) was an appointed senator—former Gov. Edwin L. Mechem (R), who had resigned, then had himself appointed—had served since the death of Sen. Dennis Chavez (D) two years earlier. Montoya won an second six-year term in 1970, then was defeated when he tried for a third one in 1976.

Previous elected public office:
New Mexico Lieutenant Governor, 1947–1949, 1955–1957
U.S. House of Representatives, 1959–1963
Subsequent elected public office: None

Hispanic U.S. Senatorial Statistics

Longest Tenure of a Hispanic U.S. Senator

Dennis Chavez (D) New Mexico, who served from May 11, 1935, through November 18, 1962: twenty-seven years, six months, and seven days.

Shortest Tenure of a Hispanic U.S. Senator

Octaviano A. Larrazolo, (R) New Mexico, who served from December 7, 1928, through March 3, 1929: two months and twenty-seven days.

Hispanic U.S. Senatorial Election Statistics

The following section provides voting statistics on those Hispanic senators who contested elections, including primaries, primary runoffs, and general elections. Names in this section appear in chronological order of senatorial service, from earliest to most recent.

Octaviano Ambrosio Larrazolo, (R) New Mexico

1928	Special	Octaviano A. Larrazolo (R)	64,623	55.7%
		Juan N. Vigil (D)	51,495	44.4%

Dennis Chavez, (D) New Mexico

1958	General	Dennis Chavez (D)	127,496	62.7%
		Forrest J. Atchley (R)	75,827	37.3%
1952	General	Dennis Chavez (D)	122,496	51.1%
		Patrick J. Hurley (R)	117,165	48.9%
1946	General	Dennis Chavez (D)	68,650	51.1%
		Patrick J. Hurley (R)	64,632	48.5%
1940	General	Dennis Chavez (D)	103,194	56.0%
		Albert K. Mitchell (R)	81,257	44.1%
1936	Special	Dennis Chavez (D)	94,585	55.7%
		Manuel A. Otero Jr. (R)	75,030	44.2%
1934	General	Bronson M. Cutting (R)	76,228	50.2%
		Dennis Chavez (D)	74,944	49.4%

Joseph Manuel Montoya, (D) New Mexico

1976	General	Harrison Schmitt (R)	234,681	57.0%
		Joseph M. Montoya (D)	176,382	43.0%
1970	General	Joseph M. Montoya (D)	151,486	52.3%
		Anderson Carter (R)	135,004	46.6%
1964	General	Joseph M. Montoya (D)	178,209	54.7%
		Edwin L. Mechem (R)	147,562	45.3%

Chronology of All Hispanic Candidates for U.S. Senate (* denotes winner)

1928	*Octaviano A. Larrazolo[1]	Republican	New Mexico
1934	*Dennis Chavez[2]	Democrat	New Mexico
1936	*Dennis Chavez	Democrat	New Mexico
	Manuel A. Otero Jr.	Republican	New Mexico
1940	*Dennis Chavez	Democrat	New Mexico
1946	*Dennis Chavez	Democrat	New Mexico

[1]Larrazolo had previously served one term (1919–1921) as governor.

[2]Chavez had previously served two terms (1931–1935) in the U.S. House.

1952	*Dennis Chavez	Democrat	New Mexico
1958	*Dennis Chavez	Democrat	New Mexico
1964	*Joseph M. Montoya[3]	Democrat	New Mexico
1970	*Joseph M. Montoya	Democrat	New Mexico
1976	Joseph M. Montoya	Democrat	New Mexico
1978	Toney Anaya[4]	Democrat	New Mexico
1986	Linda Chavez	Republican	Maryland
1990	Tom Benavides	Democrat	New Mexico
1996	Victor Morales	Democrat	Texas
	Art Trujillo	Democrat	New Mexico
1998	Paul Feleciano	Democrat	Kansas

Hispanics Serving in the U.S. House of Representatives

106th Congress (1999–2001)

State	District	Name	Party Affiliation
Arizona	2	Ed Pastor	Democrat
California	11	Richard W. Pombo	Republican
California	30	Xavier Becerra	Democrat
California	31	Matthew D. Martinez	Democrat
California	33	Lucille Roybal-Allard	Democrat
California	34	Grace Napolitano	Democrat
California	46	Loretta Sanchez (Brixley)	Democrat
Florida	18	Ileana Ros-Lehtinen	Republican
Florida	21	Lincoln Diaz-Balart	Republican
Illinois	4	Luis V. Gutierrez	Democrat
New Jersey	13	Robert Menendez	Democrat
New Mexico	3	Bill Richardson	Democrat
New York	12	Nydia M. Velasquez	Democrat
New York	16	Jose E. Serrano	Democrat
Texas	15	Ruben Hinojosa	Democrat
Texas	16	Silvestre Reyes	Democrat
Texas	20	Charles. Gonzalez	Democrat
Texas	23	Henry Bonilla	Republican
Texas	28	Ciro Rodriguez	Democrat
Texas	27	Solomon Ortiz	Democrat

---

[3]Montoya had previously served three terms (1959–1965) in the U.S. House.

[4]Anaya later served as governor of New Mexico (1983–1987).

Total Hispanics Serving

20 (16 Democrats, 4 Republicans)

Senior Hispanic Member

Matthew D. Martinez, (D) California–31st, first elected in a July 1982 special election.

Wielding Power

No Hispanics chair committees in the 106th Congress.

Female Hispanic Representation

5 Women

California	33	Lucille Roybal-Allard	Democrat
California	34	Grace Napolitano	Democrat
California	46	Loretta Sanchez (Brixley)	Democrat
Florida	18	Ileana Ros-Lehtinen	Republican
New York	12	Nydia M. Velasquez	Democrat

Hispanic Incumbents Not Returning from the 105th Congress

Henry B. Gonzalez, (D) Texas–20th, chose to retire and not seek reelection.
Esteban Torres, (D) California–34th, chose to retire and not seek reelection.

105th Congress (1997–1999)

State	District	Name	Party Affiliation
Arizona	2	Ed Pastor	Democrat
California	11	Richard W. Pombo	Republican
California	30	Xavier Becerra	Democrat
California	31	Matthew D. Martinez	Democrat
California	33	Lucille Roybal-Allard	Democrat
California	34	Esteban Torres	Democrat
California	46	Loretta Sanchez (Brixley)	Democrat
Florida	18	Ileana Ros-Lehtinen	Republican
Florida	21	Lincoln Diaz-Balart	Republican
Illinois	4	Luis V. Gutierrez	Democrat
New Jersey	13	Robert Menendez	Democrat
New Mexico	3	Bill Richardson[5]	Democrat

[5]Richardson resigned to become U.S. ambassador to the United Nations in early 1997.

New York	12	Nydia M. Velazquez	Democrat
New York	16	Jose E. Serrano	Democrat
Texas	15	Ruben Hinojosa	Democrat
Texas	16	Silvestre Reyes	Democrat
Texas	20	Henry B. Gonzalez	Democrat
Texas	23	Henry Bonilla	Republican
Texas	28	Ciro Rodriguez[6]	Democrat
Texas	28	Frank M. Tejeda	Democrat
Texas	27	Solomon Ortiz	Democrat

Total Hispanics Serving

21 (17 Democrats, 4 Republicans)

Senior Hispanic Member

Henry B. Gonzalez, (D) Texas–20th, first elected in November 1961.

Wielding Power

No Hispanics chaired committees in the 105th Congress.

Female Hispanic Representation

4 Women

California	33	Lucille Roybal-Allard	Democrat
California	46	Loretta Sanchez (Brixley)	Democrat
Florida	18	Ileana Ros-Lehtinen	Republican
New York	12	Nydia M. Velazquez	Democrat

Hispanic Incumbent Not Returning from the 104th Congress

Eligio de la Garza, (D) Texas–15th, chose to retire and not seek reelection.

104th Congress (1995–1997)

State	District	Name	Party Affiliation
Arizona	2	Ed Pastor	Democrat
California	11	Richard W. Pombo	Republican
California	30	Xavier Becerra	Democrat

[6]Ciro Rodriguez was elected on April 12, 1997, in a runoff election to replace Frank Tejeda, who had died of a brain tumor on January 30, 1997.

California	31	Matthew D. Martinez	Democrat
California	33	Lucille Roybal-Allard	Democrat
California	34	Esteban Torres	Democrat
Florida	18	Ileana Ros-Lehtinen	Republican
Florida	21	Lincoln Diaz-Balart	Republican
Illinois	4	Luis V. Gutierrez	Democrat
New Jersey	13	Robert Menendez	Democrat
New Mexico	3	Bill Richardson	Democrat
New York	12	Nydia M. Velazquez	Democrat
New York	16	Jose E. Serrano	Democrat
Texas	15	E. de la Garza	Democrat
Texas	20	Henry B. Gonzalez	Democrat
Texas	23	Henry Bonilla	Republican
Texas	26	Frank M. Tejeda	Democrat
Texas	27	Solomon Ortiz	Democrat

Total Hispanics Serving

18 (14 Democrats, 4 Republicans)

Senior Hispanic Member

Henry B. Gonzalez, (D) Texas–20th, first elected in November 1961.

Wielding Power

When the Republicans won majority control of the U.S. House of Representatives in the November 1994 elections, both Hispanic committee chairs lost their positions and assumed ranking minority member status on their committees.

Female Hispanic Representation

3 Women

California	33	Lucille Roybal-Allard	Democrat
Florida	18	Ileana Ros-Lehtinen	Republican
New York	12	Nydia M. Velazquez	Democrat

103rd Congress (1993–1995)

State	District	Name	Party Affiliation
Arizona	2	Ed Pastor	Democrat
California	11	Richard W. Pombo	Republican

California	30	Xavier Becerra	Democrat
California	31	Matthew D. Martinez	Democrat
California	33	Lucille Roybal-Allard	Democrat
California	34	Esteban Torres	Democrat
Florida	18	Ileana Ros-Lehtinen	Republican
Florida	21	Lincoln Diaz-Balart	Republican
Illinois	4	Luis V. Gutierrez	Democrat
New Jersey	13	Robert Menendez	Democrat
New Mexico	3	Bill Richardson	Democrat
New York	12	Nydia M. Velazquez	Democrat
New York	16	Jose E. Serrano	Democrat
Texas	15	E. de la Garza	Democrat
Texas	20	Henry B. Gonzalez	Democrat
Texas	23	Henry Bonilla	Republican
Texas	26	Frank M. Tejeda	Democrat
Texas	27	Solomon Ortiz	Democrat

Total Hispanics Serving

18 (14 Democrats, 4 Republicans)

Senior Hispanic Member

Henry B. Gonzalez, (D) Texas–20th, first elected in November 1961.

Wielding Power

Henry B. Gonzalez, (D) Texas–20th, was chair of the House Committee on Banking, Finance, and Urban Affairs.
E. de la Garza, (D) Texas–15th, was chair of the House Committee on Agriculture.

Achieving Power

Bill Richardson, (D) New Mexico–3rd, became chief deputy majority whip, the first Hispanic to serve in a leadership position in the party structure of the U.S. House.

Female Hispanic Representation

3 Women

California	33	Lucille Roybal-Allard	Democrat
Florida	18	Ileana Ros-Lehtinen	Republican
New York	12	Nydia M. Velazquez	Democrat

Hispanic Incumbents Not Returning from the 102nd Congress

One incumbent chose to retire and not seek reelection:

Edward H. Roybal, (D) California–25th[7]

One incumbent was defeated in the general election:

Albert G. Bustamante, (D) Texas–23rd

102nd Congress (1991–1993)

State	District	Name	Party Affiliation
Arizona	2	Ed Pastor	Democrat
California	25	Edward H. Roybal	Democrat
California	30	Matthew D. Martinez	Democrat
California	34	Esteban Torres	Democrat
Florida	18	Ileana Ros-Lehtinen	Republican
New Mexico	3	Bill Richardson	Democrat
New York	18	Jose E. Serrano	Democrat
Texas	15	E. de la Garza	Democrat
Texas	20	Henry B. Gonzalez	Democrat
Texas	23	Albert G. Bustamante	Democrat
Texas	27	Solomon Ortiz	Democrat

Total Hispanics Serving

11 (10 Democrats, 1 Republican)

Senior Hispanic Member

Henry B. Gonzalez, (D) Texas–20th, first elected in November 1961.

Wielding Power

Henry B. Gonzalez, (D) Texas–20th, was chair of the House Committee on Banking, Finance, and Urban Affairs.
E. de la Garza, (D) Texas–15th, was chair of the House Committee on Agriculture.

---

[7]Roybal was succeeded by his daughter, Lucille Roybal-Allard, in his seat, which received a new number (33) because of redistricting.

Female Hispanic Representation

1 Woman

Florida	18	Ileana Ros-Lehtinen	Republican

101st Congress (1989–1991)

State	District	Name	Party Affiliation
California	15	Tony Coelho[8]	Democrat
California	25	Edward H. Roybal	Democrat
California	30	Matthew D. Martinez	Democrat
California	34	Esteban Torres	Democrat
Florida	18	Ileana Ros-Lehtinen	Republican
New Mexico	3	Bill Richardson	Democrat
New York	18	Robert Garcia[9]	Democrat
New York	18	Jose E. Serrano	Democrat
Texas	15	E. de la Garza	Democrat
Texas	20	Henry B. Gonzalez	Democrat
Texas	23	Albert G. Bustamante	Democrat
Texas	27	Solomon Ortiz	Democrat

Total Hispanics Serving

12 (11 Democrats, 1 Republican)

Senior Hispanic Member

Henry B. Gonzalez, (D) Texas–20th, first elected in November 1961.

Wielding Power

E. de la Garza, (D) Texas–15th, was chair of the House Committee on Agriculture.

Achieving Power

Henry B. Gonzalez, (D) Texas–20th, became chair of the House Committee on Banking, Finance, and Urban Affairs.

Female Hispanic Representation

1 Woman

Florida	18	Ileana Ros-Lehtinen	Republican

---

[8]Coelho resigned in June 1989 after his involvement in an unethical "junk bond" scheme became public knowledge.

[9]Garcia resigned in December 1989 after being implicated in the Wedtech bribery scandal.

Notable First

Ileana Ros-Lehtinen (R), a Cuban American representing Florida's 18th Congressional District, became the first Hispanic woman elected to the U.S. House of Representatives. (See 68th Congress, 1923–1925.)

Hispanic Incumbent Not Returning from the 100th Congress

One incumbent chose to retire and not seek reelection:

Manual Lujan Jr., (R) New Mexico–1st

100th Congress (1987–1989)

State	District	Name	Party Affiliation
California	15	Tony Coelho	Democrat
California	25	Edward H. Roybal	Democrat
California	30	Matthew D. Martinez	Democrat
California	34	Esteban Torres	Democrat
New Mexico	1	Manual Lujan Jr.	Republican
New Mexico	3	Bill Richardson	Democrat
New York	18	Robert Garcia	Democrat
Texas	15	E. de la Garza	Democrat
Texas	20	Henry B. Gonzalez	Democrat
Texas	23	Albert G. Bustamante	Democrat
Texas	27	Solomon Ortiz	Democrat

Total Hispanics Serving

11 (10 Democrats, 1 Republican)

Senior Hispanic Member

Henry B. Gonzalez, (D) Texas–20th, first elected in November 1961.

Wielding Power

E. de la Garza, (D) Texas–15th, was chair of the House Committee on Agriculture.

99th Congress (1985–1987)

State	District	Name	Party Affiliation
California	15	Tony Coelho	Democrat
California	25	Edward H. Roybal	Democrat
California	30	Matthew D. Martinez	Democrat

California	34	Esteban Torres	Democrat
New Mexico	1	Manual Lujan Jr.	Republican
New Mexico	3	Bill Richardson	Democrat
New York	18	Robert Garcia	Democrat
Texas	15	E. de la Garza	Democrat
Texas	20	Henry B. Gonzalez	Democrat
Texas	23	Albert G. Bustamante	Democrat
Texas	27	Solomon Ortiz	Democrat

Total Hispanics Serving

11 (10 Democrats, 1 Republican)

Senior Hispanic Member

Henry B. Gonzalez, (D) Texas–20th, first elected in November 1961.

Wielding Power

E. de la Garza, (D) Texas–15th, was chair of the House Committee on Agriculture.

98th Congress (1983–1985)

State	District	Name	Party Affiliation
California	15	Tony Coelho	Democrat
California	30	Matthew D. Martinez	Democrat
California	25	Edward H. Roybal	Democrat
California	34	Esteban Torres	Democrat
New Mexico	1	Manual Lujan Jr.	Republican
New Mexico	3	Bill Richardson	Democrat
New York	18	Robert Garcia	Democrat
Texas	15	E. de la Garza	Democrat
Texas	20	Henry B. Gonzalez	Democrat
Texas	27	Solomon Ortiz	Democrat

Total Hispanics Serving

10 (9 Democrats, 1 Republican)

Senior Hispanic Member

Henry B. Gonzalez, (D) Texas–20th, first elected in November 1961.

Wielding Power

E. de la Garza, (D) Texas–15th, was chair of the House Committee on Agriculture.

97th Congress (1981–1983)

State	District	Name	Party Affiliation
California	15	Tony Coelho	Democrat
California	25	Edward H. Roybal	Democrat
California	30	Matthew D. Martinez[10]	Democract
New Mexico	1	Manual Lujan Jr.	Republican
New York	18	Robert Garcia	Democrat
Texas	15	E. de la Garza	Democrat
Texas	20	Henry B. Gonzalez	Democrat

Total Hispanics Serving

7 (6 Democrats, 1 Republican)

Senior Hispanic Member

Henry B. Gonzalez, (D) Texas–20th, first elected in November 1961.

Achieving Power

E. de la Garza, (D) Texas–15th, became chair of the House Committee on Agriculture.

96th Congress (1979–1981)

State	District	Name	Party Affiliation
California	15	Tony Coelho[11]	Democrat
California	25	Edward H. Roybal	Democrat
New Mexico	1	Manual Lujan Jr.	Republican
New York	21	Robert Garcia	Democrat
Texas	15	E. de la Garza	Democrat
Texas	20	Henry B. Gonzalez	Democrat

Total Hispanics Serving

6 (5 Democrats, 1 Republican)

---

[10]Martinez was elected in a special July 1982 election to replace a non-Hispanic incumbent who had resigned.

[11]Coelho, of Portuguese descent, might not technically be considered a Hispanic.

Senior Hispanic Member

Henry B. Gonzalez, (D) Texas–20th, first elected in November 1961.

95th Congress (1977–1979)

State	District	Name	Party Affiliation
California	25	Edward H. Roybal	Democrat
New Mexico	1	Manual Lujan Jr.	Republican
New York	21	Herman Badillo[12]	Democrat
New York	21	Robert Garcia[13]	Democrat
Texas	15	E. de la Garza	Democrat
Texas	20	Henry B. Gonzalez	Democrat

Total Hispanics Serving

5 (4 Democrats, 1 Republican)

Senior Hispanic Member

Henry B. Gonzalez, (D) Texas–20th, first elected in November 1961.

94th Congress (1975–1977)

State	District	Name	Party Affiliation
California	25	Edward H. Roybal	Democrat
New Mexico	1	Manual Lujan Jr.	Republican
New York	21	Herman Badillo	Democrat
Texas	15	E. de la Garza	Democrat
Texas	20	Henry B. Gonzalez	Democrat

93rd Congress (1973–1975)

State	District	Name	Party Affiliation
California	25	Edward H. Roybal	Democrat
New Mexico	1	Manual Lujan Jr.	Republican
New York	21	Herman Badillo	Democrat
Texas	15	E. de la Garza	Democrat
Texas	20	Henry B. Gonzalez	Democrat

---

[12]Badillo, after running for mayor of New York City and losing in the primary, resigned to join the staff of incoming Mayor Ed Koch.

[13]Garcia lost the Democratic primary to succeed Badillo but won the Republican nomination for the seat. He fought and won the general election on that ticket, then was sworn in as a Democrat.

92nd Congress (1971–1973)

State	District	Name	Party Affiliation
California	30	Edward H. Roybal	Democrat
New Mexico	1	Manual Lujan Jr.	Republican
New York	21	Herman Badillo	Democrat
Texas	15	E. de la Garza	Democrat
Texas	20	Henry B. Gonzalez	Democrat

91st Congress (1969–1971)

State	District	Name	Party Affiliation
California	30	Edward H. Roybal	Democrat
New Mexico	1	Manual Lujan Jr.	Republican
Texas	15	E. de la Garza	Democrat
Texas	20	Henry B. Gonzalez	Democrat

90th Congress (1967–1969)

State	District	Name	Party Affiliation
California	30	Edward H. Roybal	Democrat
Texas	15	E. de la Garza	Democrat
Texas	20	Henry B. Gonzalez	Democrat

89th Congress (1965–1967)

State	District	Name	Party Affiliation
California	30	Edward H. Roybal	Democrat
Texas	15	E. de la Garza	Democrat
Texas	20	Henry B. Gonzalez	Democrat

88th Congress (1963–1965)

State	District	Name	Party Affiliation
California	30	Edward H. Roybal[14]	Democrat
New Mexico	AL	Joseph M. Montoya	Democrat
Texas	20	Henry B. Gonzalez	Democrat

87th Congress (1961–1963)

State	District	Name	Party Affiliation
New Mexico	AL	Joseph M. Montoya	Democrat
Texas	20	Henry B. Gonzalez	Democrat

[14]In 1954 Roybal was the Democratic nominee for lieutenant governor of California. He lost but polled more votes than the Democratic nominee for governor on the same ticket.

86th Congress (1959–1961)

State	District	Name	Party Affiliation
New Mexico	AL	Joseph M. Montoya	Democrat

85th Congress (1957–1959)

State	District	Name	Party Affiliation
New Mexico	AL	Antonio M. Fernandez	Democrat

84th Congress (1955–1957)

State	District	Name	Party Affiliation
New Mexico	AL	Antonio M. Fernandez	Democrat

83rd Congress (1953–1955)

State	District	Name	Party Affiliation
New Mexico	AL	Antonio M. Fernandez	Democrat

82nd Congress (1951–1953)

State	District	Name	Party Affiliation
New Mexico	AL	Antonio M. Fernandez	Democrat

81st Congress (1949–1951)

State	District	Name	Party Affiliation
New Mexico	AL	Antonio M. Fernandez	Democrat

80th Congress (1947–1949)

State	District	Name	Party Affiliation
New Mexico	AL	Antonio M. Fernandez	Democrat

79th Congress (1945–1947)

State	District	Name	Party Affiliation
New Mexico	AL	Antonio M. Fernandez	Democrat

78th Congress (1943–1945)

State	District	Name	Party Affiliation
New Mexico	AL	Antonio M. Fernandez	Democrat

77th Congress (1941–1943)

No Hispanics served in the U.S. House of Representatives from 1941 to 1943.

76th Congress (1939–1941)

State	*District*	*Name*	*Party Affiliation*
Louisiana	1	Joachim Octave Fernandez	Democrat

75th Congress (1937–1939)

State	*District*	*Name*	*Party Affiliation*
Louisiana	1	Joachim Octave Fernandez	Democrat

74th Congress (1935–1937)

State	*District*	*Name*	*Party Affiliation*
Louisiana	1	Joachim Octave Fernandez	Democrat

73rd Congress (1933–1935)

State	*District*	*Name*	*Party Affiliation*
Louisiana	1	Joachim Octave Fernandez	Democrat
New Mexico	AL	Dennis Chavez	Democrat

72nd Congress (1931–1933)

State	*District*	*Name*	*Party Affiliation*
Louisiana	1	Joachim Octave Fernandez	Democrat
New Mexico	AL	Dennis Chavez	Democrat

71st Congress (1929–1931)

State	*District*	*Name*	*Party Affiliation*
Louisiana	7	Ladislas Lazaro	Democrat

70th Congress (1927–1929)

State	*District*	*Name*	*Party Affiliation*
Louisiana	7	Ladislas Lazaro	Democrat

69th Congress (1925–1927)

State	*District*	*Name*	*Party Affiliation*
Louisiana	7	Ladislas Lazaro	Democrat

68th Congress (1923–1925)

State	District	Name	Party Affiliation
Louisiana	7	Ladislas Lazaro	Democrat

Notable First: 1922

Adelina Otero-Warren, (R) New Mexico, became the first Hispanic woman to receive a major-party nomination for a seat in the U.S. House of Representatives. She garnered 45 percent of the vote in the race to fill New Mexico's lone seat in the U.S. House. (See 101st Congress, 1989–1991.)

67th Congress (1921–1923)

State	District	Name	Party Affiliation
Louisiana	7	Ladislas Lazaro	Democrat
New Mexico	AL	Nestor Montoya	Republican

66th Congress (1919–1921)

State	District	Name	Party Affiliation
Louisiana	7	Ladislas Lazaro	Democrat
New Mexico	AL	Bendigno C. Hernandez	Republican

65th Congress (1917–1919)

State	District	Name	Party Affiliation
Louisiana	7	Ladislas Lazaro	Democrat

64th Congress (1915–1917)

State	District	Name	Party Affiliation
Louisiana	7	Ladislas Lazaro	Democrat
New Mexico	AL	Bendigno C. Hernandez	Republican

63rd Congress (1913–1915)

State	District	Name	Party Affiliation
Louisiana	7	Ladislas Lazaro	Democrat

48th Congress (1883–1885) through 62nd Congress (1911–1913)

No Hispanics served in the U.S. House from 1883 to 1913 with the exception noted below.

Notable Moment: 1902

Federico Degetau, resident commissioner from the territory of Puerto Rico, was granted House floor privileges, the first Puerto Rican participant in the U.S. House of Representatives.

47th Congress (1881–1883)

State	District	Name	Party Affiliation
California	4	Romualdo Pacheco	Republican

46th Congress (1879–1881)

State	District	Name	Party Affiliation
California	4	Romualdo Pacheco	Republican

45th Congress (1877–1879)

State	District	Name	Party Affiliation
California	4	Romualdo Pacheco	Republican

Notable First: 1822

Joseph Marion Hernández, Whig of Florida, was the first Hispanic elected to the U.S. Congress. In 1822 he was selected as the territory of Florida's delegate (nonvoting) for the U.S. House of Representatives, where he served throughout 1823. Florida became a state in 1845 but did not elect another Hispanic to Congress until 1989—177 years after Hernández was elected.

Hispanic Governors in Chronological Order of Service

1. Romualdo Pacheco	Republican	California	02/27/1875–12/09/1875
2. Alonzo Garcelon	Democrat	Maine	01/08/1879–01/17/1880
3. Esequiel Cabeza de Baca	Democrat	New Mexico	01/01/17–02/16/17
4. Octaviano Ambrosio Larrazolo	Republican	New Mexico	01/01/19–01/01/21
5. Raul Hector Castro	Democrat	Arizona	01/06/75–10/01/77
6. Raymond "Jerry" Apodaca	Democrat	New Mexico	01/01/75–01/01/79
7. Toney Anaya	Democrat	New Mexico	01/01/83–01/01/87
8. Robert "Bob" Martinez	Republican	Florida	01/05/87–01/03/91

How They Assumed Office

1. **Romualdo Pacheco**, (R) California (Born: 1831; Died: 1899)
   Served: 02/27/1875–12/09/1875

   Succeeded on February 27, 1875, after the incumbent resigned. As lieutenant governor, Pacheco moved up to the governorship to complete the term of Newton Booth (R), who resigned after being elected to the U.S. Senate by the state legislature.

   Previous elected public office:
   California Lieutenant Governor, 1871–1875
   California Treasurer, 1863–1867
   Subsequent elected public office:
   U.S. House of Representatives, 1877–1883

2. **Alonzo Garcelon**, (D) Maine (Born: 1813; Died: 1906)
   Served: 01/08/1879–01/17/1880

   Elected in 1878 for a one-year term by the state legislature. Maine's constitution provided for election by the legislature if no candidate received a majority of the popular vote. Even though Garcelon placed third, his Democratic allies in the state legislature joined forces with the Greenback Party, whose candidate came in second, to award the governorship to him. Garcelon sought reelection in 1879 for an additional one-year term, and again no candidate received a majority, sending the choice to the legislature once more. Disputes arose this time about which party had elected the most members of the legislature. The state supreme court finally decided in favor of the Republicans, as they had more newly elected members seated. The Republican-dominated legislature then voted their gubernatorial candidate—who had received the most votes in the general election—into the statehouse. Shortly thereafter, Maine dropped its one-year gubernatorial term, also providing that only a plurality was necessary to win the governorship.

   Previous elected public office:
   Maine House of Representatives, 1853–1854, 1857–1858
   Maine Senate, 1854–1856
   Subsequent elected public office: None

3. **Esequiel Cabeza de Baca**, (D) New Mexico (Born: 1864; Died: 1917)
   Served: 01/01/17–02/16/17

   Elected on November 7, 1916, to a two-year term. De Baca died in office in February 1917, only forty-seven days after his inauguration.

   Previous elected public office:
   New Mexico Lieutenant Governor, 1912–1915
   Subsequent elected political office: None (died in office)

4. **Octaviano Ambrosio Larrazolo**, (R) New Mexico (Born: 1859; Died: 1930)
   Served: 01/01/19–01/01/21

Elected on November 5, 1918, to a two-year term. Since New Mexico did not permit governors to run for consecutive terms, Larrazolo was ineligible to run again in 1920.

Previous elected public office:
    El Paso, Texas, District Attorney
    El Paso, Texas, School Board
Subsequent elected political office:
    New Mexico State Legislature, 1927–1928
    U.S. Senate, 1928–1929

5. **Raul Hector Castro**, (D) Arizona (Born: 1916)
Served: 01/06/75–10/01/77

Elected on November 5, 1974, to a four-year term. Castro resigned the governorship on October 1, 1977, after he was confirmed as U.S. ambassador to Argentina. Previously, during the 1960s, he had also served as U.S. ambassador to El Salvador and Bolivia.

Previous elected public office:
    Pima County, Arizona, District Attorney, 1954–1958
    Judge of the Superior Court, Arizona, 1958–1964
Subsequent elected public office: None

6. **Raymond "Jerry" Apodaca**, (D) New Mexico (Born: 1934)
Served: 01/01/75–01/01/79

Elected on November 5, 1974, to a four-year term. Since New Mexico did not permit governors to serve consecutive terms, Apodaca was ineligible to seek reelection in 1978. He did return to the ballot in 1982 as a candidate in the Democratic Senate primary, where he finished second.

Previous elected public office:
    New Mexico State Senate, 1967–1974
Subsequent elected public office: None

7. **Toney Anaya**, (D) New Mexico (Born: 1941)
Served: 01/01/83–01/01/87

Elected on November 2, 1982, to a four-year term. Since New Mexico did not permit governors to serve consecutive terms, Apodaca was ineligible to run for reelection in 1986. Previously, Anaya had been the Democratic nominee for U.S. Senate in 1978, but he lost that contest to Sen. Peter Domenici (R).

Previous elected public office:
    New Mexico Attorney General, 1975–1978
Subsequent elected public office: None

8. **Robert "Bob" Martinez**, (R) Florida (Born: 1934)
Served: 01/05/87–01/03/91

Elected on November 4, 1986, to a four-year term. After what most observers thought was a rocky first term, Martinez sought a second one in 1990 but was defeated in the general election.

Previous elected public office:
   Mayor, Tampa, Florida, 1979–1986
Subsequent elected public office: None

Hispanic Gubernatorial Statistics

Longest Tenure of a Hispanic Governor

Raymond "Jerry" Apodaca, (D) New Mexico, **Toney Anaya**, (D) New Mexico, and **Robert Martinez**, (R) Florida, all of whom served one full four-year term.

Shortest Tenure of a Hispanic Governor

Esequiel C. de Baca, (D) New Mexico, who served one month and fifteen days, from his swearing-in on January 1, 1917, until his death on February 16, 1917.

Hispanic Gubernatorial Election Statistics

The following section provides voting statistics on those Hispanic governors who contested elections, including primaries, primary runoffs, and general elections. Names in this section appear in chronological order of gubernatorial service, from earliest to most recent.

Esequiel Cabeza de Baca, (D) New Mexico

1916	General	Esequiel C. de Baca (D)	32,875	49.4%
		Holm C. Bursum (R)	31,552	47.4%

Octaviano Ambrosio Larrazolo, (R) New Mexico

1918	General	Octaviano A. Lazzarolo (R)	23,752	50.5%
		Felix Garcia (D)	22,433	47.7%

Raul Hector Castro, (D) Arizona

1974	General	Raul H. Castro (D)	278,375	50.4%
		Russell Williams (R)	273,674	49.6%
1974	Democratic Primary	Raul H. Castro	115,268	67.0%
		Jack Ross	31,250	18.0%
		Two others	24,986	14.0%
1970	General	Jack Williams (R)	209,356	50.9%
		Raul H. Castro (D)	202,053	49.1%

Raymond "Jerry" Apodaca, (D) New Mexico

1974	General	Raymond "Jerry" Apodaca (D)	164,172	50.0%

		Joe Skeen (R)	160,430	48.8%
1974	Democratic Primary	Raymond "Jerry" Apodaca	35,090	24.0%
		Odis Echols Jr.	25,760	17.0%
		B. M. Mayfield	22,806	15.0%
		Two others	19,505	13.0%

Toney Anaya, (D) New Mexico

1982	General	Toney Anaya (D)	215,840	53.0%
		John Irick (R)	190,626	47.0%
1982	Democratic Primary	Toney Anaya	101,077	57.0%
		Aubrey L. Dunn	60,866	34.0%
		Fabian Chavez Jr.	11,874	7.0%

Robert "Bob" Martinez, (R) Florida

1990	General	Lawton Chiles (D)	1,988,341	57.0%
		Robert "Bob" Martinez (R)	1,526,738	43.0%
1986	General	Robert "Bob" Martinez (R)	1,847,525	55.0%
		Steve Pajcic (D)	1,538,620	45.0%
1986	Primary Runoff	Robert "Bob" Martinez	259,333	56.0%
		Lou Frey Jr.	244,499	44.0%
1986	Republican Primary	Robert "Bob" Martinez	244,499	44.0%
		Lou Frey Jr.	138,017	25.0%
		Tom Gallagher	127,709	23.0%

Chronology of All Hispanic Candidates for Governor (denotes winner)*

1878	Alonzo Garcelon	Democrat	Maine
1879	*Alonzo Garcelon	Democrat	Maine
1916	*Esequiel C. de Baca	Democrat	New Mexico
1918	*Octaviano A. Larrazolo	Republican	New Mexico
	Felix Garcia	Democrat	New Mexico
1924	Manuel B. Otero Jr.	Republican	New Mexico
1940	Maurice Miera	Republican	New Mexico
1942	Joseph Tondre	Republican	New Mexico
1948	Manuel Lujan	Republican	New Mexico
1968	Fabian Chavez Jr.	Democrat	New Mexico
1970	Raul H. Castro	Democrat	Arizona
1974	*Raul H. Castro	Democrat	Arizona
	*Raymond "Jerry" Apodaca	Democrat	New Mexico
1982	*Toney Anaya	Democrat	New Mexico
1986	*Robert "Bob" Martinez	Republican	Florida

| 1990 | Robert "Bob" Martinez | Republican | Florida |
| 1998 | Martin J. Chavez | Democrat | New Mexico |

Hispanics Who Have Held Other State Executive Offices[15]

California

Lieutenant Governor
Cruz Bustamante (D), 1999–
Romualdo Pacheco (R), 1871–1875[16]

Treasurer
Romualdo Pacheco (R), 1863–1867

Colorado

Attorney General
Ken Salazar (R), 1999–

New Mexico

Lieutenant Governor
Casey Luna (D), 1991–1995
Roberto Mondragon (D), 1971–1975,
   1979–1983
Joseph M. Montoya (D), 1947–1951,
   1955–1957[17]
Tibo J. Chavez (D), 1951–1955
Ceferino R. Quintana (D), 1941–1943
Luis C. de Baca (D), 1935–1937
Jose A. Baca (D), 1923–1925
Esequiel C. de Baca (D), 1912–1915[18]

Attorney General
Patricia A. Madrid (D), 1999–
Toney Anaya (D), 1975–1979[19]
Joe L. Martinez (D), 1949–1953
Filo Sedillo (D), 1939–1941
Miguel A. Otero Jr. (R), 1929–1931

Auditor
Domingo Martinez (D), 1999–
Robert E. Vigil (D), 1991–1999
Albert Romero (D), 1983–1987
Alvino Castillo (D), 1979–1983
Max Sanchez (D), 1975–1979
Alex J. Armijo (D), 1963–1967
Ben Chavez (D), 1957–1959
E. D. Trujillo (D), 1939–1943, 1947–1951
Jose O. Garcia (D), 1935–1939
Arsenio Velarde (D), 1931–1935
Victoriano Ulibarri (R), 1929–1931
Miguel A. Otero Jr. (R), 1927–1929
Juan N. Vigil (D), 1923–1927

Secretary of State
Stephanie Gonzales (D), 1991–1999
Rebecca Vigil-Giron (D), 1987–1991, 1999–
Clara Padilla Jones (D), 1983–1987
Ernestine Evans (D), 1967–1971, 1975–1979
Alicia M. Romero (D), 1947–1951
Jessie M. Gonzales (D), 1939–1943
Elizabeth F. Gonzales (D), 1935–1939
Marguerite P. Baca (D), 1931–1935
Soledad C. Chacon (D), 1923–1927
Manual Martinez (R), 1919–1921
Antonio Lucero (D), 1912–1919

Treasurer
Michael A. Montoya (D), 1995–

Rhode Island

Treasurer
Paul J. Tavares (D), 1999–

---

[15]These offices are a combination of election by popular vote, election by the state legislature, and appointment by the governor.

[16]Pacheco also served as governor for ten months in 1875 and three terms in the U.S. House (1877–1883).

[17]Montoya later served for three terms (1959–1965) in the U.S. House and two terms (1965–1977) in the U.S. Senate.

[18]De Baca also served one month as governor, dying shortly after his inauguration.

[19]Anaya later served as governor (1983–1987).

Texas

Attorney General
  Dan Morales (D), 1991–1999

Secretary of State
  Alberto R. Gonzales (R), 1997–
  Antonio O. Garza (R), 1995–1997
  Roy Barrera Sr. (D), 1967

Hispanics in State Legislatures

Notable First: 1978

Polly Baca, (D) Colorado, was the first Hispanic woman elected to a state senate.

Notable First: 1941

Concha Ortiz y Pino, (D) New Mexico, became the majority whip in New Mexico's house of representatives, the first Hispanic woman to hold a leadership position in a state legislature.

Notable First: 1937

Oscar Garcia Rivera, (D) New York, was the first Puerto Rican elected to a state legislature.

Notable First: 1932

Marta Luisa Arcelay, Puerto Rico, was the first Puerto Rican woman elected to a state/territorial legislature.

Notable First: 1930

Fedelina Lucero Gallegos, (R) New Mexico, was the first Hispanic woman elected to a state legislature.

Notable First: 1912

Roman L. Baca, (R) New Mexico, became speaker of New Mexico's house of representatives, the first Hispanic to hold that position in a state legislature.

Notable First

Casimiro Bareia of Colorado, who served in that state's senate 1876–1916, was the first Hispanic to achieve the post of president pro tem of a state senate, holding the position twice.

Hispanic Speakers of State Lower Legislative Chambers

Antonio Villaraigosa, (D) California, 1997–
Cruz Bustamante, (D) California, 1996–1997

Raymond G. Sanchez, (D) New Mexico, 1983–1984, 1987–
Walter K. Martinez, (D) New Mexico, 1971–1978
George W. Armijo, (D) New Mexico, 1939–1940
A. A. Sedillo, (R) New Mexico, 1919–1920
Sucundino Romero, (R) New Mexico, 1915
Roman L. Baca, (R) New Mexico, 1912–1913, 1927–1929

Hispanics in the Judiciary

U.S. Supreme Court Justice

1932–1938   **Benjamin N. Cardozo,** (D) New York, appointed by Pres. Herbert Hoover Although primarily thought of as being a "Jewish" Supreme Court justice, Cardozo was actually a descendant of a well-known Sephardic family that dated back to colonial times. As such, he was therefore the first—and so far only—Hispanic appointed to the U.S. Supreme Court.

Notable Firsts: 1992

Irma Gonzalez and **Lourdes G. Baird**, both of California, and **Sonia Sotomayor**, New York, were the first female Hispanics appointed federal judges. Baird, of Guatemalan American descent, was also probably the first Guatemalan American appointed to the federal bench.

Notable First: 1987

Dorothy Comstock Riley, Michigan, was the first Hispanic female chief justice of a state supreme court.

Notable First: 1983

Irma Vidal Santaella, New York, was the first female Puerto Rican to sit on a state supreme court.

Notable First: 1979

Jose A. Cabranes, (D) Connecticut, appointed by Pres. Jimmy Carter, was the first Puerto Rican federal judge in the continental United States.

Notable First: 1964

Phillip Newman, appointed by Gov. Pat Brown to a Los Angeles municipal judgeship, was the first Mexican American appointed as a judge in the U.S.

Hispanics at the Local Level

Notable First: 1988

Gilda Oliveros (R) was elected mayor of Hialeah Gardens, Florida, the first Cuban American woman elected mayor in the U.S.

Notable First: 1981

Henry Cisneros (D) was elected mayor of San Antonio, Texas, the first Mexican American mayor of a large American city.

Asian Americans in American Politics

A Brief Chronology

1907 First Asian Americans to serve in the U.S. House of Representatives

Benito Legarda and **Pablo Ocampo**, both of the Philippines, were elected resident commissioners from that territory to the U.S. House of Representatives.

1912 First Chinese American woman to vote in a presidential election

Tye Leung, San Francisco, California, voted in the 1912 presidential election. She was able to do so because California had granted women the right to vote in 1911.

1926 First Asian American elected to the lower house of a legislative assembly

Yew Char, (R) Hawaii, was elected to Hawaii's territorial legislature; he was also the first Chinese American elected to the lower house of a territorial legislative assembly.

1929 First Asian American elected to a territorial senate

Paul A. Low, (R) Hawaii, was elected to the senate of the territory of Hawaii; he was also the first Chinese American elected to a territorial senate.

1946 First Asian American elected to public office on the U.S. mainland

Wing F. Ong, Democrat, was elected to Arizona's house of representatives. He was also the first Chinese American elected to public office on the U.S. mainland.

1949 First Asian American speaker of a state or territorial house of representatives

Hiram Fong, Republican, was elected speaker of Hawaii's territorial house of representatives; he was also the first Chinese American to hold the position of speaker in a state or territorial house of representatives.

1950 First Chinese American judge on the U.S. mainland

Chuck Mau, California, was appointed to a state circuit court seat.

1956 First Japanese American state/territorial supreme court justice

Masaji Marumoto, Hawaii, was appointed an associate justice of the territory of Hawaii's supreme court.

1957 **First Asian American member of Congress**

Dalip Singh Saund, (D) California, was sworn in as the first Asian American (and Asian Indian–American) member of the U.S. House of Representatives.

1959 **First Asian American member of the U.S. Senate**

Hiram Fong, (R) Hawaii, was elected to the U.S. Senate in the first election after Hawaii was admitted as a state; he was also the first Chinese American member of the U.S. Senate.

First Japanese American chief justice of a state supreme court

Wilfred C. Tsukiyama, (R) Hawaii, became chief justice of the supreme court in that state.

1965 **First Asian American woman sworn into the U.S. House of Representatives**

Patsy Takemoto Mink, (D) Hawaii, was sworn into the U.S. House of Representatives.

1968 **First Asian American to deliver the keynote address at the national convention of a major political party**

Daniel K. Inouye, U.S. senator from Hawaii, delivered the keynote address at the 1968 Democratic National Convention.

1971 **First Japanese American mayor of a large American city**

Norman Mineta, Democrat, was elected mayor of San Jose, California.

1973 **First Asian American governor**

George Ariyoshi, Democrat, assumed the governorship of Hawaii after the incumbent became ill and resigned. He was also the first Japanese American to serve as governor of a U.S. state.

1974 **First Asian American woman elected to a statewide position**

March Fong, Democrat, was elected California's secretary of state. She was also the first Chinese American elected to statewide office in the U.S.

1978 **First Asian American female lieutenant governor**

Jean Sadako King, (D) Hawaii, was elected lieutenant governor of that state. She was also the first Japanese American woman elected lieutenant governor in the U.S.

1987 **First Asian American to head a standing committee of the U.S. Senate**

Daniel K. Inouye, (D) Hawaii, became chair of the Select Committee on Indian Affairs.

1989 **First Asian American woman to serve as a state supreme court justice**

Joyce Kennard, (R) California, was appointed associate justice of that state's supreme court.

1993   First Asian American to chair a standing committee in the U.S. House of Representatives

Norman Mineta, (D) California, became chair of the Transportation and Infrastructure Committee.

Asian Americans and Political Power

The following chart (by state) details the number of Asian Americans who have served their states in three of the most powerful positions in U.S. politics: governor, U.S. Senate (both appointed and elected), and U.S. House of Representatives.

State	Governor	U.S. Senate	U.S. House
California	-	1	4
Hawaii	2	3	4
Oregon	-	-	1
Washington	1	-	-
Total Asian Americans Who Have Served	3	4	9

Best and Worst States for Asian Americans Achieving Power

Hawaii, undoubtedly, must be considered the best state for Asian Americans in exercising their political power. **California**, because of its large Asian American population and the scarcity of Asian American officeholders, must be considered the worst.

Asian Americans constitute the fastest growing minority in the United States. They already constitute 10 percent of California's population, and by the turn of the century they will probably make up 10 percent of the U.S. population. Some experts have even estimated that by the year 2020 Asian Americans may outnumber African Americans.

As their numbers increase we can expect to see more and more Asian Americans entering the political ring. One of the biggest factors that has prevented a larger number of Asian Americans from reaching political office has been the assimilation and dispersal of the overall community plus the lack of cohesiveness between its components. Asian Americans have integrated more cohesively into communities than have other minorities; thus it becomes almost impossible to arrange political boundaries to create "predominately" Asian American electoral districts. Another factor in their political impotence is low voter registration from the community as a whole. Those who are registered to vote, with one exception, do not do so as a monolithic bloc, as do African Americans, for example. Japanese Americans are usually Democratic voters, as are Filipino Americans, whereas Korean Americans, Chinese Americans, and Taiwanese Americans tend to favor Republicans over Democrats.

The increasingly larger Southeast Asian community now residing in the United States, especially Vietnamese Americans, is a particularly interesting minority group to begin tracking politically.

Many members are now entering their second decade of American residency. They have begun to achieve some economic stability along with their American citizenship. Their first ventures in American political life are now beginning to occur. For instance, 1992 saw the first three Vietnamese Americans seeking political office (on the city councils of two small California cities). As the children of this community, especially American-born ones, mature and achieve a higher socioeconomic status than their parents, they can be expected to move into contention for more political offices. Vietnamese Americans tend to support and vote more Republican than do other Asian Americans. Of those registered to vote in Southern California, for example, fully two-thirds considered themselves to be Republican.

Vietnamese Americans, along with Laotian Americans and Khmer Americans, have tended to gather in certain areas of the U.S. Undoubtedly it is in these areas where their first political stirrings will be felt. The Vietnamese American communities in San Jose, California, and several smaller cities farther south in Orange County, California, will soon see more and more Vietnamese Americans entering political life. Khmer Americans have concentrated in Long Beach, California, and Lowell, Massachusetts, and many Laotian Americans have settled in Stockton and Merced, California, and Minneapolis, Minnesota; many Hmong Americans, from Laos, moved to Wausau, Wisconsin (where they already make up 15 percent of that small city's population), and other small cities throughout Wisconsin and Minnesota.

Until now the political power of this fragmented ethnic group has been solely concentrated in the two states with the largest Asian American populations: California and Hawaii. But in the last several years Asian Americans have also sought political office in other states (for example, in Colorado, Georgia, Delaware, Nevada, and Utah) where relatively few Asian Americans reside, occasionally even winning. For example, Washington elected an Asian American governor in 1996.

Asian Americans in the U.S. Cabinet

Thus far no Asian Americans have been appointed to the secretary level of a president's cabinet. For the last several administrations, however, they have held subcabinet-level positions in different departments. **Elaine Chao** achieved the highest rank thus far when Pres. George Bush named her deputy secretary of transportation in 1989, the second-ranking position in the department. Later, Bush named Chao to head the Peace Corps.

Asian Americans in the Executive Branch

Notable First: 1991

Patricia F. Saiki, (R) Hawaii, appointed by Pres. George Bush as head of the Small Business Administration, was the first Asian American to head that agency.

Notable First: 1989

Julia Chang Bloch, appointed U.S. ambassador to Nepal by Pres. George Bush, was the first female Asian American to hold the rank of ambassador.

Notable First: 1988

Elaine Chao became the first Asian American woman to chair a federal commission when Pres. Ronald Reagan named her as head of the Federal Maritime Commission.

Notable First: 1987

Joy Cherian, (R) Washington, D.C., appointed by Pres. Ronald Reagan, was the first Asian American (Asian Indian–American) to sit on the Equal Employment Opportunity Commission.

Notable First: 1977

Patsy Takemoto Mink, (D) Hawaii, appointed by Pres. Jimmy Carter, was the first Asian American woman to serve as assistant secretary of state.

Asian Americans at the National Party Level

As shown by the sparse statistics below, the involvement of Asian Americans on the national scene of American politics has thus far been dismal. This can be certain to change, however, as both major political parties seek to increase their share of minority voters in an increasingly less white United States.

Notable First: 1972

Patsy Takemoto Mink, Hawaii, a four-term member of the U.S. House of Representatives, formally entered the presidential race and appeared on the ballot for the Oregon Democratic presidential primary. She withdrew from the race shortly after winning less than 2 percent of the vote in the Oregon primary.

Notable First: 1968

Daniel K. Inouye, Hawaii, a first-term U.S. senator of Japanese American descent, delivered the keynote address at the Democratic National Convention, the first Asian American accorded that honor by either major political party.

Notable First: 1964

Hiram L. Fong, Hawaii, a two-term U.S. senator of Chinese American descent, had his name placed in nomination for president at the Republican National Convention, the first Asian American to be nominated.

Asian American U.S. Senators in Chronological Order of Service

Senator	*Party*	*State*	*Ethnic Background*	*Dates Served*
1. Hiram Leong Fong	Republican	Hawaii	Chinese American	08/21/59–01/01/77

2. Daniel Ken Inouye	Democrat	Hawaii	Japanese American	01/03/63–
3. Samuel Ichiye Hayakawa	Republican	California	Japanese American	01/01/77–01/01/83
4. Masayuki "Spark" Matsunaga	Democrat	Hawaii	Japanese American	01/01/77–04/15/90

How They Assumed Office

1. Hiram Leong Fong, (R) Hawaii (Born: 1907)
Served: 08/21/59–01/01/77

Elected on August 1, 1959, in a special election after Hawaii was admitted to statehood. The new state was entitled to two U.S. senators, and both were selected in this special election. Fong won the "toss" to serve the longer term of the two victors, or until January 1, 1965. He won full six-year terms in 1964 and 1970 but declined to seek a third term in 1976 and retired.

Previous elected public office:
    Hawaii Territorial House of Representatives, 1938–1954
Subsequent elected public office: None

2. Daniel Ken Inouye, (D) Hawaii (Born: 1924)
Served: 01/03/63–

Elected on November 6, 1962, to a full six-year term. Inouye won additional six-year terms in 1968, 1974, 1980, 1986, 1992, and 1998.

Previous elected public office:
    Hawaii Territorial House of Representatives, 1954–1958
    Hawaii Territorial Senate, 1958–1959
    U.S. House of Representatives, 1959–1963

3. Samuel Ichiye Hayakawa, (R) California (Born: 1906; Died: 1992)
Served: 01/01/77–01/01/83

Elected on November 2, 1976, to a full six-year term. Hayakawa, who earned the nickname "Sleeping Sam" for his tendency to doze off on the floor of the U.S. Senate during debates, did not seek reelection to a second term.

Previous and subsequent elected public office: None

4. Masayuki "Spark" Matsunaga, (D) Hawaii (Born: 1916; Died: 1990)
Served: 01/01/77–04/15/90

Elected on November 2, 1976, to a full six-year term. Matsunaga won additional six-year terms in 1982 and 1988 before dying in office in 1990.

Previous elected public office:
  Hawaii Territorial House of Representatives, 1954–1959
  U.S. House of Representatives, 1963–1977

Asian American U.S. Senatorial Statistics

Longest Tenure of an Asian American Senator

Daniel K. Inouye, (D) Hawaii, who was sworn in on January 3, 1963, has served six complete six-year terms and is beginning his seventh term.

Shortest Tenure of an Asian American Senator

Samuel I. Hayakawa, (R) California, who served only one six-year term (January 1, 1977–January 1, 1983).

First Asian American Senator to Chair a U.S. Senate Committee

Daniel K. Inouye, (D) Hawaii, was the first Asian American to chair a committee in the U.S. Senate, when he assumed the chairmanship of the U.S. Select Committee on Indian Affairs in 1987. The committee was later made a "permanent" committee, named the U.S. Senate Committee on Indian Affairs.

First Succession of One Asian American Senator by Another

Masayuki "Spark" Matsunaga, (D) Hawaii, was sworn in on January 1, 1977, to the seat formerly held by **Hiram Fong**, (R) Hawaii, which marked the first succession of one Asian American U.S. senator by another.

Two Asian American Women Who Tried to Become U.S. Senators but Failed

Patsy Takemoto Mink, (D) Hawaii, who held one of the state's two seats in the U.S. House of Representatives, ran as a candidate for the U.S. Senate nomination in the 1976 Democratic primary. She lost the nomination to Masayuki "Spark" Matsunaga, who held Hawaii's other U.S. House seat. After her senatorial primary defeat, Mink served on the Honolulu city council, then returned again to a seat in the U.S. House in 1990.

Patricia F. Saiki, (R) Hawaii, who had been elected to the U.S. House in 1986, was the Republican candidate in 1990 for the U.S. Senate seat left open by the death of Sen. Masayuki "Spark" Matsunaga in 1989. After she failed in that election, Saiki competed as the Republican nominee in the 1994 Hawaii gubernatorial race, where she lost again.

Asian American U.S. Senatorial Election Statistics

The following section provides voting statistics on those Asian American senators who contested elections, including primaries, primary runoffs, and general elections. Names in this section appear in chronological order of senatorial service, from earliest to most recent.

Hiram Leong Fong, (R) Hawaii

1970	General	Hiram L. Fong (R)	124,163	51.6%
		Cecil Heftel (D)	116,597	48.4%
1964	General	Hiram L. Fong (R)	110,747	53.0%
		Thomas P. Gill (D)	96,789	46.4%
1959	General	Hiram L. Fong (R)	81,161	52.9%
		Frank Fasi (D)	77,647	47.1%

Daniel Ken Inouye, (D) Hawaii

1998	General	Daniel K. Inouye (D)	305,410	79.0%
		Crystal Young (R)	68,371	18.0%
		Others		3.0%
1998	Democratic Primary	Daniel K. Inouye	109,128	89.0%
		Richard Thompson	8,484	7.0%
		Others		4.0%
1992	General	Daniel K. Inouye (D)	208,266	57.0%
		Rick Reed (R)	97,928	27.0%
		Linda B. Martin (Green)	49,921	14.0%
1992	Democratic Primary	Daniel K. Inouye	94,827	79.0%
		Wayne K. Nishiki	25,782	21.0%
1986	General	Daniel K. Inouye (D)	241,887	74.0%
		Frank Hutchinson (R)	86,910	26.0%
1980	General	Daniel K. Inouye (D)	224,485	78.0%
		Cooper Brown (R)	53,068	18.0%
1974	General	Daniel K. Inouye (D)	207,454	82.9%
		Minor parties only	42,767	17.1%
1968	General	Daniel K. Inouye (D)	189,248	83.4%
		Wayne Thiessen (R)	34,008	15.0%
1962	General	Daniel K. Inouye (D)	136,294	69.4%
		Ben Dillingham (R)	60,067	30.6%

Samuel Ichiye Hayakawa, (R) California

1976	General	Samuel I. Hayakawa (R)	3,748,973	52.0%
		John V. Tunney (D)	3,502,862	48.0%
1976	Republican Primary	Samuel I. Hayakawa	886,743	38.0%
		Robert "Bob" Finch	614,240	27.0%
		Alonzo Bell	532,969	23.0%

Masayuki "Spark" Matsunaga, (D) Hawaii

1988	General	Masayuki "Spark" Matsunaga (D)	247,941	77.0%
		Maria Hustace (R)	66,987	21.0%
1982	General	Masayuki "Spark" Matsunaga (D)	245,386	80.0%
		Clarence J. Brown (R)	52,071	17.0%
1976	General	Masayuki "Spark" Matsunaga (D)	162,305	66.0%
		William F. Quinn (R)	122,724	34.0%
1976	Democratic Primary	Masayuki "Spark" Matsunaga	109,731	52.0%
		Patsy Takemoto Mink	84,732	40.0%

Chronology of All Asian American Candidates for U.S. Senate (denotes winner)*

1959	*Hiram L. Fong	Republican	Hawaii	Chinese American
	Wilfred C. Tsukiyama	Republican	Hawaii	Japanese American
1962	*Daniel K. Inouye[1]	Democrat	Hawaii	Japanese American
1964	*Hiram L. Fong	Republican	Hawaii	Chinese American
1968	*Daniel K. Inouye	Democrat	Hawaii	Japanese American
1970	*Hiram L. Fong	Republican	Hawaii	Chinese American
1974	*Daniel K. Inouye	Democrat	Hawaii	Japanese American
1976	*Samuel I. Hayakawa	Republican	California	Japanese American
	*Masayuki "Spark" Matsunaga[2]	Democrat	Hawaii	Japanese American
1980	*Daniel K. Inouye	Democrat	Hawaii	Japanese American
1982	*Masayuki "Spark" Matsunaga	Democrat	Hawaii	Japanese American
1986	*Daniel K. Inouye	Democrat	Hawaii	Japanese American
1988	*Masayuki "Spark" Matsunaga	Democrat	Hawaii	Japanese American
	Shien-Biau (S. B.) Woo	Democrat	Delaware	Chinese American
1990	Patricia F. Saiki[3]	Republican	Hawaii	Japanese American
1992	*Daniel K. Inouye	Democrat	Hawaii	Japanese American
1998	Matthew Fong	Republican	California	Chinese American
	*Daniel K. Inouye	Democrat	Hawaii	Japanese American
	John Lim	Republican	Oregon	Korean American

---

[1]Inouye had previously served two terms (1959–1963) in the U.S. House.

[2]Matsunaga had previously served seven terms (1963–1977) in the U.S. House.

[3]Saiki had previously served two terms (1987–1991) in the U.S. House.

Asian Americans Serving in the U.S. House of Representatives

106th Congress (1999–2001)

State	District	Name	Party Affiliation	Ethnic Background
California	5	Robert Matsui	Democrat	Japanese American
Hawaii	2	Patsy Takemoto Mink	Democrat	Japanese American
Oregon	1	David Wu	Democrat	Chinese American

Asian American Incumbent Not Returning from the 105th Congress

Jay Kim, (R) California–41st, was defeated in the Republican primary.

105th Congress (1997–1999)

State	District	Name	Party Affiliation	Ethnic Background
California	5	Robert Matsui	Democrat	Japanese American
California	41	Jay Kim	Republican	Korean American
Hawaii	2	Patsy Takemoto Mink	Democrat	Japanese American

104th Congress (1995–1997)

State	District	Name	Party Affiliation	Ethnic Background
California	5	Robert Matsui	Democrat	Japanese American
California	15	Norman Mineta[4]	Democrat	Japanese American
California	41	Jay Kim	Republican	Korean American
Hawaii	2	Patsy Takemoto Mink	Democrat	Japanese American

Notable First: 1995

In the December 12, 1995, special election to fill Norman Mineta's seat, which was based in San Jose, California, home of one of the largest concentrations of Vietnamese Americans in the U.S., **Linh Dao**, a businesswoman running as an Independent, became the first Vietnamese American to run for a seat in the U.S. House of Representatives. Although she ran far behind the Democratic and Republican nominees, she still managed to win 5 percent of the vote.

103rd Congress (1993–1995)

State	District	Name	Party Affiliation	Ethnic Background
California	5	Robert Matsui	Democrat	Japanese American
California	15	Norman Mineta	Democrat	Japanese American

---

[4]Mineta resigned on October 10, 1995, to accept a position in private industry.

| California | 41 | Jay Kim | Republican | Korean American |
| Hawaii | 2 | Patsy Takemoto Mink | Democrat | Japanese American |

Achieving Power

Norman Mineta, (D) Hawaii, became chair of the U.S. House Committee on Public Works and Transportation, the first Asian American to chair a House committee.

102nd Congress (1991–1993)

State	District	Name	Party Affiliation	Ethnic Background
California	5	Robert Matsui	Democrat	Japanese American
California	15	Norman Mineta	Democrat	Japanese American
Hawaii	2	Patsy Takemoto Mink	Democrat	Japanese American

Asian American Incumbent Not Returning from the 101st Congress

Patricia F. Saiki, (R) Hawaii–1st, lost her bid for a U.S. Senate seat.

101st Congress (1989–1991)

State	District	Name	Party Affiliation	Ethnic Background
California	5	Robert Matsui	Democrat	Japanese American
California	15	Norman Mineta	Democrat	Japanese American
Hawaii	1	Patricia F. Saiki	Republican	Japanese American
Hawaii	2	Patsy Takemoto Mink[5]	Democrat	Japanese American

100th Congress (1987–1989)

State	District	Name	Party Affiliation	Ethnic Background
California	5	Robert Matsui	Democrat	Japanese American
California	15	Norman Mineta	Democrat	Japanese American
Hawaii	1	Patricia F. Saiki	Republican	Japanese American

99th Congress (1985–1987)

State	District	Name	Party Affiliation	Ethnic Background
California	5	Robert Matsui	Democrat	Japanese American
California	15	Norman Mineta	Democrat	Japanese American

---

[5]Mink was selected in a special September 1990 election to fill the seat of an incumbent who had resigned; she had previously served six terms (1965–1977) in the U.S. House.

98th Congress (1983–1985)

State	District	Name	Party Affiliation	Ethnic Background
California	5	Robert Matsui	Democrat	Japanese American
California	15	Norman Mineta	Democrat	Japanese American

97th Congress (1981–1983)

State	District	Name	Party Affiliation	Ethnic Background
California	5	Robert Matsui[6]	Democrat	Japanese American
California	15	Norman Mineta	Democrat	Japanese American

96th Congress (1979–1981)

State	District	Name	Party Affiliation	Ethnic Background
California	5	Robert Matsui	Democrat	Japanese American
California	15	Norman Mineta	Democrat	Japanese American

95th Congress (1977–1979)

State	District	Name	Party Affiliation	Ethnic Background
California	15	Norman Mineta	Democrat	Japanese American

Asian American Incumbents Not Returning from the 94th Congress

Masayuki "Spark" Matsunaga, (D) Hawaii–1st, won a U.S. Senate seat.
Patsy Takemoto Mink, (D) Hawaii–2nd, lost the Democratic primary for the U.S. Senate nomination.

94th Congress (1975–1977)

State	District	Name	Party Affiliation	Ethnic Background
California	15	Norman Mineta	Democrat	Japanese American
Hawaii	1	Masayuki "Spark" Matsunaga	Democrat	Japanese American
Hawaii	2	Patsy Takemoto Mink	Democrat	Japanese American

93rd Congress (1973–1975)

State	District	Name	Party Affiliation	Ethnic Background
Hawaii	1	Masayuki "Spark" Matsunaga	Democrat	Japanese American
Hawaii	2	Patsy Takemoto Mink	Democrat	Japanese American

---

[6]In 1971, when he was elected mayor of San Jose, California, Matsui became the first Japanese American elected mayor of a larger American city.

92nd Congress (1971–1973)

State	District	Name	Party Affiliation	Ethnic Background
Hawaii	1	Masayuki "Spark" Matsunaga	Democrat	Japanese American
Hawaii	2	Patsy Takemoto Mink	Democrat	Japanese American

91st Congress (1969–1971)

State	District	Name	Party Affiliation	Ethnic Background
Hawaii	1	Masayuki "Spark" Matsunaga	Democrat	Japanese American
Hawaii	2	Patsy Takemoto Mink	Democrat	Japanese American

90th Congress (1967–1969)

State	District	Name	Party Affiliation	Ethnic Background
Hawaii	1	Masayuki "Spark" Matsunaga	Democrat	Japanese American
Hawaii	2	Patsy Takemoto Mink	Democrat	Japanese American

89th Congress (1965–1967)

State	District	Name	Party Affiliation	Ethnic Background
Hawaii	AL	Masayuki "Spark" Matsunaga	Democrat	Japanese American
Hawaii	AL	Patsy Takemoto Mink	Democrat	Japanese American

88th Congress (1963–1965)

State	District	Name	Party Affiliation	Ethnic Background
Hawaii	AL	Masayuki "Spark" Matsunaga	Democrat	Japanese American

Asian American Incumbents Not Returning from the 87th Congress

Daniel K. Inouye, (D) Hawaii–AL, won a seat in the U.S. Senate.
Dalip S. Saund, (D) California–31st, was defeated in the general election.

87th Congress (1961–1963)

State	District	Name	Party Affiliation	Ethnic Background
California	29	Dalip S. Saund	Democrat	Asian Indian–American
Hawaii	AL	Daniel K. Inouye	Democrat	Japanese American

86th Congress (1959–1961)

State	District	Name	Party Affiliation	Ethnic Background
California	29	Dalip S. Saund	Democrat	Asian Indian–American
Hawaii	AL	Daniel K. Inouye[7]	Democrat	Japanese American

85th Congress (1957–1959)

State	District	Name	Party Affiliation	Ethnic Background
California	29	Dalip S. Saund	Democrat	Asian Indian–American

Notable First

Dalip S. Saund, (D) California–29th, an Asian Indian–American, became the first Asian American to serve as a full member of the U.S. House. Previously, he had been the first Asian Indian–American judge in the U.S.

Notable First: 1907

Benito Legarda and **Pablo Ocampo**, both elected as resident commissioners from the Philippine Islands, were the first Asian Americans to serve in the U.S. Congress.

Asian American Governors in Chronological Order of Service

1. George Ryoichi Ariyoshi	Democrat	Hawaii	Japanese American	10/01/73–12/02/86
2. Benjamin Jerome Cayetano	Democrat	Hawaii	Filipino American	12/03/94–
3. Gary Faye Locke	Democrat	Washington	Chinese American	01/15/97–

How They Assumed Office

1. George Ryoichi Ariyoshi, (D) Hawaii (Born: 1926)
Served: 10/01/73–12/02/86

Succeeded on October 1, 1973, to the governorship after the resignation of ailing Gov. John Burns (D). Ariyoshi had a long history of service within Hawaii's Democratic Party and had been lieutenant governor for three years when he became governor. In 1974 and again in 1978 he was easily elected to full four-year terms. But in 1982 he was challenged in the Democratic primary by the female lieutenant governor, Jean Sadako King. Ariyoshi beat her, then triumphed

---

[7]Inouye was elected in a special election in September 1959 when Hawaii was admitted as the fiftieth state.

again in the general election to win a third term. He retired to private life after the third full term ended in 1986.

Previous elected public office:
  Hawaii Territorial House of Representatives, 1954–1958
  Hawaii Territorial Senate, 1958–1959
  Hawaii State Senate, 1959–1970
  Hawaii Lieutenant Governor, 1970–1974
Subsequent elected political office: None

2. Benjamin Jerome Cayetano, (D) Hawaii (Born: 1939)
Served: 12/03/94–

Elected on November 8, 1994, to a four-year term. Reelected to another term in 1998.

Previous elected political office:
  Hawaii House of Representatives, 1975–1978
  Hawaii State Senate, 1979–1986
  Hawaii Lieutenant Governor, 1986–1994

3. Gary Faye Locke, (D) Washington (Born: 1950)
Served: 01/15/97–

Elected on November 5, 1996, to a four-year term.

Previous elected political office:
  Washington State House of Representatives, 1981–1993
  King County, Washington, Chief Executive, 1993–1997

Asian American Gubernatorial Statistics

Longest Tenure of an Asian American Governor

George R. Ariyoshi, (D) Hawaii, who served thirteen years, two months, and one day during 1973–1986.

Asian American Gubernatorial Election Statistics

The following section provides voting statistics on those Asian American governors who contested elections, including primaries, primary runoffs, and general elections. Names in this section appear in chronological order of gubernatorial service, from earliest to most recent.

George Ryoichi Ariyoshi, (D) Hawaii

1982	General	George R. Ariyoshi (D)	141,043	45.0%
		Frank Fasi (I)	89,303	29.0%
		D. G. Anderson (R)	81,507	26.0%

1982	Democratic Primary	George R. Ariyoshi	128,993	54.0%
		Jean S. King	106,935	45.0%
1978	General	George R. Ariyoshi (D)	153,394	55.0%
		John R. Leopold (R)	124,610	45.0%
1978	Democratic Primary	George R. Ariyoshi	130,527	51.0%
		Frank Fasi	126,903	49.0%
1974	General	George R. Ariyoshi (D)	136,262	54.6%
		Randolph Crossley (R)	113,388	45.4%
1974	Democratic Primary	George R. Ariyoshi	71,319	36.0%
		Frank Fasi	62,023	31.0%
		Thomas P. Gill	59,280	30.0%

Benjamin Jerome Cayetano, (D) Hawaii

1998	General	Benjamin J. Cayetano (D)	197,639	50.0%
		Linda C. Lingle (R)	192,582	49.0%
		Others		1.0%
1998	Democratic Primary	Benjamin J. Cayetano	unopposed	
1994	General	Benjamin J. Cayetano (D)	134,978	37.0%
		Frank Fasi (I)	113,158	31.0%
		Patricia F. Saiki (R)	107,908	29.0%
1994	Democratic Primary	Benjamin J. Cayetano	110,489	55.0%
		John "Jack" Lewin	76,606	38.0%

Gary Faye Locke, (D) Washington

1996	General	Gary F. Locke (D)	1,038,108	58.0%
		Ellen Craswell (R)	721,994	42.0%
1996	Primary[8]	Gary F. Locke (D)	192,886	24.0%
		Norm Rice (D)	146,705	18.0%
		Ellen Craswell (R)	121,337	15.0%
		Dale Foreman (R)	108,960	14.0%
		Jay Inslee (D)	81,355	10.0%
		Norm Maleng (R)	60,839	8.0%
		Others		11.0%

Chronology of All Asian American Candidates for Governor
(denotes winner)*

1974	*George R. Ariyoshi	Democrat	Hawaii	Japanese American
1978	*George R. Ariyoshi	Democrat	Hawaii	Japanese American
1982	*George R. Ariyoshi	Democrat	Hawaii	Japanese American
1994	*Benjamin J. Cayetano	Democrat	Hawaii	Filipino American
	Patricia F. Saiki[9]	Republican	Hawaii	Japanese American

[8]Washington uses a variety of the "jungle" primary, where all candidates, regardless of party, are listed on one ballot. The holder of the highes vote in each party advances to the general election.

[9]Saiki had previously served two terms (1987–1991) in the U.S. House; she was also unsuccessful as the Republican nominee for the U.S. Senate in 1990.

| 1996 | *Gary F. Locke | Democract | Washington | Chinese American |
| 1998 | *Benjamin J. Cayetano | Democrat | Hawaii | Filipino American |

Asian American Who Have Held Other State Executive Offices[10]

California

Secretary of State
March Fong Eu (D), 1974–1994[11]

Treasurer
Matthew K. Fong (R), 1995–1999[12]

Delaware

Lieutenant Governor
Shien-Biau (S. B.) Woo (D), 1985–1989[13]

Hawaii

Lieutenant Governor
Mazie K. Hirono (D), 1994–

Benjamin Jerome Cayetano (D),
     1986–1994[14]
Jean Sadako King (D), 1978–1982[15]
Nelson K. Doi (D), 1974–1978
George R. Ariyoshi (D), 1970–1973[16]
Andrew Ing (D), 1966

Attorney General
Shiro Kashiwa (D), 1959–1963

Nevada

Secretary of State
Cheryl Lau (R), 1991–1995[17]

Asian Americans in State Legislatures

Completely reliable statistics on Asian Americans serving in state legislatures are difficult to obtain, since few are serving at present outside of Hawaii, which has reportedly quit keeping such ethnic statistics. Usually most tallies in the other states do not even list Asian Americans as a separate category, instead lumping them with other minorities under "Other."

---

[10]These offices are a combination of election by popular vote, election by the state legislature, and appointment by the governor.

[11]Eu resigned in 1994 to accept an appointment as U.S. ambassador to Micronesia.

[12]Fong is the son of March Fong Eu, but they belong to different political parties.

[13]Woo was unsuccessful in 1988 as the Democratic nominee for U.S. Senate.

[14]Cayetano was elected governor in 1994.

[15]In 1982 King challenged incumbent Governor Ariyoshi in the gubernatorial primary in an effort to deny him renomination; she lost.

[16]Ariyoshi also served as governor (1973–1986).

[17]Lau was unsuccessful in the 1994 Republican primary for the gubernatorial nomination.

Notable First: 1994

Nimi McConigley (R), elected to Wyoming's house of representatives, the first female Asian Indian–American elected to a state legislature.

Notable First: 1991

Kumar P. Barve (D), elected to the Maryland house of assembly, the first Asian Indian–American elected to a state legislature.

Notable First: 1990

David Valderrama (D), elected to the Maryland house of assembly, the first Filipino American elected to a state legislature on the U.S. mainland.

Notable First: 1974

Thelma Garcia Buchholdt (D), elected to Alaska's house of representatives, the first Filipino American woman elected to a state legislature in the U.S. The second was probably **Elizabeth "Liz" Allan-Hodge** (R), who served as an Idaho state representative (1985–1991).

Notable First: 1966

Moni Minn (R), elected to Hawaii's house of representatives, the first Korean American woman elected to a state legislature in the U.S. Minn had been appointed earlier in the year to fill the seat of her deceased husband.

Notable Firsts: 1962

Alfred H. Song (D), elected to the California senate, the first Korean American elected to a state legislature. He was also the first Asian American to sit in that state's upper chamber.

Benjamin Menor (D), elected to the Hawaii senate, the first Filipino American elected to a state senate in the U.S.

Seiji Horiuchi, elected to the Colorado legislature, the first Japanese American elected to a state legislative seat in the continental U.S.

Notable First: 1956

Patsy T. Mink (D), elected to Hawaii's house of representatives, the first Japanese American woman to serve in a territorial legislature.

Notable First: 1955

William Heen (R), elected president pro tem of the Hawaii territorial senate, the first Chinese American elected to head a state/territorial senate.

Notable First: 1954

Peter Ajúda (D), elected to Hawaii's house of representatives, the first Filipino American elected to serve in a territorial legislature.

Notable First: 1949

Hiram Fong (R), elected as speaker of Hawaii's house of representatives, the first Chinese American to head a territorial legislature.

Notable First: 1946

Wing F. Ong (D), elected to Arizona's house of representatives, the first Chinese American elected official in the continental United States and the first Asian American elected to a state legislative house.

Notable Firsts: 1930

Tasaku Oka (R) and **Masayoshi "Andy" Yamashiro** (R), elected to Hawaii's territorial house of representatives, the first Japanese Americans elected to a territorial legislature.

Notable First: 1929

Paul A. Low (R), elected to Hawaii's territorial senate, the first Chinese American elected to a territorial senate.

Notable First: 1926

Yew Char (R), elected to Hawaii's territorial house of representatives, the first Chinese American elected to a territorial legislative body.

Notable First: 1922

James Handa (R), a candidate for Hawaii's territorial house of representatives, the first Asian American to seek a legislative seat in the U.S.

Asian American Speakers of State Lower Legislative Chambers

Calvin Say, (D) Hawaii, 1998–
Richard Kawakami, (D) Hawaii, 1987
James Wakatsuki, (D) Hawaii, 1975–1980
Tadao Beppu, (D) Hawaii, 1968–1974

Asian Americans in the Judiciary

Notable First: 1997

Thang Nguyen Barrett, California, became the first Vietnamese American judge in the U.S., when he assumed his position on the bench in the Santa Clara County municipal court.

Notable First: 1993

Paula Nakayama, Hawaii, was appointed justice on the Hawaii Supreme Court, the first Japanese American woman to reach that position on a state supreme court.

Notable First: 1993

Ronald T. Y. Moon, Hawaii, was appointed chief justice of the Hawaii Supreme Court, the first Korean American to reach that position on a state supreme court.

Notable First: 1989

Joyce Kennard, (R) California, of part Indonesian descent, was appointed by Gov. George Deukmejian (R) to the California Supreme Court, the first Asian American woman to serve on a state supreme court.

Notable First: 1974

Benjamin Menor, (D) Hawaii, was appointed to that state's supreme court, the first Filipino American to be named a state supreme court justice in the U.S.

Notable First: 1972

Shiro Kashiwa, Hawaii, was appointed to the U.S. Court of Claims in Washington, D.C., the first Japanese American federal judge.

Notable First: 1971

Herbert Y. C. Choy, (R) Hawaii, was appointed by Pres. Richard Nixon to the U.S. Court of Appeals for the Ninth Circuit and became the first Korean American federal judge. Having discounted William Heen (see **Notable First: 1917**), many also credit Choy as being the first Asian American federal judge.

Notable Firsts: 1959

Delbert F. Wong, (D) California, was appointed by Gov. Edmund Brown (D) to the Los Angeles municipal court, becoming the first Chinese American judge in the continental United States.
Wilfred C. Tsukiyama, (R) Hawaii, was appointed chief justice of Hawaii's supreme court, the first Japanese American to become chief justice of a state supreme court.

Notable First: 1956

Masaji Marumoto was appointed as a justice on Hawaii's supreme court, the first Japanese American to become justice on a state or territorial supreme court.

Notable First: 1953

John Aiso, (R) California, was appointed to the Los Angeles municipal court, the first Japanese American judge in the mainland United States.

Notable First: 1950

Chuck Mau was appointed as a state circuit court judge, the first Chinese American state judge.
Dalip Singh Saund, (D) California, was elected judge of the Westmoreland, California, judicial district, the first Asian Indian–American judge in the U.S. Six years later Saund became the first Asian Indian–American (and Asian American) elected to the U.S. House of Representatives.

Notable First: 1917

William H. Heen, of Chinese-Hawaiian heritage, was appointed judge of the first circuit court in Hawaii by Pres. Woodrow Wilson, becoming the first Asian American federal judge.

Asian Americans at the Local Level

Notable First: 1993

Somsanith Khamuongsa, Virginia, became the first Laotian American appointed to public office in the U.S. when he was made a county magistrate of Fairfax County, Virginia.

Notable First: 1994

Gary F. Locke (D) became head of King County (Seattle), Washington, the first Chinese American to lead a county government in the U.S.

Notable First: 1992

Tony Lam (R) was elected to the city council of Westminster, California, the first Vietnamese American elected to public office in the U.S.

Notable Firsts: 1992

Arun Jhaveri was elected mayor of Burien, Washington, by his fellow city councilmembers, and **John Abraham** (R) was elected mayor of Teaneck Township, New Jersey, by his fellow councilmembers; they became the first Asian Indian–American mayors in the U.S.

Notable Firsts: 1991

Jay Kim (R) was elected mayor of Diamond Bar, California, becoming the first Korean American mayor in the U.S.

Choua Lee won an at-large seat on the St. Paul, Minnesota, school board, becoming the first female Hmong American elected to public office in the U.S.

Notable First: 1983

Lily Chen (D) served as mayor of Monterey Park, California, becoming the first female Chinese American mayor in the U.S.

Notable First: 1980

Carol Kawanami was elected mayor of Villa Park, California, becoming the first female Japanese American to hold that post in the U.S.

Notable First: 1975

Eduardo E. Malaprit was elected mayor of Kauai, Hawaii, becoming the first Filipino American mayor in the U.S.

Notable First: 1964

Shunichi Kimura was elected mayor of Hawai'i County, Hawaii, becoming the first Japanese American mayor in the U.S.

Notable First: 1948

Daniel Liu was appointed chief of police in Honolulu, Hawaii, becoming the first Chinese American police chief in the U.S.

Notable First: 1930

Noboru Miyake (D) was elected county supervisor in Kauai, Hawaii, becoming the first Japanese American elected to the governing body of a county jurisdiction.

Native Minorities in American Politics

Comments on Native Minorities

This section includes information on native minorities such as Native Americans, Native Hawaiians, and Native Alaskans. Several states did not permit Native Americans to vote in state and local elections, claiming that due to their unique federal status they were noncitizens. Barriers in the last two states (Arizona in 1948, New Mexico in 1962) that had limited Native American suffrage were finally removed as a result of successful lawsuits.

A Brief Chronology

1853 First Native American governor

William Walker, a member of the Wyandot Huran tribe is appointed to serve as governor of the Nebraska territory

1887 First native minority U.S. senator

Matthew S. Quay, (R) Pennsylvania, is credited by some authorities as being the first native minority U.S. senator because of some possible Native American ancestry. Others debunk that as unsubstantiated legend, saying he was merely honorably inducted into a "tribe."

1892 First Native American elected to the U.S. House of Representatives

Charles B. Curtis, (R) Kansas, was elected to his first term in the U.S. House of Representatives.

1903 First Native Hawaiian member of the U.S. House of Representatives

Prince Jonah Kuhio Kalanianaole, (R) Hawaii, was elected as a delegate from that territory.

This section includes only brief mention of native minority people elected in the territories of Guam and American Samoa, because they are not states.

227

1907 First undisputed Native American elected to the U.S. Senate

Charles B. Curtis, (R) Kansas, a seven-term member of the U.S. House, was elected to his first term in the U.S. Senate.

1922 First Native American woman appointed as tribal chief

Alice Brown Davis, Florida, appointed as chief of the Seminole Nation in Florida by Pres. Warren G. Harding.

1924 First Native American woman elected to a state legislature

Cora Reynolds Anderson, (R) Michigan, was elected to Michigan's house of representatives.

1925 First Native Hawaiian woman elected to a state/territorial legislature

Rosalie Enos Lyons Keliinoi, (R) Hawaii, was elected to the territory of Hawaii's lower legislative house.

1950 First Native American elected governor

Johnston Murray, Democrat, was elected governor of Oklahoma.

1973 First Native Guamanian (Chamorro) to serve in the U.S. House of Representatives

Antonio Borja Won Pat, (D) Guam, elected as delegate from that territory.

First Inuit (Native Alaskan) to receive a congressional nomination from a major political party

Emil Notti, (D) Alaska, was nominated for the U.S. House of Representatives.

1976 First Native Hawaiian elected U.S. representative

Daniel Akaka, (D) Hawaii, was elected to the U.S. House of Representatives.

1981 First Samoan to serve in the U.S. House of Representatives

Fofo I. F. Sunia, (D) American Samoa, elected as delegate from that territory.

1986 First Native Hawaiian elected governor

John D. Waihee III, (D) Hawaii, was elected governor.

1990 First Native Hawaiian member of the U.S. Senate

Daniel Akaka, (D) Hawaii, a seven-term member of the U.S. House, was appointed to the U.S. Senate.

1992 First Native American woman to receive a congressional nomination from a major party

Ada Deer, (D) Wisconsin, was nominated for a seat in the U.S. House of Representatives.

Native Minorities and Political Power

The following chart (by state) details the total number of native minorities who have served their states in three of the most powerful positions in U.S. politics: governor, U.S. Senate (both appointed and elected), and U.S. House of Representatives.

State	Governor	U.S. Senate	U.S. House
California	-	-	1
Colorado	-	1	1
Hawaii	1	1	1
Kansas	-	1	1
Oklahoma	1	1	5
Pennsylvania	-	1	-
South Dakota	-	-	1
Total Native Minorities Who Have Served	2	5	10

Best and Worst States for Native Minorities Achieving Political Power

Oklahoma would have to be considered the best state for native minorities in achieving political power. **Alaska**, where they compose almost 16 percent of the population but exert little political power, would have to be considered the worst.

Native Minorities in the U.S. Cabinet

No person of recorded native minority descent has yet served in a presidential cabinet.

Native Minorities in the Executive Branch

Notable First: 1993

Ada Deer, a Menominee from Wisconsin, became the first female Native American to be appointed assistant secretary for Indian affairs in the U.S. Department of the Interior.

Notable First: 1869

Ely Samuel Parker, a Seneca, was appointed commissioner of Indian affairs in the U.S. Department of the Interior, the first Native American to hold the position.

Native Minorities at the National Party Level

Notable First: 1928

Charles B. Curtis, (R) Kansas, a four-term U.S. senator of Native American descent (Kaw), was elected vice president on the Republican ticket with Herbert Hoover. He and Hoover were defeated for reelection in 1932 by the Democratic duo of Franklin D. Roosevelt and John Nance Garner.

Native Minority U.S. Senators

1. Matthew Stanley Quay[1]	Republican	Pennsylvania	Native American (Abenaki or Seneca)	03/04/1887–03/03/1899, 01/17/01–05/28/04
2. Charles Brent Curtis	Republican	Kansas	Native American (Kaw)	03/20/07–03/20/13, 03/04/15–03/03/29
3. Robert Latham Owen	Democrat	Oklahoma	Native American (Cherokee)	12/11/07–03/03/25
4. Daniel Kahikina Akaka	Democrat	Hawaii	Native Hawaiian	04/28/90–
5. Ben Nighthorse Campbell	Republican	Colorado	Native American (Northern Cheyenne)	01/05/93–

Note: A few references on prominent Native Americans include Hiram Rhodes Revels, (R) Mississippi, who was reputed to have Lumbee-Croatan ancestry. He appears in this book under the listings for African Americans, where he most commonly appears in other reference material.

How They Assumed Office

1. **Matthew Stanley Quay**, (R) Pennsylvania (Born: 1833; Died: 1904)
   Served: 03/04/1887–03/03/1899, 01/17/01–05/28/04

Elected in 1887 by the Pennsylvania legislature for a full six-year term and again in 1893 for a second one. When the legislature adjourned in 1899 without electing a senator for the new term beginning March 4, 1899, Quay was appointed by the governor on April 21, 1899, to fill the vacancy. He presented his credentials for what would have been his third term when the U.S. Senate convened on December 25, 1899, but was not permitted to take his seat. On April 24, 1900, the seat was finally declared vacant. Quay was again elected by the state legislature to fill the vacancy and resumed his seat on January 17, 1901, this time being seated by the U.S. Senate without any problem.

Previous elected political office:
   Pennsylvania House of Representatives, 1865–1867

---

[1]As the United States Senate Historical Office states, "Pinning down Senator Quay's ancestry has posed a longstanding problem for historians. His immediate forbears were apparently of Scotch-Irish descent; one biographer, while not discounting the possibility that some of the Senator's ancestors were of Native American descent, has stated that Quay's Indian ancestry is an 'unsubstantiated legend.'"

Pennsylvania Secretary of Commonwealth, 1872–1878, 1879–1882
Pennsylvania State Treasurer, 1885–1887
Subsequent elected political office: None

2. **Charles Brent Curtis**,[2] (R) Kansas (Born: 1860; Died: 1936)
Served: 03/20/07–03/20/13, 03/04/15–03/03/29

Elected in 1906 by the Kansas legislature for a full six-year term. Due to a change in party control of the Kansas legislature, Curtis was not reelected for a second term. In 1915 he was appointed by the governor of Kansas to another full six-year term. He won reelection by popular vote to full terms in 1920 and 1926. Curtis resigned his Senate seat in 1929 after he was elected vice president under Herbert Hoover on the Republican ticket in 1928.

Previous elected political office:
    U.S. House of Representatives, 1893–1906
Subsequent elected political office:
    Vice President, 1929–1933

3. **Robert Latham Owen**, (D) Oklahoma (Born: 1856; Died: 1947)
Served: 12/11/1907–03/03/1925

Elected in 1907 by the Oklahoma legislature as one of that state's first two U.S. senators. He received the "short term," which was for five years. Owen was reelected by the state legislature again in 1912 for another full term, then won a third full term in 1918 by popular vote. He retired and did not seek reelection for a fourth term.

Previous elected and subsequent political office: None

4. **Daniel Kahikina Akaka**, (D) Hawaii (Born: 1924)
Served: 04/28/90–

Received an interim appointment in late April 1990 from Gov. George R. Ariyoshi (D) to fill the seat of deceased Sen. Masayuki "Spark" Matsunaga (D). A special election was scheduled for November 1990 to fill the remainder—four years—of Matsunaga's term. Akaka won the special election, then won a full six-year term of his own in 1994.

Previous elected political office:
    U.S. House of Representatives, 1977–1990

5. **Ben Nighthorse Campbell**, (R) Colorado (Born: 1933)
Served: 01/05/93–

---

[2]It is an interesting historical note that Curtis, America's first Native American U.S. senator, was also the first senator to support an Equal Rights Amendment. He introduced the bill in the U.S. Senate in 1923. His cosponsor in the U.S. House of Representatives was Rep. Daniel R. Anthony Jr., (R) Kansas, a direct descendent of feminist Susan B. Anthony.

Elected on November 3, 1992, to a full six-year term as a Democrat. After the Republicans won control of the U.S. Senate in the November 1994 elections, Campbell waited until March 5, 1995, then switched his party affiliation to Republican. His move was rumored to have been brought about more because of personal conflicts with certain Democratic leaders in Colorado than because of ideology. Reelected to another term in 1998.

Previous elected political office:
    Colorado House of Representatives, 1982–1986
    U.S. House of Representatives, 1987–1992

Native Minority U.S. Senatorial Statistics

Longest Tenure of a Native Minority Senator

Charles B. Curtis, (R) Kansas, who served a total of twenty years.

Only Male Senator to Have Exclusively Had Female Challengers

Daniel K. Akaka, (D) Hawaii, is the only U.S. senator who has faced only female challengers in his U.S. Senate elections. In 1990, when he ran in the special election to retain his appointed seat and complete the remaining balance (four years) of Sen. Masayuki "Spark" Matsunaga's term, Akaka's challenger was U.S. Rep. Patricia F. Saiki, (R) Hawaii, who had served two terms in the U.S. House (1987–1991). Maria Hustace (R), a seventy-six-year-old rancher from the island of Molokai, was Akaka's challenger for the 1994 general election when he sought a full six-year term.

Native Minority U.S. Senatorial Election Statistics

The following section provides voting statistics on those native minority senators who contested elections, including primaries, primary runoffs, and general elections. Names in this section appear in chronological order of senatorial service, from earliest to most recent.

Robert Latham Owen, (D) Oklahoma

1918	General	Robert L. Owen (D)	105,050	58.0%
		Johnson (R)	77,188	42.0%
1912	General	Robert L. Owen (D)	126,407	60.0%
		Dickerson (R)	83,488	40.0%

Charles Brent Curtis, (R) Kansas

1926	General	Charles B. Curtis (R)	308,222	63.6%
		George Stephens (D)	168,446	34.7%
1920	General	Charles B. Curtis (R)	327,072	64.0%
		George H. Hodges (D)	170,443	33.4%
1914	General	Charles B. Curtis (R)	180,823	35.5%

		George A. Neeley (D)	176,929	34.8%
		Victor Murdoch (Prog.)	116,755	22.9%

Daniel Kahikina Akaka, (D) Hawaii

1994	General	Daniel K. Akaka (D)	256,189	72.0%
		Maria Hustace (R)	86,320	24.0%
1990	General	Daniel Akaka (D)	188,901	54.5%
		Patricia F. Saiki (R)	155,978	45.5%
1990	Democratic Primary	Daniel K. Akaka	180,235	91.0%
		Paul Snider	18,427	9.0%

Ben Nighthorse Campbell, (R)[3] Colorado

1998	General	Ben N. Campbell (R)	802,125	62.0%
		Dottie V. Lamm (D)	451,680	35.0%
		Others		3.0%
1998	Republican Primary	Ben N. Campbell	153,134	71.0%
		Bill Eggert	63,489	29.0%
1992	General	Ben N. Campbell (D)	803,725	52.0%
		Terry Considine (R)	662,893	43.0%
1992	Democratic Primary	Ben N. Campbell	117,634	46.0%
		Richard Lamm	93,599	36.0%
		Josie Heath	47,418	18.0%

Chronology of All Native Minority Candidates for U.S. Senate
(denotes winner)*

1912	*Robert L. Owen	Democrat	Oklahoma	Native American (Cherokee)
1914	*Charles B. Curtis	Republican	Kansas	Native American (Kaw)
1918	*Robert L. Owen	Democrat	Oklahoma	Native American (Cherokee)
1920	*Charles B. Curtis	Republican	Kansas	Native American (Kaw)
1926	*Charles B. Curtis	Republican	Kansas	Native American (Kaw)
1946	Will Rogers Jr.	Democrat	California	Native American (Cherokee)
1986	Frank Hutchinson[4]	Republican	Hawaii	Native American
1990	*Daniel K. Akaka	Democrat	Hawaii	Native Hawaiian
1992	*Ben N. Campbell	Democrat	Colorado	Native American (Northern Cheyenne)
1994	*Daniel K. Akaka	Democrat	Hawaii	Native Hawaiian
1998	*Ben N. Campbell	Republican	Colorado	Native American (Northern Cheyenne)

---

[3]Campbell switched to the Republican Party in 1995.

[4]When he was fourteen years old, Hutchinson became the first Native American to serve as a page in the U.S. Senate.

Native Minorities Serving in the U.S. House of Representatives

State	District	Name/Years Served	Party Affiliation	Ethnic Background
Kansas	4	Charles B. Curtis/ 1893–1907	Republican	Native American (Kaw)
Oklahoma	4, 3	Charles D. Carter/ 1907–1915, 1915–1927	Democrat	Native American (Choctaw)
Oklahoma	2	W. W. Hastings/ 1915–1921, 1923–1935[5]	Democrat	Native American (Cherokee)
Oklahoma	AL	Will Rogers/ 1933–1943	Democrat	Native American (Cherokee)
California	16	Will Rogers Jr./ 1943–1945	Democrat	Native American (Cherokee)
Oklahoma	2	William G. Stigler/ 1945–1953	Democrat	Native American (Choctaw)
South Dakota	1	Ben Reifel/ 1961–1971	Republican	Native American (Rosebud Sioux)
Oklahoma	2	Clem Rogers McSpadden/1973–1975	Democrat	Native American (Cherokee)
Hawaii	2	Daniel K. Akaka/ 1977–1990	Democrat	Native Hawaiian
Colorado	3	Ben N. Campbell/ 1987–1993	Democrat	Native American (Northern Cheyenne)

Notable Firsts: 1973 and 1974

In Alaska's special 1973 election to replace deceased U.S. Rep. Nick Begich (D), the unsuccessful Democratic candidate was **Emil Notti**, an Inuit leader. Again in the 1974 general election the Democratic candidate for the U.S. House was another Inuit, a state senator named **William L. Hensley**. Both Notti and Hensley lost their races, yet this was the first time that Native Alaskans had received major-party congressional nominations.

Notable First: 1981

Fofo I. F. Sunia, (D) American Samoa, elected as a delegate from that territory, the first Samoan American to serve in the U.S. Congress.

Notable First: 1973

Antonio Borja Won Pat, (D) Guam, elected as a delegate from that territory, the first Native Guamanian (Chamorro) to serve in the U.S. House.

---

[5]The break in Hastings's congressional service was caused by his defeat in the 1920 general election by Republican Alice Mary Robertson, the second woman elected to the U.S. House of Representatives. Hastings returned to the seat in the House after a rematch in 1922, when he defeated Robertson.

Notable First: 1903

Prince Jonah Kuhio Kalanianaole, (R) Hawaii, elected as a delegate from that territory, the first Native Hawaiian to serve in the U.S. House.

Native Minority Women and the U.S. House of Representatives

A Native American woman has yet to be elected to the U.S. House of Representatives. In fact, only two such women have ever received a major-party nomination to contest a seat in that body. The first was **Ada Elizabeth Deer** (D) of the Menominee tribe, who contested the 2nd Congressional District of Wisconsin in the November 1992 election. In 1996 **Georgianna Lincoln** (D), an Athabascan, unsuccessfully sought Alaska's single at-large seat.

Native Minority Governors

1. Johnston Murray	Democrat	Oklahoma	Native American (Chickasaw)	01/08/51–01/10/55
2. John David Waihee III	Democrat	Hawaii	Native Hawaiian	01/01/86–01/01/95

How They Assumed Office

1. **Johnston Murray**, (D) Oklahoma (Born: 1902; Died: 1974)
   Served: 01/08/51–01/10/55

Elected on November 7, 1950, for a four-year term. Murray was the son of flamboyant Oklahoman William H. "Alfalfa Bill" Murray, a U.S. representative (1913–1917) and governor (1931–1935). Constitutionally barred from a second consecutive term, Murray's wife, Willie Emerson Murray, ran in his stead in the 1954 Democratic primary for the gubernatorial nomination. Their attempted succession ploy did not prove popular with voters, and she finished seventh out of a field of sixteen candidates.

Previous and subsequent elected political office: None

2. **John David Waihee III**, (D) Hawaii (Born: 1946)
   Served: 01/01/86–01/01/95

Elected on November 4, 1986, for a four-year term. Waihee was reelected to a second term in 1990. He retired to private life after being ineligible to run for a third term in 1994.

Previous elected political office:
    Hawaii Lieutenant Governor, 1982–1986
    Hawaii House of Representatives, 1980–1982
Subsequent elected political office: None

Native Minority
Gubernatorial Statistics

Longest Tenure of a Native Minority Governor

John D. Waihee III, (D) Hawaii, who served for eight years (1986–1994).

Native Minority Gubernatorial
Election Statistics

The following section provides voting statistics on those native minority governors who contested elections, including primaries, primary runoffs, and general elections. Names in this section appear in chronological order of gubernatorial service, from earliest to most recent.

Johnston Murray, (D) Oklahoma

1950	General	Johnston Murray (D)	329,308	51.1%
		Jo O. Ferguson (R)	313,205	48.6%

John David Waihee III, (D) Hawaii

1990	General	John D. Waihee III (D)	203,491	61.0%
		Fred Hemmings (R)	131,310	39.0%
1990	Democratic Primary	John D. Waihee III	179,383	88.0%
		Benjamin Hopkins	9,735	5.0%
		Robert H. Garner	9,112	4.0%
		Two others	4,517	2.0%
1986	General	John D. Waihee III (D)	173,655	52.0%
		D. G. Anderson (R)	160,460	48.0%
1986	Democratic Primary	John D. Waihee III	105,579	46.0%
		Cecil Heftel	83,939	36.0%
		Patsy Takemoto Mink	37,998	16.0%

Chronology of All Native Minority
Candidates for Governor
(* denotes winner)

1950	*Johnston Murray	Democrat	Oklahoma	Native American (Chickasaw)
1986	*John D. Waihee III	Democrat	Hawaii	Native Hawaiian
1990	*John D. Waihee III	Democrat	Hawaii	Native Hawaiian
1994	Larry EchoHawk	Democrat	Idaho	Native American (Pawnee)

Native Minorities Who Have Held
Other State Executive Offices[6]

Hawaii

Lieutenant Governor
    John D. Waihee III (D), 1982–1986[7]   (Native Hawaiian)
    Bill Richardson (D), 1962–1966   (Native Hawaiian)
    James Kealoha (R), 1959–1962   (Native Hawaiian)

Idaho

Attorney General
    Larry EchoHawk (D), 1991–1995[8]   (Native American—Pawnee)

New Mexico

Attorney General
    Hal Stratton (R), 1987–1991   (Native American—Cherokee)

Pennsylvania

Secretary of the Commonwealth
    Matthew Stanley Quay (R),
    1872–1878, 1879–1882[9]   (Native American—Abenaki or Seneca)

Treasurer
    Matthew Stanley Quay (R), 1885–1887   (Native American—Abenaki or Seneca)

Native Minorities in State Legislatures

Completely reliable statistics on native minorities serving in state legislatures are difficult to obtain. Few serve at present and most tallies of the ethnicity of state legislators simply have a category ti-

---

[6]These offices are a combination of election by popular vote, election by the state legislature, and appointment by the governor.

[7]Waihee also served as governor (1986–1994).

[8]EchoHawk was unsuccessful in 1994 as the Democratic nominee for governor.

[9]Quay also served as U.S. senator (1887–1899 and 1901–1904). But as the United States Senate Historical Office states, "Pinning down Senator Quay's ancestry has posed a longstanding problem for historians. His immediate forbears were apparently of Scotch-Irish descent; one biographer, while not discounting the possibility that some of the Senator's ancestors were of Native American descent, has stated that Quay's Indian ancestry is an 'unsubstantiated legend.'"

tled "Other," without further definition. It can probably be surmised that in states with sizeable Native American residents the "Other" category does refer to them. In Alaska, that category probably refers to the Inuit, Aleut, and other Native Alaskans, whereas in Hawaii it would refer to Native Hawaiians or other Pacific Islanders.

Notable First: 1992

Georgianna Lincoln, (D) Alaska, an Athabascan, was elected to the state senate, the first Native American woman to sit in a state senate.

Notable First: 1959

Eben Hopson (D), an Inuit, and **Frank Peratrovich** (D), a Tlingit, both of Alaska, were elected to the state house of representatives in Alaska's first vote after achieving statehood, the first Native Alaskans elected to a state legislature in the U.S.

Notable First: 1948

Percy Ipalook and **William Beltz**, both Inuits of Alaska, became the first two Native Alaskans elected to a territorial legislature.

Frank Peratrovich (D), a Tlingit, was elected president of Alaska's territorial senate, the first Native Alaskan to assume that position in the U.S. Earlier, in 1946, he had been the first elected to a territorial senate.

Notable First: 1934

William Paul, a Tlingit of Alaska, was elected to the territorial house, the first Native Alaskan to sit in a state or territorial legislature.

Notable Second: 1930

Dolly Smith Cusker (Akers), (D) Montana and an Assiniboine, was elected to that state's house of representatives and became the second Native American woman elected to a state legislature. Mrs. Cusker is often erroneously identified as having been the *first* Native American woman elected.

Notable First: 1925

Rosalie Enos Lyons Keliinoi, (R) Hawaii, was elected to a seat in Hawaii's territorial house, the first female Native Hawaiian elected to a state or territorial legislature.

Notable First: 1924

Cora Reynolds Anderson, (R) Michigan and a Chippewa, was elected to Michigan's house of representatives, the first Native American woman elected to a state legislature.

Native Minority Speakers of State Lower Legislative Chambers

Daniel Kihano, (D) Hawaii, 1987–1992
William A. Durant, (D) Oklahoma, 1910–1912

Native Minorities in the Judiciary

Notable First: 1953

Napoleon B. Johnson, a Cherokee from Oklahoma, became chief justice of that state's supreme court, the first Native American to attain that position on a state supreme court.

Native Minorities at the Local Level

Notable First: 1985

Wilma Mankiller of Oklahoma was elected principal chief of the Cherokee Nation, the first Native American woman elected chief.

Notable First: 1922

Alice Brown Davis of Florida was appointed chief of the Seminole Nation by Pres. Warren G. Harding, the first Native American woman appointed chief.

Gays and Lesbians in American Politics

Comments on Gays and Lesbians

Beginning in the 1970s gays and lesbians flung open their closet doors and began seeking political offices in a variety of states across America. At first their candidacies were local. They sought positions—on city councils and in state legislatures—generally representing small areas where large numbers of homosexual voters were concentrated. By the mid-1990s they were winning major-party nominations to contest statewide posts, were serving in Congress, and had even been appointed to positions in the executive branch of the federal government and to federal judgeships.

A Brief Chronology

1961 First openly gay person to seek public office

Jose Sarria, (D) California, contested a seat on the San Francisco board of supervisors.

1974 First openly gay/lesbian elected to public office

Elaine Noble, a Democrat, was elected to a seat in the state legislature of Massachusetts.

1980 First openly gay mayor elected

Gene Ulrich was elected mayor of Bunceton, a small town in Missouri.

1984 First openly gay elected to the U.S. House of Representatives

Gerry Studds, (D) Massachusetts, was elected to his seventh term in the U.S. House of Representatives. Although first elected in 1972, Studds didn't proclaim his sexual orientation until midway through his sixth term.

1992 First openly gay/lesbian elected to a statewide position

Edward S. Flanagan, (D) Vermont, was elected to the post of state auditor of accounts.

1993 First openly lesbian to serve in a subcabinet-level position

Roberta Achtenberg, (D) California, was appointed as an assistant secretary in the U.S. Department of Housing and Urban Development.

1994   First openly gay/lesbian federal judge appointed

Deborah Batts was appointed to the U.S. District Court for the Southern District of New York.

1998   First openly lesbian elected to U.S. House of Representatives

Tammy Baldwin, (D) Wisconsin, was elected to the U.S. House of Representatives, the first openly lesbian to win a seat in that body.

Gays and Lesbians and Political Power

The following chart (by state) details the total number of gays and lesbians who have served their states in three of the most powerful positions in U.S. politics: governor, U.S. Senate (both appointed and elected), and U.S. House of Representatives.

State	Governor	U.S. Senate	U.S. House
Arizona	-	-	1
Connecticut	-	-	1
Maryland	-	-	1
Massachusetts	-	-	2
Mississippi	-	-	1
New York	-	-	1
Texas	-	-	2
Wisconsin	-	-	2
Total Gays and Lesbians Who Have Served	0	0	11

Best and Worst States for Gay and Lesbians Achieving Political Power

Massachusetts, because it regularly elected two gay representatives, would have to be considered the best state for gays and lesbians in achieving political power. **California**, where numerous gays and lesbians have been unable to translate their numbers into political power far beyond the local level, would have to be considered the worst.

The National Level

The 1998 congressional elections did not see as many gay and lesbian candidates running for the U.S. House (in either primaries or the general election) as had competed just two years earlier. One of the most significant things about this election was that lesbian candidates far outnumbered gay candidates. The most notable candidates were:

Tammy Baldwin, a state senator, won her race as Democratic nominee in Wisconsin's 2nd Congressional District.

Paul Barby, who was the losing 1996 Democratic nominee in Oklahoma's 6th Congressional District, tried again in 1998, but still came out the loser.

Margarethe Cammermeyer, famed for her dismissal from the military because she was a lesbian, lost her race as the Democratic nominee in Washington's 2nd Congressional District.

Christine Kehoe, a member of San Diego's city council, lost her race as the Democratic nominee for California's 49th Congressional District.

Two other gay members of the U.S. House, who won reelection in 1998 are:

Barney Frank, (D) Massachusetts–4th, who was first elected in 1980. He finally admitted—almost casually during an interview—his homosexuality in 1987. In July 1990 the U.S. House reprimanded him by a vote of 409–18 on two minor charges involving his past relationship with a male prostitute. During his tenure in Congress, Frank has remained extremely popular in his district, rarely winning less than 60 percent of the vote.

Jim Kolbe, (R) Arizona–5th, who was first elected in 1984, finally admitted his homosexuality during the summer of 1996, when he was threatened with being "outed" by a national gay publication. Despite their votes against legislation favored by gay rights organizations (votes in which Kolbe had joined them), his House colleagues from Arizona—plus the conservative Republican governor—all staunchly supported Kolbe after his announcement. He went on to win his November 1998 reelection race by a 52–45 percent margin.

The 1996 elections also saw a record number of openly gay/lesbian candidates entering the primaries of both parties for seats in the U.S. House of Representatives:

Patrick Baikauskas sought the Republican nomination in Illinois's 20th Congressional District to fill the seat of incumbent Richard Durbin, who was seeking a U.S. Senate seat, and placed third in the race.

Paul Barby won the Democratic nomination for Oklahoma's 6th Congressional District, then made his homosexuality known. He lost the general election by a 64–36 percent margin.

David "Skip" Koontz unsuccessfully sought the Democratic nomination in Maryland's 6th Congressional District to run against incumbent Roscoe Bartlett.

Dale McCormick, the only open lesbian in the 1996 group of candidates, sought the Democratic nomination in Maine's 1st Congressional District and lost narrowly.

Justin Raimundo won the Republican nomination in California's 8th Congressional District—primarily based in San Francisco—but lost the general election overwhelmingly. His candidacy most likely did not catch fire with the large number of gay/lesbian voters in the district because he was a strong supporter of presidential candidate Pat Robertson.

Eric Resnick unsuccessfully sought the Democratic nomination in Ohio's 16th Congressional District.

Richard Zbur won the Democratic nomination in California's 38th Congressional District but lost the general election by a 53–43 percent margin. Had he won, Zbur, who has a Hispanic mother, would have been the nation's first gay Hispanic representative.

Prior to the 106th Congress, two other openly gay men had also served in the U.S. House:

Steve Gunderson, (R) Wisconsin–3rd, who was first elected in 1980. He finally admitted his homosexuality in November 1994 after a magazine article was published about him. Although Gunderson had announced it would be his last term if he won in November 1994, he came close to mounting a last-minute write-in candidacy for his seat again. He finally abandoned the effort, with many claiming that he was pressured by the more conservative members of the U.S. House Republican leadership.

Gerry Studds, (D) Massachusetts–10th, who was first elected in 1972. His homosexuality came to light in 1983 after a sex scandal involving the House pages and several House members. Studds was the only member accused of having had sex with a male page. Although many thought that he might have trouble winning reelection, Studds has persevered since then, rarely winning less than 60 percent of the vote in his district. Studds announced in late 1995 that he would retire at the end of his eighth term in 1996.

Undoubtedly other "closeted" gays and lesbians have served in the U.S. Congress. For example, in the early 1990s a congresswoman (or perhaps a former congresswoman like Barbara Jordan of Texas; see below) granted an interview in which she admitted her lesbianism—off the record, of course. Five other congressmen are worth noting because of their involvement in sexual matters:

Robert Bauman, (R) Maryland–1st, was first elected in a special election in August 1973 and defeated for reelection in November 1980. Married and conservative, Bauman was a critic of the U.S. House Democratic leadership, which had worked hard to help keep his seat in Congress. In October 1980 he was charged with soliciting sex from a sixteen-year-old male. He told the press, "I have been plagued by two afflictions, alcoholism and homosexual tendencies." Bauman's constituents turned him out of office the next month. By August 1983 Bauman finally came out, causing his wife of twenty-one years to have their marriage annulled. He has not sought electoral office since then.

Jon Hinson, (R) Mississippi–4th, was first elected in November 1978 and resigned in April 1981. Single and conservative, Hinson was first arrested in 1976 for committing an obscene act at the Iwo Jima Memorial, but the incident was kept quiet. In 1980 he admitted to the incident and also told how he had been one of the survivors of a 1977 fire at a homosexual movie house in the nation's capital in which several people had been killed. He had recently married—and claimed a religious conversion, both factors undoubtedly helping his successful reelection campaign. His luck was not to last long, however. During February 1981 Hinson was arrested in the restroom of a House office building and charged with attempted oral sodomy. He resigned from his seat two months later and has not sought electoral office since.

Stewart B. McKinney, (R) Connecticut–4th, was first elected in November 1970 and died in office in May 1987. Liberal and married, McKinney was the second-ranking Republican on the House Banking, Finance, and Urban Affairs Committee when he died—the first member of Congress to succumb to AIDS. Shortly after his death a man came forward to announce that he and McKinney had had a long-standing affair, and he was soon embroiled in a legal contest with McKinney's family.

Frederick Richmond, (D) New York–14th, was first elected in May 1974 and retired at the end of his fifth term in 1983. Liberal, wealthy, and single, Richmond was charged in 1978 with having solicited a young man for sex acts. He pleaded not guilty, and the charges were dropped after he participated in a program of the Washington, D.C., courts for first offenders. Richmond's wealth—he personally pumped large amounts of his fortune into special programs in his district—undoubtedly helped him to overcome any doubts his constituents may have had about his arrest, and he won reelection in 1974 only a few months after his arrest. By 1982 two different problems faced Richmond: His seat had been redistricted to have a slight African American majority, and there were charges that he had helped a onetime convict obtain a position unethically. He chose to retire and not contest the November 1982 election.

Joe Wyatt Jr., (D) Texas–14th, was first elected in 1978. Shortly after being sworn into office in 1979, Wyatt, a conservative, was arrested on homosexual charges. He entered an alcohol rehabilitation program and withdrew from the 1980 race. In 1982 he ran again in the same district— this time as a Republican—but garnered only 39 percent of the vote.

In early 1996 a national gay paper revealed after the death of one of the most distinguished women to serve in the U.S. House that she had been a "closet" lesbian during her tenure there.

Barbara Jordan, (D) Texas–18th, was first elected in 1972 and retired in 1978. Jordan, an outspoken liberal and noted eloquent speaker, began her remarkable political journey in 1967, when she was thirty-one years old, by becoming the first African American woman elected to the Texas legislature. Taking her seat as the only female and the first African American in the state senate, Jordan was soon president pro tem of the body, acting on several occasions as Texas's governor during the absence from the state of the governor and lieutenant governor. In 1972 she moved to national politics with her entry into the U.S. House, being the first African American woman elected from the South. After three terms Jordan retired to pursue a teaching career. After her death in 1995 rumors were confirmed that Jordan indeed had been a lesbian. She chose never to publicize her sexual orientation, possibly figuring that it would detract from her legislative career.

Notable First: 1997

James C. Hormel, (D) California, was appointed ambassador to Luxembourg, the first openly gay ambassador nominated to represent the U.S. abroad diplomatically. At the time of publication, the U.S. Senate still had not confirmed the appointment.

Notable First: 1993

Roberta Achtenberg, (D) California, was appointed assistant secretary for fair housing and equal opportunity in the U.S. Department of Housing and Urban Development by Pres. Bill Clinton, the first openly gay/lesbian official appointed to a federal position that required confirmation by the U.S. Senate.

Notable First: 1954

Lester Hunt, (D) Wyoming, first elected to the U.S. Senate in 1948, committed suicide, the fourth sitting senator to take his own life. Hunt had learned that his political opponents planned to reveal the homosexuality of one of his children during his fall 1954 reelection campaign in an attempt to mar his chance for a second term.

Notable First: 1857

James Buchanan, (D) Pennsylvania, was inaugurated president. A lifelong bachelor, Buchanan was widely rumored to have had a lengthy relationship with William Rufus King, a former senator from Alabama and vice president under Franklin Pierce.

Notable First: 1853

William Rufus King, (D) Alabama, was inaugurated vice president. A lifelong bachelor, King was the reputed lover of Sen. James Buchanan of Pennsylvania, which led to his being dubbed "Miss Nancy" among those who were aware of the relationship. King, who was the only vice president to take his oath of office while on foreign soil (Cuba, where he had gone because of poor health), died a few months later at his home in Alabama.

The State Level

Only two openly gay/lesbian officials currently serve in statewide office:

Edward S. Flanagan, (D) Vermont, won the Democratic nomination for the post of state auditor of accounts in 1992. He subsequently won the general election that November, then won reelection in 1996 and 1998.

Dale McCormick, (D) Maine, an unsuccessful congressional candidate in the 1996 Democratic primary for Maine's 1st Congressional District, was elected by the state legislature on December 4, 1996, as state treasurer.

The November 1994 elections saw two other openly gay/lesbian candidates win major-party nominations for statewide office. They were:

Tony Miller, (D) California, succeeded to the office of California secretary of state in early 1994 when the incumbent—an Asian American female, March Fong Eu—resigned to become a U.S. ambassador. Miller sought and narrowly won the Democratic nomination for a full four-year term. He was defeated by his Republican challenger, Bill Jones, in November 1994.

Karen Burstein, (D) New York, after serving in the New York legislature, sought and won the Democratic nomination for state attorney general when the incumbent chose not to seek reelection. She was defeated in November 1994 by her Republican opponent, Dennis C. Vacco.

Notable First: 1993

Allan Spear (D) became president of the Minnesota senate. He won his first election to that body in 1972, then publicly revealed his sexual orientation two years later after the first openly lesbian state representative was elected.

Notable First: 1974

Elaine Noble (D), a lesbian, was elected to a seat in the Massachusetts legislature even though she had openly acknowledged her sexual orientation.

The Judiciary

Notable Firsts: 1994

Marcy Kahn was elected to New York's highest court, the first openly lesbian state supreme court justice in the U.S.

Deborah Batts was appointed by Pres. Bill Clinton to the U.S. District Court for the Southern District of New York, the first openly gay/lesbian federal judge.

Notable First: 1979

Steven Lachs was appointed to the Los Angeles, California, superior court, becoming the first openly gay judge in the U.S.

Notable First: 1978

Abby Soven was appointed to the Los Angeles, California, municipal court, the first openly lesbian judge in the U.S.

The Local Level

Notable First: 1997

Margarita Lopez (D) was elected to the city council of New York City, becoming the first Puerto Rican lesbian elected to office in the mainland U.S.

Notable First: 1996

Margo Frasier (D), elected as sheriff of Travis County (San Antonio), Texas, was the first open gay/lesbian elected a county sheriff in the U.S.

Notable Firsts: 1994

Susan Leal (D), elected to the San Francisco board of supervisors, was the first openly lesbian Hispanic elected in the U.S.

Lawrence Wong (D), elected to the San Francisco community college board, was the first openly gay Asian American elected in the U.S.

Notable First: 1992

Kenneth Reeves (D), elected mayor of Cambridge, Massachusetts, was the first openly gay African American mayor.

Notable First: 1991

Sherry Harris (D), elected to the Seattle city council, was the first openly lesbian African American elected official in the U.S.

Notable First: 1989

Keith St. John (D), elected alderman in Albany, New York, was the first openly gay African American elected official in the U.S.

Notable First: 1988

Richard Wagner (D), elected chair of the Dane County, Wisconsin, board of supervisors, was the first open gay/lesbian to head a county governing unit in the U.S.

Notable First: 1984

Valerie Terrigno (D), elected mayor of West Hollywood, California, was the first openly lesbian elected mayor in the U.S.

Notable First: 1983

John Laird (D), elected mayor of Santa Cruz, California, was the first open gay elected mayor of a medium-sized (45,000+ population) city in the U.S.

Notable First: 1982

Richard Wagner (D), elected to the Dane County, Wisconsin, board of supervisors, was the first open gay/lesbian elected to a county governing board in the U.S.

Notable First: 1980

Gene Ulrich, elected mayor of Bunceton, Missouri, was the first openly gay/lesbian mayor in the U.S.

Notable Firsts: 1977

Steve Camara (D), elected to the Fall River, Massachusetts, school committee office, was the first open gay/lesbian elected to a public school governing board.

Harvey Milk (D), elected to the San Francisco board of supervisors, was the first gay/lesbian elected to public office in a large city in the U.S. In 1978 Milk was the victim of one of the most notorious political assassinations in American history when both he and Mayor George Moscone were gunned down in City Hall by Dan White, a disturbed fellow member of the board of supervisors who had resigned only days before the shooting.

Notable First: 1974

Kathy Kozachenko (Human Rights Party), elected to the Ann Arbor, Michigan, city council, was the first open gay/lesbian elected to public office in the United States.

Notable Firsts: 1972

Nancy Weshster and **Jerry Degrieck** (both Human Rights Party) were elected to the Ann Arbor, Michigan, city council; both proclaimed their homosexuality soon after their elections.

Notable First: 1961

Jose Sarria contested a seat on the San Francisco board of supervisors, becoming the first openly gay candidate to run for public office in the U.S.

Significant Political Milestones for Various Ethnic and Religious Groups

African American

First Elected Governor

L. Douglas Wilder, (D) Virginia, elected in 1989

First Elected to U.S. Senate

Hiram R. Revels, (R) Mississippi, elected in 1870

First Female Elected to U.S. Senate

Carol Moseley-Braun, (D) Illinois, elected in 1992

First Elected to U.S. House of Representatives

John Willis Menard,[1] (R) Louisiana, elected in 1868

First Female Elected to U.S. House of Representatives

Shirley Chisholm, (D) New York, elected in 1968

First Federal Cabinet Member

Robert C. Weaver, (D) Washington, D.C., appointed in 1967 by Pres. Lyndon Johnson

---

[1]Menard was elected, but the U.S. House of Representatives refused to seat him. The first two African Americans elected and seated were Jefferson F. Long, (R) Georgia, and Joseph H. Rainey, (R) South Carolina; both were seated in 1869.

First Female Federal Cabinet Member

Patricia Roberts Harris, (D) Washington, D.C., appointed in 1977 by Pres. Jimmy Carter

First U.S. Supreme Court Justice

Thurgood Marshall, (D) New York, appointed by Pres. Lyndon Johnson in 1967

Albanian American

First Elected to U.S. House of Representatives

Joseph J. DioGuardi, (R) New York, elected in 1984

First Elected Mayor of a Large City

Victor H. Schiro (D), elected mayor of New Orleans, Louisiana, in 1962

Arab American

First Elected Governor

Victor Atiyeh, (R) Oregon, elected in 1978

First Female Elected to U.S. House of Representatives

Mary Rose Oakar, (D) Ohio, elected in 1976

First Elected Mayor of a Large City

Michael J. Damas, (D) Cleveland, Ohio, elected in 1959

Armenian American

First Elected Governor

George Deukmejian, (R) California, elected in 1982

First Elected to U.S. House of Representatives

Steven B. Derounian, (R) New York, elected in 1952

Asian Indian–American

First Elected to U.S. House of Representatives

Dalip S. Saund, (D) California, elected in 1956

Austrian American

First U.S. Supreme Court Justice

Felix Frankfurter, (D) Massachusetts, appointed in 1939 by Pres. Franklin D. Roosevelt

First Elected to U.S. House of Representatives

Julius Goldzier, (D) Illinois, elected in 1892

Basque American

First Elected Governor

Paul Laxalt, (R) Nevada, elected in 1966

First Elected to U.S. Senate

Paul Laxalt, (R) Nevada, elected in 1974

Bulgarian American

First Elected to a State Legislature

Stoyan Christowe, (R) Vermont, elected in 1960

First Elected Mayor of a Large City

Ivan Lebamov (D), elected in 1974 in Ft. Wayne, Indiana

Cape Verdean–American

First Elected to Statewide Office

Francisco Borges, (D) Connecticut, elected as state treasurer in 1986

Chamorro (Native Guamanian)

First Elected Delegate to U.S. House of Representatives

Antonio Borja Won Pat, (D) Guam, elected delegate in 1972

Chinese American

First Elected to U.S. Senate

Hiram L. Fong, (R) Hawaii, elected in 1959

First Elected to U.S. House of Representatives

David Wu, (D) Oregon, elected in 1998

First Elected Governor

Gary F. Locke, (D) Washington, elected in 1996

Croatian American

First Elected Governor

Rudy Perpich, (D) Minnesota, elected in 1983[2]

Cuban American

First Elected to U.S. House of Representatives

Ileana Ros-Lehtinen, (R) Florida, elected in 1990

First Male Elected to U.S. House of Representatives

Lincoln Diaz-Balart, (R) Florida, elected in 1992

Czech American

First Elected to U.S. Senate

Roman Hruska, (R) Nebraska, elected in 1954

First Elected to U.S. House of Representatives

John Wilkes Kittera, (Federalist) Pennsylvania, elected in 1791

First Elected Governor

Otto Kerner, (D) Illinois, elected in 1960

First Federal Cabinet Member

Madeleine Korbel Albright (D), appointed in 1997 by Pres. Bill Clinton as Secretary of State

First Female Elected to a State Legislature

Pauline Davis, (D) California, elected in 1952

---

[2]Perpich had succeeded to the governorship in 1976 when the incumbent resigned, but he lost the following election. He was "first" elected to the office in 1982. Mike Stepovich was the first Croatian American governor, but he was appointed by President Eisenhower in 1957 as Alaska's territorial governor. When Alaska achieved statehood in 1959, he continued in office—temporarily—and ran for the office in the new state's first general election but was defeated.

First Elected Mayor of Large City

Anton J. Cermak, (D) Chicago, elected in 1931

Danish American

First Elected Governor

Hjalmar Petersen, (Farmer-Labor) Minnesota, succeeded to office in 1936

First Elected to U.S. House of Representatives

Jacob Johnson, (R) Utah, elected in 1912

Dominican American

First Elected to a State Legislature

Adriano Espaillat, (D) New York, elected in 1996

Dutch American

First Elected President

Martin Van Buren, (D) New York, elected in 1836

First Elected to U.S. Senate

Nicholas Van Dyke, (Federalist) Delaware, elected in 1817

First Elected to U.S. House of Representatives

Alexander Gillon, South Carolina, elected in 1793

First Elected Governor

Cornelius P. Van Ness, (Democrat-Republican) Vermont, elected in 1823

Filipino American

First Elected Governor

Benjamin Jerome Cayetano, (D) Hawaii, elected in 1994

First Elected Resident Commissioners to U.S. House of Representatives

Benito Legarda and **Pablo Ocampo**, Philippine Islands, elected resident commissioners in 1907

First Female elected Mayor

Tess Santiago, Dalano, California, elected in 1994

Finnish American

First Elected to U.S. House of Representatives

Oscar J. Larson, (R) Minnesota, elected in 1920

French American

First Elected to U.S. Senate

Eligius Fromentin, (Democrat-Republican) Louisiana, elected in 1812

First Elected to U.S. House of Representatives

John Baptiste Charles Lucas, Pennsylvania, elected in 1802

First Elected Governor

Jacques Philippe Viller, Louisiana, elected in 1816

German American

First Elected to U.S. Senate

John P. G. Muhlenberg, (Democrat-Republican) Pennsylvania, elected in 1801

First Elected Governor

Peter Muhlenberg, Pennsylvania, elected in 1787

Greek American

First Elected Vice President

Spiro T. Agnew, (R) Maryland, elected in 1968

First Elected Governor

Spiro T. Agnew, (R) Maryland, elected in 1966

First Elected to U.S. Senate

Paul Sarbanes, (D) Maryland, elected in 1976

First Female Elected to U.S. Senate

Olympia J. Snowe, (R) Maine, elected in 1994

First Elected to U.S. House of Representatives

Lucas Miller,[3] (D) Wisconsin, elected in 1890

First Female Elected to U.S. House of Representatives

Olympia J. Snowe, (R) Maine, elected in 1978

First Federal Cabinet Member

Pete Peterson, (R) Illinois, appointed in 1972 by Pres. Richard Nixon as secretary of commerce

First Elected Mayor

Antonios Protos, Nogales, Arizona, elected in 1895

First Female Elected Mayor

Helen Boosalis, (D) Lincoln, Nebraska, elected in 1975

Hungarian American

First Elected to U.S. House of Representatives

Joseph Pulitzer, (R) New York, elected in 1884

Irish American (Catholic)

First Elected to U.S. Senate

Daniel Carroll, (Federalist) Maryland, 1789

---

[3]Miller was brought to the U.S. as an infant orphan from Greece and adopted by an American family, which accounts for his decidedly non-Greek surname.

First Elected to U.S. House of Representatives

Michael Walsh, (D) New York, elected 1852

First Federal Cabinet Member

Joseph McKenna, (R) California, appointed in 1897 by Pres. William McKinley as attorney general

First U.S. Supreme Court Justice

Joseph McKenna, (R) California, appointed in 1898 by Pres. William McKinley

Italian American

First Elected Governor

John O. Pastore, (D) Rhode Island, elected in 1946

First Female Elected Governor

Ella T. Grasso, (D) Connecticut, elected in 1974

First Elected to U.S. Senate

Frederick B. Balzar, (R) Nevada, elected in 1926

First Elected to U.S. House of Representatives

Francis B. Spinola, (D) New York, elected in 1886

First Female Elected to U.S. House of Representatives

Ella T. Grasso, (D) Connecticut, elected in 1970

First Federal Cabinet Member

Anthony J. Celebrezze, (D) Ohio, appointed in 1963 by Pres. John F. Kennedy as secretary of health, education, and welfare

First U.S. Supreme Court Justice

Antonin Scalia, (R) Virginia, appointed in 1986 by Pres. Ronald Reagan

First Federal Judge

Matthew Abruzzo, appointed in 1936 by Pres. Franklin D. Roosevelt

Japanese American

First Elected Governor

George R. Ariyoshi, (D) Hawaii, elected in 1974

First Elected to U.S. Senate

Daniel K. Inouye, (D) Hawaii, elected in 1962

First Elected to U.S. House of Representatives

Daniel K. Inouye, (D) Hawaii, elected in 1959

First Female Elected to U.S. House of Representatives

Patsy Takemoto Mink, (D) Hawaii, elected in 1964

First Female Elected Mayor of a Large City

Eunice Sato, (D) Long Beach, California, elected in 1980

Jewish American

First Elected to Office in Colonial America

Francis Salvador, South Carolina Provincial Congress, elected in 1775

First Elected Governor

David Emanuel, (Democrat-Republican) Georgia, elected in 1801[4]

First Elected to U.S. Senate

David Levy Yulee, (D) Florida, elected in 1845

---

[4]The next Jewish governors were not until many, many years later: Moses Alexander, (D) Idaho, in 1914 and Arthur Seligman, (D) New Mexico, and Julius L. Meier, (I) Oregon, both in 1930.

First Female(s) Elected to U.S. Senate

Dianne G. Feinstein, (D) California, and **Barbara L. Boxer**, (D) California, both elected in 1992

First Elected to U.S. House of Representatives

Lewis C. Levin, (American) Pennsylvania, elected in 1844

First Female Elected to U.S. House of Representatives

Florence P. Kahn, (R) California, elected in 1925

First Federal Cabinet Member[5]

Oscar S. Straus, (R) New York, appointed in 1906 by Pres. Theodore Roosevelt as secretary of commerce and labor

First U.S. Supreme Court Justice

Louis D. Brandeis, (D) Massachusetts, appointed in 1916 by Pres. Woodrow Wilson

First Female U.S. Supreme Court Justice

Ruth Bader Ginsburg, (D) Washington, D.C., appointed in 1993 by Pres. Bill Clinton

Korean American

First Elected to U.S. House of Representatives

Jay S. Kim, (R) California, elected in 1992

Lebanese American

First Elected to U.S. Senate

James G. Abourezk, (D) South Dakota, elected in 1972

---

[5]It is interesting to note that the cabinet of the Confederacy inaugurated in 1861 had a Jewish member, Judah P. Benjamin, who held the position of attorney general, forty-five years before the federal cabinet had its first Jewish member. Benjamin later served in the Confederate cabinet in the additional posts of secretary of war and secretary of state. Prior to his service to the Confederacy, Benjamin had been a Democratic U.S. senator from Louisiana; when he was elected to his first senate term in 1852, Benjamin was only the second Jew to serve in that body. He was held in such high renown that Whig Pres. Zachary Taylor nominated him as attorney general, but he declined the honor. A contemporary admirer of Benjamin's said he was "Hebrew in blood, English in tenacity of grasp and purpose, and French in taste."

First Elected to U.S. House of Representatives

Abraham Kazan Jr., (D) Texas, elected in 1966

First Elected Lieutenant Governor

Elias "Eddie" Francis, (R) Arizona, elected in 1966

Lithuanian American

First Elected to U.S. House of Representatives

Samuel Dickstein, (D) New York, elected in 1922

Mexican American

First Elected Governor

Raul H. Castro, (D) Arizona, elected in 1974

First Elected to U.S. House of Representatives

Henry B. Gonzalez, (D) Texas, elected in 1961

First Female Elected to U.S. House of Representatives

Lucille Roybal-Allard, (D) California, elected in 1992

Mormon

First Elected Governor

Heber T. Wells, (R) Utah, elected in 1896

Muslim

First Elected Mayor

Charles Bilal, Kountze, Texas, elected in 1991

First to Win the Nomination of a Major Party for a Congressional Seat

Eric Carlson, who won the Republican nomination for California's 35th Congressional District in 1996

First Muslim Cleric to Offer the Opening Prayer at a Session of the U.S. Senate

Deen Mohammed (Wallace) Warith, of Chicago, Illinois, on February 6, 1992

First Muslim Cleric to Offer the Opening Prayer at a Session
of the U.S. House of Representatives

Siraj Wahhaj, of Brooklyn, New York, on January 15, 1991

Norwegian American

First Elected Vice President

Walter F. Mondale, (D) Minnesota, elected in 1976

First Elected Governor

Knute Nelson, (R) Minnesota, elected in 1892

First Elected to U.S. Senate

Knute Nelson, (R) Minnesota, elected in 1894

First Elected to U.S. House

Nils Pederson Haugen, (R) Wisconsin, elected in 1887

First Female Elected to U.S. House of Representatives

Coya Gjesdal Knutson, (D) Minnesota, elected in 1954

Polish American

First Elected Governor

Edmund S. Muskie, (D) Maine, elected in 1954

First Elected to U.S. Senate

Edmund S. Muskie, (D) Maine, elected in 1958

First Female Elected to U.S. Senate

Barbara A. Mikulski, (D) Maryland, elected in 1986

First Elected to U.S. House of Representatives

George Sea Shanklin, (Conservative) Kentucky, elected in 1865

First Female Elected to U.S. House of Representatives

Barbara A. Mikulski, (D) Maryland, elected in 1976

First Federal Cabinet Member

John A. Gronouski, (D) Wisconsin, appointed in 1963 by Pres. John F. Kennedy as postmaster general

First Elected Mayor of Large City

Joseph Mruk, Buffalo, New York, elected in 1949

First Federal Judge

Arthur A. Koscinski, appointed by Pres. Harry S. Truman

Portuguese American

First Elected to U.S. House of Representatives

Tony Coelho, (D) California, elected 1978

First U.S. Supreme Court Justice

Benjamin N. Cardozo, (R) New York, appointed in 1932 by Pres. Herbert Hoover

First Elected to a State Legislature

João G. Mattos Jr., California, elected in 1900

First Female Elected Mayor

Helen L. C. Silveira Lawrence, San Leandro, California, elected in 1941

Puerto Rican American

First Elected Resident Commissioner to U.S. House of Representatives

Federico Degetau, Puerto Rico, elected resident commissioner in 1901

First Elected to U.S. House of Representatives

Herman Badillo, (D) New York, elected in 1970

First Female Elected to U.S. House of Representatives

Nydia M. Velazquez, (D) New York, elected in 1992

First Female Elected to a State Legislature

Olga A. Mendez, (D) New York, elected in 1978

Roman Catholic

First Elected to U.S. Senate

Charles Carroll, (Federalist) Maryland, elected in 1789

First Priest Elected to U.S. House of Representatives

Robert F. Drinan, (D) Massachusetts, elected in 1970

First Elected Governor

John E. Howard, (Federalist) Maryland, elected in 1788

First U.S. Supreme Court Justice

Roger B. Taney, (D) Maryland, appointed in 1836 as chief justice by Pres. Andrew Jackson

First Nun Elected Mayor

Carolyn Farrell, elected in Dubuque, Iowa, in 1980

Russian American

First Elected to U.S. House of Representatives

Meyer London, (Socialist) New York, elected in 1914

Salvadorean American

First Elected to a State Legislature

Elizabeth "Liz" Figueroa, (D) California, elected in 1994

Samoan

First Elected Delegate to U.S. House of Representatives

Fofo I. F. Sunia, (D) American Samoa, elected delegate in 1980

Serbian American

First Elected Governor

George V. Voinonich, (R) Ohio, elected in 1994

First Elected to U.S. Senate

Tom Harkin, (D) Iowa, elected in 1984

First Elected to U.S. House of Representatives

Tom Harkin, (D) Iowa, elected in 1974

First Female Elected to U.S. House of Representatives

Helen Delich Bentley, (R) Maryland, elected in 1984

Sikh American

First Elected to U.S. House of Representatives

Dalip Singh Saund, (D) California, elected in 1956

Slovak American

First Elected to U.S. House of Representatives

Joseph M. Gaydos, (D) Pennsylvania, elected in 1958

Slovenian American

First Elected Governor

Frank Lausche, (D) Ohio, elected in 1944

First Elected to U.S. Senate

Frank Lausche, (D) Ohio, elected in 1950

First Elected to U.S. House of Representatives

John Blatnik, (D) Minnesota, elected in 1946

Swedish American

First Elected Governor

John Lind, (D)[6] Minnesota, elected in 1898

---

[6]After three terms in the U.S. House as a Republican, Lind changed parties and became a Democrat before winning his gubernatorial seat.

First Elected to U.S. House of Representatives

John Lind, (R) Minnesota, elected in 1886

First Federal Cabinet Member

Thomas F. Bayard, (D) Delaware, appointed in 1885 by Pres. Grover Cleveland as secretary of state

Swiss American

First Elected President

Herbert Hoover, (R) California, elected in 1928

First Federal Cabinet Member

Albert Gallatin, (Democrat-Republican) Pennsylvania, appointed in 1801 by Pres. Thomas Jefferson as secretary of the treasury

First Elected Governor

Albert Gallatin, (Democrat-Republican) Pennsylvania, elected in 1793

First Female Elected Governor

Madeleine M. Kunin, (D) Vermont, elected in 1984

Syrian American

First Elected to U.S. House of Representatives

George A. Kasem, (D) California, elected in 1958

First Female Elected to U.S. House of Representatives

Anna G. Eshoo, (D) California, elected in 1992

First Federal Cabinet Member

Donna E. Shalala, (D) Wisconsin, appointed in 1993 by Pres. Bill Clinton as secretary of health and human services

Ukrainian American

First Elected to a State Legislature

O. Malena, Pennsylvania, elected in 1932

Notable First

Dr. Nicholas Konstantinowich Sudzylovsky-Russel, first president of the Hawaii territorial senate, 1898

West Indian–American

First Elected to U.S. House of Representatives

Shirley B. Chisholm, (D) New York, elected in 1968

First Male Elected to U.S. House of Representatives

Mervyn Dymally, (D) California, elected in 1980

Other Interesting Political Milestones

U.S. Senate

Youngest Senator Seated

John Henry Eaton, (Democrat-Republican) Tennessee, who was sworn in as a U.S. senator when he was 28 years, 4 months, and 20 days old. Eaton, a friend of Andrew Jackson's, was appointed to his seat by the governor of Tennessee. Although the U.S. Constitution sets thirty years as the minimum age for a senator, it was ignored in Eaton's case because no one came forward to challenge his credentials when he presented himself for the oath of office. Two other senators were also sworn in before the minimum age of thirty: Armistead T. Mason, (Democrat-Republican) Virginia, at 28 years, 5 months, and 18 days; and Henry Clay, (Democrat-Republican) Kentucky, at 29 years, 8 months, and 17 days.

Youngest Female Senator Seated

Blanche L. Lincoln, (D) Arkansas, who was sworn in on 01/05/99 at the age of 38 years, 3 months and 6 days.

Only Person to Represent Three Different States in the Senate

James Shields (D)
   Illinois—03/04/1849–03/15/1849, 12/03/1849–03/03/1855

Minnesota—05/11/1858–03/03/1859
Missouri—01/27/1879–03/02/1879

Shields also served as governor (appointed) of the Oregon Territory and as a justice on the Illinois Supreme Court.

Only Person to Represent Two Different States in the Senate

Waitman T. Willey (Unionist-Republican)
Virginia—07/13/1861–03/03/1863
West Virginia—08/04/1863–03/03/1871

Willey was first elected by a "rump" legislature that supported the Union after Virginia's secession and represented essentially territory that became the state of West Virginia two years later.

Only Father and Son to Serve Concurrently in the Senate

Henry Dodge, (D) Wisconsin, who served 06/08/1848–03/03/1857, and his son,
Augustus C. Dodge, (D) Iowa, who served 12/07/1848–02/22/1855.

Heaviest Senator

Dixon H. Lewis, (D) Alabama, who served 04/22/1844–10/25/1848 and weighed more than 500 pounds. Lewis was so heavy his seat in the U.S. Senate had to be specially constructed.

Blind

Thomas P. Gore, (D) Oklahoma, elected in 1907.

House of Representatives

Blind

Thomas D. Schall, (Progressive) Minnesota, elected in 1914.

Governor

Youngest Elected Governor

Harold Stassen, (R) Minnesota, elected in 1938 at age 31

Only Person Elected Governor of Two Different States

Sam Houston (Democrat-Republican)
Tennessee—10/01/1827–04/16/1829
Texas—12/21/1859–03/16/1861

Houston also served a term as president of the Republic of Texas and in the U.S. Senate, (D) Texas, from 02/21/1846–03/03/1859.

Only Governors Elected Under the Banners of Both Major Parties for Different Terms

Mills O. Godwin, Virginia
   Democrat—01/16/66–01/17/70
   Republican—01/12/74–01/14/78

Forrest "Fob" James, Alabama
   Democrat—01/18/79–01/23/83
   Republican—01/15/95–01/21/99

Suicides

Five U.S. senators have committed suicide while in office:

   James H. Lane, (R) Kansas—July 11, 1866
   Frank B. Brandegee, (R) Connecticut—October 14, 1924
   Joseph Medill McCormick, (R) Illinois—February 25, 1925
   Lester C. Hunt, (D) Wyoming—June 19, 1954
   John P. East, (R) North Carolina—June 29, 1986

Lester C. Hunt was the only one to have actually committed the act in his senate office, doing so in the Senate Office Building, now named the Richard Russell Senate Office Building.

Bibliography

Bacon, Donald, Roger Davidson, and Morton Keller, eds. *The Encyclopedia of the United States Congress*. Simon and Schuster, 1995.

Baker, Richard A. *The Senate of the United States: A Bicentennial History*. Krieger, 1988.

Baker, Ross K. *House and Senate*. W. W. Norton, 1995.

Barber, James David, and Barbara Kellerman, eds. *Women Leaders in American Politics*. Prentice-Hall, 1986.

Barone, Michael, Douglas Matthews, and Grant Ujifusa. *The Almanac of American Politics*. Gambit, 1973, 1971.

_____. *The Almanac of American Politics*. Dutton, 1979, 1977, 1975.

Barone, Michael, and Grant Ujifusa. *The Almanac of American Politics*. Barone, 1981.

_____. *The Almanac of American Politics*. National Journal, 1997, 1995, 1993, 1991, 1989, 1987, 1985, 1983.

Baxter, Sandra. *Women and Politics*. University of Michigan Press, 1983.

Bayes, Jane H. *Minority Politics and Ideologies in the United States*. Chandler and Sharp, 1982.

Bennett, Lerone Jr. *Black Power U.S.A.: The Human Side of Reconstruction, 1867–1877*. Johnson, 1967.

Bernardo, Stephanie. *The Ethnic Almanac*. Doubleday, 1981.

Bingham, Clara. *Women on the Hill*. Times Books, 1997.

Bone, Hugh A. *Party Committees and National Politics*. University of Washington Press, 1958.

Boxer, Barbara. *Strangers in the Senate: Politics and the New Revolution of Women in America*. National Press Books, 1996.

Breckinridge, Sophonisha P. *Women in the Twentieth Century: A Study of Their Political, Social, and Economic Activities*. McGraw-Hill, 1933.

Byrd, Robert C. *The Senate, 1789–1989: Addresses on the History of the United States Senate*. Government Printing Office, 1989–1994 [Volume One: Chronological; Volume Four: Historical Statistics].

Carpenter, Allan, and Carl Provorse. *The World Almanac of the U.S.A.* World Almanac Books, 1996.

Carroll, Susan J. *Women as Candidates in American Politics*. Indiana University Press, 1994.

Cassara, Beverly, ed. *American Women: The Changing Image*. Beacon Press, 1962.

Chamberlin, Hope. *A Minority of Members*. New American Library, 1973.

Christian, Charles M. *Black Saga*. Houghton Mifflin, 1995.

Christopher, Maurine. *Black Americans in Congress*. Thomas Y. Crowell, 1976.

Clem, Alan L. *Prairie State Politics*. Public Affairs Press, 1967.

Congressional Quarterly. *Congress A to Z*. Congressional Quarterly, 1988.

Cook, Elizabeth Adell, ed. *The Year of the Woman*. Westview Press, 1994.

Corbin, Raymond M. *1999 Facts About Blacks*. Beckham House Publishers, 1986.

Cotter, Cornelius P., and Bernard C. Hennessy. *Politics Without Power: The National Party Committees*. Atherton, 1964.

Cowan, Tom, and Jack Maguire. *Timelines of Afro-American History*. Perigee Books, 1994.

Cox, Elizabeth M. *Women and Territorial Legislators, 1895–1995*. McFarland, 1996.

_____. *Women in Modern American Politics*. Congressional Quarterly, 1997.

Crystal, David, ed. *The Cambridge Factfinder*. Cambridge University Press, 1993.

D'Amico, Francine, and Peter R. Beckman, eds. *Women in World Politics*. Bergin and Garvey, 1995.

Darcy, Robert. *Women, Elections, and Representation*. Longman, 1987.

David, Paul T., Ralph N. Goldman, and Richard C. Bain. *The Politics of National Party Conventions*. Brookings Institution, 1960.

Davis, Mary B. *Native America in the Twentieth Century: An Encyclopedia*. Garland Publishers, 1994.

Davis, Rebecca Howard. *Women and Power in Parliamentary Democracies*. University of Nebraska Press, 1997.

DeBold, Kathleen, ed. *Out for Office: Campaigning in the Gay '90s*. Gay/Lesbian Victory Fund, 1994.

Dennis, Henry C. *The American Indian, 1492–1976*. Oceana Publications, 1976.

Diamond, Robert A., ed. *Guide to U.S. Elections*. Congressional Quarterly Press, 1976.

Dohen, Dorothy. *Women in Wonderland*. Sheed and Ward, 1960.

Dole, Bob. *Historical Almanac of the United States Senate*. Government Printing Office, 1989.

Douglas, William A., and Jon Bilbao. *Amerikanuak: Basques in the New World*. University of Nevada Press, 1975.

Duncan, Phil, ed. *Politics in America 1992*. Congressional Quarterly Press, 1991.

_____. *Politics in America 1994*. Congressional Quarterly Press, 1993.

_____. *Politics in America 1996*. Congressional Quarterly Press, 1995.

_____. *Politics in America 1998*. Congressional Quarterly Press, 1997.

Edds, Margaret. *Free at Last*. Adler and Adler, 1987.

Estell, Kenneth. *African America: Portrait of a People*. Visible Ink Press, 1994.

Famighetti, Robert, ed. *World Almanac and Book of Facts*. World Almanac Books, 1996.

Fenton, John H. *Midwest Politics*. Holt, Rinehart, and Winston, 1966.

Flexnor, Eleanor. *Century of Struggle: The Women's Rights Movement in the United States*. Belknap Press of Harvard University Press, 1959.

Foner, Eric. *Freedom's Lawmakers*. Louisiana State University Press, 1996.

Francis, Lee. *Native Time*. St. Martin's Press, 1996.

Furer, Howard B. *The Scandinavians in America, 986–1970*. Oceana Publications, 1972

Gertzog, Irwin N. *Congressional Women*. Praeger, 1984.

Good, Josephine L. *The History of Women in Republican National Conventions and Women in the Republican National Committee*. Women's Division of the Republican National Committee, 1963.

Government Printing Office. *Biographical Directory of the American Congress*. Various editions.

Gruberg, Martin. *Women in American Politics*. Academia Press, 1968.

Gunther, John. *Inside U.S.A.* Harper and Brothers, 1947.

Hartner, Susan. *From Margin to Mainstream: American Women in Politics Since 1960*. McGraw-Hill, 1996.

Heinemann, Sue. *Timelines of American Women's History*. Berkley Publishing Group, 1996.

Herman, Masako. *The Japanese in America, 1843–1973*. Oceana Publications, 1974.

Hine, Darlene Clark, Elsa Barkley Brown, and Rosalyn Terborg-Penn, eds. *Black Women in America: An Historical Encyclopedia*. Indiana University Press, 1993.

Holmes, Jack E. *Politics in New Mexico*. University of New Mexico Press, 1967.

Holt, Thomas. *Black Over White: Negro Political Leadership in South Carolina During Reconstruction*. University of Illinois Press, 1977.

Irwin, Inez Haynes. *Angels and Amazons: A Hundred Years of American Women*. Doubleday Doran, 1933.

Jackson, Bryan O., ed. *Social and Ethnic Politics in California*. IGS Press, 1991.

Jackson, Kendall. *America Is Me*. HarperCollins, 1996.

Johnson, Otto, ed. *Information Please Almanac*. Houghton Mifflin, 1996.

Jonas, Frank H., ed. *Politics in the American West*. University of Utah Press, 1969.

Kanellos, Nicolás. *Hispanic Firsts*. Visible Ink Press, 1997.

_____. *The Hispanic Almanac.* Visible Ink Press, 1994.

Key, V. O., Jr. *American State Politics.* Knopf, 1956.

Kirkpatrick, Jeanne. *The New Presidential Elite: Men and Women in National Politics.* Russell Sage Foundation, 1976.

Konnyu, Leslie. *Hungarians in the U.S.A.* American Hungarian Review, 1967.

Lakeville Press Inc. *American Jewish Biographies.* Facts on File, 1982.

Lamson, Peggy. *Few Are Chosen.* Houghton-Mifflin, 1968.

Lanigan, Esther F. *American Political Women: Contemporary and Historical Profiles.* Libraries Unlimited, 1980.

Lankevich, George, Jr. *Ethnic America: 1978–1980.* Oceana Publications, 1981.

Le Veness, Frank P., and Jane P. Sweeney, eds. *Women Leaders in Contemporary U.S. Politics.* Lynne Rienner, 1987.

Lindop, Laurie. *Political Leaders.* Twenty-First Century Books, 1996.

Ljungmark, Lars. *Swedish Exodus.* Southern Illinois University Press, 1979.

Lowe, C. H. *The Chinese in Hawaii.* Privately published, 1972.

Magill, Frank N., ed. *Great Lives from History: American Women Series.* Salem Press, 1995.

Malinkowski, Sharon, ed. *Notable Native Americans.* Gale Research, 1995.

Mandel, Ruth B. *In the Running: The New Woman Candidate.* Beacon Press, 1983.

Marable, Manning. *Black American Politics.* Verso, 1985.

McCarty, Kathryn Shane. *Women in Municipal Government.* National League of Cities, 1986.

Medhi, Beverlee Turner. *The Arabs in America.* Oceana Publications, 1978.

Melendy, Howard Brett. *Asians in America.* Twayne Publishers, 1977.

Mikulski, Barbara. *Capitol Offense.* Dutton, 1996.

Morgan, Neil. *Westward Tilt: The American West Today.* Random House, 1963.

Morris, Dan, and Inez Morris. *Who Was Who in American Politics.* Hawthorn Books, 1974.

Mullaney, Marie Marmo, ed. *Biographical Directory of the American Governors, 1983–1988.* Meckler Books, 1989.

_____. *Biographical Directory of the American Governors, 1988–1994.* Greenwood Press, 1994.

Myrdal, Gunnar. *An American Dilemma: The Negro Problem and American Democracy.* Harper and Row, 1944.

Nakanishi, Don T., supv. *National Asian Pacific American Political Roster and Resource Guide.* UCLA Asian American Studies Center, 1995.

Natella, Arthur. *The Spanish in America.* Oceana Publications, 1980.

National Museum and Archive of Lesbian and Gay History, comp. *The Gay Almanac.* Berkley Books, 1996.

Neill, Lois Decker, ed. *The Women's Book of World Records and Achievements.* Anchor Press/Doubleday, 1979.

Ng, Franklin, ed. *The Asian-American Encyclopedia.* Marshall Cavendish, 1995.

Niiya, Brian, ed. *Japanese American History.* Facts on File, 1993.

Odegard, Peter H., and Hans H. Baerwald. *The American Republic: Its Government and Politics.* Harper and Row, 1964.

Olsen, Kirstin. *The Chronology of Women's History.* Greenwood Press, 1994.

Olson, James Stuart. *Native Americans in the Twentieth Century.* Brigham Young University Press, 1984.

Opfell, Olga. *Women Prime Ministers and Presidents.* McFarland, 1993

Ornstein, Norman J., et al., eds. *Vital Statistics on Congress.* Congressional Quarterly, 1995.

Owens, John R., Edmund Costantin, and Louis F. Weschler. *California Politics and Parties.* Macmillan, 1970.

Palmer, Albert Wentworth. *Orientals in American Life.* R and E Research Associates, 1972.

Pap, Leo. *The Portuguese-Americans.* Twayne Publishers, 1981.

Paxton, Annabel. *Women in Congress.* Dietz Press, 1945.

Peirce, Neal R. *The Great Plains States of America*. W. W. Norton, 1973.

_____. *The Mountain States of America*. W. W. Norton, 1972.

_____. *The New England States of America*. W. W. Norton, 1976.

Peirce, Neal R., and John Keefe. *The Great Lakes States of America*. W. W. Norton, 1980.

Peirce, Neal R., and Michael Barone. *The Mid-Atlantic States of America*. W. W. Norton, 1977.

Perry, Troy. *Profiles in Gay and Lesbian Courage*. St. Martin's Press, 1991.

Peterson, Barbara Bennett, ed. *Notable Women in Hawaii*. University of Hawaii Press, 1984.

Pollack, Jill. *Women on the Hill: A History of Women in Congress*. Franklin Watts, 1996.

Prpic, George J. *The Croatian Immigrants in America*. Philosophical Library, 1971.

Rajoppi, Joanne. *Women in Office: Getting There and Staying There*. Bergin and Garvey, 1993.

Randall, Vicky. *Women and Politics*. Tavistock, 1981.

Ritchie, Donald A. *The Young Oxford Companion to the Congress of the United States*. Oxford University Press, 1993.

Romney, Ronna. *Momentum: Women in American Politics Now*. Crown, 1988

Rosenthal, Alan, ed. *The Political Life of the American States*. Praeger Publishers, 1984.

Rutledge, Leigh. *Gay Book of Lists*. Alyson Publications, 1988.

Sheldon, Suzanne Eaton. *Women in Government*. GGM Career/Horizons, 1984.

Sinclair, Andrew. *The Better Half: The Emancipation of the American Woman*. Harper and Row, 1965.

Skerry, Peter. *Mexican Americans: The Ambivalent Minority*. The Free Press, 1993.

Smith, Jessie Carney, ed. *Black Firsts*. Visible Ink Press, 1994.

Smith, Samuel Denny. *The Negro in Congress, 1870–1901*. Kennikat Press, 1966.

Sobel, Robert, and John Raimo, eds. *Biographical Directory of the American Governors, 1789–1978*. Meckler Books, 1978.

_____. *Biographical Directory of the American Governors, 1978–1983*. Meckler Books, 1983.

Stanwick, Kathy, proj. staff. *Women in Public Office: A Biographical Directory and Statistical Analysis*. Scarecrow Press, 1978.

Stewart, Debra W., ed. *Women in Local Politics*. Scarecrow Press, 1980.

Stewart, Jeffrey C. *1001 Things Everyone Should Know About African-American History*. Doubleday, 1996.

Stone, Chuck. *Black Political Power in America*. Dell Publishing, 1970.

Swain, Carol M. *Black Faces, Black Interests: The Representatives of Black Americans in Congress*. Harvard University Press, 1993.

Telgen, Diane, and Jim Camp, eds. *Notable Hispanic Women*. Gale Research, 1993.

Thernstrom, Stephan, ed. *Harvard Encyclopedia of American Ethnic Groups*. Harvard University Press, 1980.

Tiger, Harriet, ed. *Who's Who in America in 1996*. Reed Reference Publishing, 1996.

Trager, James. *The Women's Chronology*. Henry Holt, 1994.

Tung, William L. *The Chinese in America: 1820–1973*. Oceana Publications, 1974.

Tunnell, Ted. *Crucible of Reconstruction: War Radicalism and Race in Louisiana, 1862–1877*. Louisiana State University Press, 1984.

Tyrkus, Michael J., ed. *Gay and Lesbian Biography*. St. James Press, 1997.

Unterburger, Amy L., ed. *Who's Who Among Asian Americans*. Gale Research, 1995.

Utter, Jack. *American Indians*. National Woodlands Publishing, 1993.

Vigil, Maurilio. *Hispanics in American Politics*. University Press of America, 1987.

Waldman, Carl. *Who Was Who in Native American History*. Facts on File, 1990.

Walton, Haynes, Jr. *Invisible Politics: Black Political Behavior*. State University of New York Press, 1985.

Weatherford, Doris. *American Women's History*. Prentice-Hall, 1994.

Wertsman, Vladimir. *The Ukrainians in America: 1608–1975*. Oceana Publications, 1976.

_____. *The Russians in America: 1727–1970*. Oceana Publications, 1977.

Weyl, Nathaniel. *The Jew in American Politics*. Arlington House, 1968.

Wharton, Vernon Lane. *The Negro in Mississippi, 1865–1890*. Harper and Row Publishers, 1947.

Whitney, Susan, and Tom Raynor. *Women in Politics*. Franklin Watts, 1986.

Wigoder, Geoffrey. *Dictionary of Jewish Biography*. Simon and Schuster, 1991.

Williams, Barbara. *Breakthrough: Women in Politics*. Walker, 1979.

Witt, Lynn, Sherry Thomas, and Eric Marcus, eds. *Out in All Directions: The Almanac of Gay and Lesbian America*. Warner Books, 1995.

Women Elected Officials: A Fifty State Resource. Center for the American Woman and Politics, 1996.

Wright, John W., ed. *The Universal Almanac*. Andrews and McMeel, 1994.

Young, Louise M. *The Political Role of Women in the United States*. Report to the International Political Science Association, 1953.

_____. *Understanding Politics*. Pellegrini and Cudahy, 1950.

Zaykowski, Dorothy Ingersoll. *Native American Women of North America*. Tudor Publishers, 1997.

Zeller, Belle, ed. *American State Legislatures*. Crowell, 1954.

Zia, Helen, and Susan B. Gall, eds. *Notable Asian Americans*. Gale Research, 1995.

Special Internet Research Sites

http://www.allpolitics.com/1997/index.html	AllPolitics
http://osiris.colorado.edu/POLSCI/RES/amer.html	American Politics Resources
http://www.clark.net/ccentral/	CampaignCentral
http://www.stardot.com/ce/	Campaigns and Elections Online
http://www.capweb.net/campaign.html	Campaigns and Politics
http://www-rci.rutgers.edu/~cawp/	Center for the American Woman and Politics
http://www.sas.upenn.edu/African_Studies/Govern_Political/	Congressional Black Caucus Guide
http://www.electnet.org/	ElectNet—The State Election Watch
http://www1.pitt.edu/~lmitten/indians.html	Guide to Native America Sites
http://www.headwaymag.com/	Headway (formerly National Minorities) Magazine
http://www.neta.com/~1stbooks/gov.htm	Hispanic Contributions to the USA
http://assets.wharton.upenn.edu/~rajiv98/iapac.html	Indian-American Political Awareness Committee
http://www.latimes.com/HOME/NEWS/POLITICS/	Los Angeles Times—Online Politics and Government
http://www.lib.umich.edu/libhome/Documents.center/	Minority Political Site Links
http://www.nando.net/nt/politics/	Nando Times—Politics
http://www.naleo.org/index.htm	National Association of Latino Elected Officials
http://www.cloakroom.com/	National Journal—The Cloakroom
http://www.politicalindex.com/	National Political Index
http://www.feminist.com/nwpc.htm	National Women's Political Caucus
http://www.mstm.okstate.edu/students/jjohnson2/ok-native.htm	Native America
http://scuish.scu.edu/SCU/Programs/Diversity/natref.html	Native American Reference Sources
http://www.nytimes.com/yr/mo/day/politics/	New York Times Online—Politics
http://www.tiac.net/users/parallax/	Notable Citizens of Planet Earth Database
http://www.potifos.com/tpg/index.html	Political Graveyard

http://PoliticalResources.com/ — Political Resources Online
http://www.geocities.com/CapitolHill/2533/pprissue.html — Price Political Review
http://www.vote-smart.org/ — Project Vote Smart
http://www.lsu.edu/guests/poli/public_html/research.html — Research Links in Political Science
http://www.rollcall.com/ — RollCall Magazine
http://www.soci.swt.edu/areas/multicltrlinks.htm — Selected Multicultural Links on the WWW Directory

http://members.aol.com/thecitadel/sopol/index.html — Southern Politics Page
http://www.political.com/ — Texas Political Resource Page
http://www.hillnews.com/ — The Hill—The Capitol Newspaper
http://www.senate.gov/history/intro.htm — United States Senate—Historical Office
http://www.washingtonpost.com/ — Washington Post
http://www.washtimes.com/politics/inside.html — Washington Times—Inside Politics
http://socialstudies.com/mar/womenpolitics.html — Women in American Politics
http://www.glue.umd.edu/~cliswp/ — Women in Politics
http://wizard.ucr.edu/~charmer/womens.html — Women in Politics
http://wlo.org/ — Women Leaders Online
http://wlo.org/ — Women Leaders Online/Women Organizing for Change

http://www.wic.org/ — Women's International Center
http://www.inform.umd.edu/EdRes/Topic/WomensStudies/ — Women's Studies

Special Research Contacts

Anderson, Anita, Law Librarian, Office of the Attorney General, Minnesota
Bennett, Dana, State of Nevada
Bender, John F., Chief Elections Counsel, Secretary of State of Ohio
Borreca, Richard, *Honolulu Star-Bulletin*
Burrowes, Dr. Carl P., Marshall University, West Virginia
Cargot, Pat, *Detroit Free Press*
Carino, Brenda, Media Contact, Lt. Governor's Office, State of Alaska
Carter, Don, Reference and Information Services, National Library of Canada
Castillo, Quemardo, Elections Bureau, Mississippi Secretary of State Office
Chargot, Pat, *Detroit Free Press*
Christian, Sarah, Constituent Services Supervisor, Office of the Governor of Texas
Clayton, Bridgett, Elections Bureau, Mississippi Secretary of State Office
Cook, Rebecca McDowell, Secretary of State, Missouri
Davis, Janice, British House of Commons
Dennis, Carol, Assistant Secretary, Oklahoma State Election Board
Dwyer, Bonnie, Reference Librarian, Maine State Library
Gashi, Dr. Mithat
Gillespie, Missy, Elections Specialist, Office of the Governor of Utah
Golden, Priscilla, Librarian, Wyoming State Library
Greene, Brian, Librarian, Wyoming State Library
Karam, Mary T., National Field Coordinator, Arab American Institute
Kawasaki, Jodee, Librarian, Montana State University Library

Locy, Steve, Oklahoma State University Library
Lupp, Robert E., Supervising Librarian, New Jersey State Government Publications
McDiarmid, Hugh, *Detroit Free Press*
McDonald, Janice P., Elections Specialist, Office of the Secretary of State of Alabama
Miller, Tamara G., Assistant Editor, Papers of Elizabeth Cady Stanton and Susan B. Anthony Project, Rutgers University
Mitten, Lisa, Librarian, University of Pittsburgh Library
Preston, Sherry, City of Burien, Washington
Quatannens, Dr. Jo Anne McCormick, Asst. Historian, United States Senate Historical Office
Shah, Rajiv, Indian American Political Awareness Committee
Souki, Joseph M., Speaker, Hawaii State House of Representatives
Spartz, India, Librarian, Alaska State Library
Suleiman, Dr. Michael, Department of Political Science, Kansas State University
Tabella, Pat, Public Information Coordinator, Office of the Secretary of State of Rhode Island
Taylor, Connie, Office of the Secretary of State of Iowa
Thompson, Shelley L., Research Analyst, Office of the Secretary of State of Arizona
Tsuji, Marian E., Chief of Staff, Lt. Governor of Hawaii
Watchke, Gary A., Research Analyst, Legislative Reference Bureau, Wisconsin
West, Eugene, Rasmuson Library, University of Alaska–Fairbanks
Wittman, Bradley S., Bureau of Elections, Michigan

Additional Special Research Sources

American Muslim Council
Center for the American Woman and Politics
Congressional Black Caucus
Democratic National Committee
Hmong National Development Group
International Parliamentary Union
Joint Center for Political Studies
Library of Congress
National Association Latino Elected/Appointed Officials
National Women's Political Caucus
Republican National Committee
San Francisco Public Library: Special African-American, Chinese, Filipino, Gay/Lesbian Archives
UCLA Asian-American Studies Center
United States Senate Historical Office
The offices of the secretaries of state and official election statistical offices or bureaus of the fifty states.

Reader Submissions for the Next Edition

Submissions for inclusion in the next edition of *The Almanac of Women and Minorities in American Politics* are welcomed. Please complete as much of the following information as possible, then submit it to:

Mail: *Almanac of Women and Minorities in American Politics*
          c/o Westview Press
          5500 Central Avenue
          Boulder, CO 80301-2877

or

E-mail: jhm@sirius.com

Name of person, event, or year for inclusion:

Notable achievement or event that happened:

Pertinent facts (be as specific as possible):

References available (please list books, articles, etc., that will provide additional information):

Submitted by:

Address:

Phone: (   )   E-mail address:

May we contact you for further information on this submission?   Yes   No

Index